2016   5   Keep 7/18
Le 12/18

S0-BZE-604

The Letter - A Family's Tale Unplugged

by T.M. Guldan

To my father and mother,
May they be resting peacefully with their son.

To my brothers and sisters,
May your memories of 1970 finally rest in peace.

To my sister and brother-in-law,
Whose son went off to war.

To my Kelly and Kevin,
May your children never know war.

To all parents,
With children involved in a war...

The Letter
A Family's Tale Unplugged

SHARED PEN Edition

www.SharedPen.com

SHARED PEN

The "*Pieta*" by Michelangelo

Michelangelo felt the lives within each block of marble as he chipped away, trying to set them free. Writing non-fiction is like this. It is a process of chipping away to find that story within a block of life and setting it free.

The Letter
A Family's Tale Unplugged
by T.M. Guldan

Table of Contents

i. To the Reader

I began writing at about the age of eleven. I don't know if this was an escape for me or just something to do with my time. I was obsessed with it until one day my mother said to me, "You're going to write our family story."

Faced with this expectation, my enthusiasm faded; or maybe I had grown older and was more involved in other activities and gave up writing. I didn't pick it up again until I was forty-one years old, when I became an empty-nester. It was a few years later when my sister said to me, "Look at this, Terri."

And the story of our family finally began.

My research for this book included dozens of interviews, reading books, and traveling to Vietnam. I interviewed eleven of my siblings, Denise, a relative by heart, aunts, uncles, cousins, close friends, neighbors, and Vietnam veterans. They were all generous and honest in sharing their emotions, reaching back into a painful time to recall feelings of sorrow and confusion. I often use just their memories rather than researching facts because it is these memories that help to understand what they were feeling. You will find quotations from these interviews throughout this book. They are a testament to the battle scars, from the Vietnam War, we have all carried for more than forty years.

While in Vietnam, I walked on Hill 55 and toured the surrounding area of Da Nang. This is where my brother Johnny spent the last few months of his life. I gathered dirt from the spot where he died, urged to do so by a sibling. Many have given me letters they had received from Johnny. Portions of those letters and quotations from tape recordings Johnny sent home are found throughout this book as well. I didn't correct the spelling or grammar in Johnny's letters. I use Johnny's actual letters to capture events, emotions, family dynamics, and historic detail. I include bits of the political and social atmosphere of the time.

Some of the towns or areas in Vietnam had very similar names so it wasn't clear if Johnny was speaking of the same place when he writes Bic Bah in one letter and Bich Bac in another. In my research I found only a town called Bich Bac. This led me to believe they were one and the same town, and that Johnny learned the proper spelling once he had spent more time in the area.

As a ten year old I was pretty oblivious to my parents agonizing over my brother's decision to go to war and with their worries once he had left. I didn't understand what was going on in Vietnam. I didn't understand why my neighbor called my brother—who was my hero—a "baby killer." We didn't talk about it and I didn't ask. Then, at eleven years old, I watched my parents suffer when my brother didn't make it back home. We all suffered—silently. However, thirty-three years later my sister Margie and I discovered a letter my father had left behind, which helped my siblings, myself, and others to find our voices so that we were finally able to talk about this tragedy.

My story focuses on the year 1970. By focusing on one year, while intertwining current emotions, memories of decades ago, and historic details, I hope to display how war and loss have affected us all, not only at the time of loss but decades later. This book is a merging of personal memoirs and history. I call it a *memumentory*.

I. Introduction

"It is the silence that betrayed us."

—Barack Obama,
Dreams from My Father

My sister Margie and I were cleaning out the second bedroom of my parents' modest, Orland Park condo. It was March of 2003. Dad had passed away the month before at the age of seventy-four, after a five-month battle with cancer. We were told he went quickly for a bone cancer victim. I believe he was in a hurry to be with Mom again. My mother died suddenly in December 1998, a few months after my parents had celebrated their fiftieth wedding anniversary. I read somewhere that many older couples die within five years of each other.

The room Margie and I were packing up had been my father's office. It was a small, square bedroom with one metal framed window, which looked out onto a knoll that was kept company by a curvy, paved walking path. As usual for the Chicago area, the knoll was barren this time of year. Yet in summer it was filled with tall prairie grass, exuding peacefulness when the wind rustled through it. Margie was sorting through papers, receipts, and various office supplies in the small wooden desk that sat adjacent to the window. Behind us were shelves bulging with hard and softcover books displaying titles from Scott Turow, Louis L'Amour and the American Medical Association. My mother didn't mind that she didn't get to claim a part of that office with her sewing machine and knitting projects. The contents of this little room kept Dad out of her hair. She would have rather been knitting in the living room, looking out to the street, feeling one with the neighbors as they walked their dogs and got in their cars. She wasn't one to spend time alone in a small room like my father. She would usually be out visiting with one of the twelve of us or her close friends.

Although it was just Margie and I in the second bedroom of the condo my parents had shared in the last years of their life together, the others were not far away, busy in each of the few remaining rooms, packing things up and throwing things away. We worked well together as a family when we set our minds to it. This was cultivated throughout our upbringing by the regimented Saturday chores scheduled by my mother and the laborious summer chores at our farm, governed by both Mom and Dad. I was going through a box on the floor next to the desk, a few feet from my sister, trying to determine which papers were valuable and which weren't.

Margie was a triplet. She had shared the womb with our brother, Jim, and sister, Eileen. Margie's stature of five feet one inch and ninety pounds seems a contradiction of her nature. She was the first of her triplet siblings to enter the world and that innate determination to push her way out has stuck with her throughout her life. She was diagnosed with diabetes in 1987, which has wreaked havoc on her eyesight and circulation over the years, but she just keeps going. We had been concentrating on the task at hand and not talking much save for a few comments or chuckles on the things my father had kept, when Margie suddenly said, "Look at this, Terri."

I looked over to see that Margie had a small envelope in her hand. I wondered why this letter, one among many in the pile of papers we had been tossing out, made my sister call it out to me. I saw that the letter had not been opened. I watched as she carefully pried at its sealed flap and removed a couple of sheets of thin, yellowed stationery. I gently took the fragile papers my sister offered me, as we stood amidst a jungle of boxes and a large plastic garbage bag we had been feeding at our discretion. The cursive writing on the letter lay in a neat, consistent rhythm across each of the delicate pages.

Dear John,

The letter began, written in black ink on the small pages. At the top of each page, in the same black ink, were page numbers, now barely visible. I marveled at the meticulous organization of this simple letter. At the same time I was perplexed. Who had sent this, I wondered. My thoughts swirled. Since there were postal markings on it indicating it had come from Vietnam, I immediately thought it had come from my brother, Johnny, years and years ago. No, that couldn't be. Johnny would have begun with, "Dear Dad" rather than "Dear John." And my father would have opened it, for sure.

The date, "7/28/70," was written in the upper right corner of the first page. This date was immediately significant to me. Six days later, on August 3, 1970, my brother was killed. Between reading the address on the envelope and the "Love, Dad" on its last page, I realized that this letter had traveled to Vietnam and back, unopened—until now, thirty-three years later. It was returned because the recipient, my brother Johnny, had been mortally wounded before my father's letter ever reached him.

1970, a turbulent time for all Americans, was especially tumultuous for my family. While war waged in the combat zones, our family suffered in the noncombat zones and continued after the war ended. Johnny's death nearly tore my family apart and yet, we never talked about it. We never talked about our feelings about his death, implying to each of us that our feelings were not important. The Vietnam War and its impact on our family loomed large, yet we did our best to ignore it.

And so perhaps it is not surprising that my father put the letter Johnny never received away, keeping it sealed all these years as if it was still in transit. My father was forty-three years old when he wrote this last letter to his twenty-year-old son. It was now 2003 and I had a twenty-year-old son who was looking for a purpose while a war was waging in a remote, hostile land. I read this letter with the dread that some day I could be writing a similar letter to my son. I became acutely aware of what my father must have been feeling all those years ago.

Although the topics discussed in this letter were mundane—domestic activities in which any Midwest, middle-class family might participate—I absorbed a parent's agony carrying the words that lay across those small pages. At the same time, I felt the fear of a child reaching back through the letter for some degree of normalcy. A story appeared before my eyes, as if a long, heavy stage curtain were being pulled back to reveal our family's tragedy. The handwriting, the paper, the dated and numbered pages are all physical, tangible elements of our story. It is the story of us, of those left behind. It is about individuals, families, war, the processing of trauma and loss. More importantly, it is about courage and loyalty, love and faith in the midst of one of the most interesting periods of U.S. history.

II. The Happening

"Stay with me
The world is dark and wild..."
—*Into the Woods*, song lyrics,
Disney

The Vietnam War began for me on a crisp and cold January evening in 1970. Stars were in the sky. I sat in the back of our toasty Oldsmobile Vista Cruiser station wagon, peering out the window as it pulled into the small, almost unnoticeable parking lot of the tiny 91st Street Beverly train station. The frozen snow popped under the tires as our heavy car moved slowly over it, sounding like the bubbles bursting on plastic packing wrap when you squeeze them. My father was driving. I had all the confidence in the world in my father's driving. I knew he could maneuver us through this dark parking lot, find what we needed to find, and get us back home safely on this dark, freezing night. Dad had safely driven us to our farm and back hundreds of times. Now, I think back and cringe at how we all slept in the back, no seat belts, as the cars traveled at the speed limit of seventy miles per hour. Once we drove past another family's station wagon that was off the road, down in a ditch. There were several bodies lying still in the grass, covered head to toe with blankets. I could hear my mom gasp and there were a few words from my older brothers and sisters in the middle seat. I looked up to the front of the car and studied my dad. He didn't flinch. He kept his eyes on the road and joined my mother in saying the rosary.

Mom did not come with us to the train station that evening. She was manning the homestead, eight city blocks away, with Patti, Mariann, Bill, Margie, Eileen, Joe, Mimi, and Bonnie all waiting excitedly for us to return home. I am the tenth of thirteen children. Mom affectionately referred to me as their "five-and-dime," the fifth girl, tenth child. When it was all said and done, there were six boys and seven girls. Four brothers preceded me, so Mom prayed to St. Therese for a girl. This is where I got my name, although saintly I was not. I scared my little sister at night, called my brothers names, and didn't help my older sisters fold the laundry. By the age of eleven, I had gotten in fights with two of the neighbor boys. I once called my brother, Bill, a name in front of his friends. It was a word I had heard him use before. It caused him to cuss and swear. I didn't even know what it meant.

That night, I peered out the car window, into the train station parking lot. The thick, crusty coat of two-day-old snow adhered to the ground. Being the tenth, I was enjoying the rare privilege of a window seat only because I was second oldest in the car, not counting my dad. My brother Mickey, two years older than me, got the other back seat window and Chris, my younger brother sat in the middle. We were saving the front seat for our oldest brother, Johnny. The oldest gets the front seat, the first choice at all times, and the last chocolate chip cookie. These are the unwritten laws one must abide by in a large family. The youngest is an exception to these rules. The youngest tends to get whatever she wants. Bonnie was the youngest.

Most often Dad followed the Bible's guidance: "If you spare the rod, you spoil the child." However, when it came to Bonnie, he was a heathen. Bonnie, whose name was determined by the day she arrived, July 14, one day before Saint Bonaventure Day, could bring the soft spot out in Dad. One time when Bonnie had done something that caused Dad to threaten a spanking, she ran from him. He followed after her, from one room to the next until she promptly sat down on the ground. Sitting on her hands, to protect her bottom from a spanking, she shouted, "I love you Dad, I love YOU!" She proclaimed this at his feet, looking up at him towering above her, with her pleading big blue eyes. All he could do was laugh. Those who witnessed this were amazed, and this scene went down in infamy. She had tamed the beast.

The train rolled into the darkness surrounding the station without much fanfare, aside from the occasional squeaking of its brakes as it came to a stop. The 91st Street station was the only train station I knew at ten years old, having lived only in Beverly, a small neighborhood on the southwest side of Chicago. Beverly Hills, my neighborhood, was a predominantly Irish Catholic. Most people know Beverly Hills as the city in California but few have heard of the neighborhood on the southwest side of Chicago. While spending the previous summer at the farm, I had written to my best friend, Lyn, who lived across the street from me my whole life (all ten years of it, at that point). My letters were returned because I had addressed them to Beverly, Illinois.

I could see the doors of the train open and a few people file out as if a gumball machine was dispensing a handful of gumballs. Dark figures moved steadily, some disappearing behind the small depot building. Then the train rolled off, as inconspicuously as it had arrived.

My eyes darted here and there, squinting as I eagerly peered through the steamed-up glass of the back seat window, competing to be the first one to spot him. It was quiet in the car. I don't know if that was due to the fact we were all concentrating so hard to be the first to spot Johnny or whether it was the thickness of night that surrounded us. Winter nights seem to do that—make everyone quiet. I focused my attention back to the droplets racing down the window, one eating another, gobbling up its clone opponents. I tried to guess which of the droplets would be the first to reach the bottom of the window. They never ended their run in the direction they had started out, and so it was impossible to know which drop would consume another or be consumed. But that didn't stop me from trying to figure it out.

It was Friday, January 9, 1970. Johnny was arriving home for a thirty-day leave after graduating from the Marine Corps boot camp in San Diego, California and several weeks of training at Camp Pendleton, north of San Diego. The Vietnam War had been raging for several years by the time Johnny had enlisted at the age of nineteen. He wanted to do the right thing, like his hero, Dr. Tom Dooley, whom he read about in high school. Dr. Dooley was a Navy doctor focused on helping the children in Laos and Vietnam in the 1950s.

My guess was wrong again. A raindrop came out of nowhere and consumed the one I had my eye on as the winner. I pulled my focus away from the window pane and looked out into the hazy parking lot. I spotted a husky soldier, all dressed up in a uniform with gold buttons marching up and down his chest and a white cap. He was walking toward our car. The droplet-studded window and the twilight blurred the image of this figure.

My father got out of the car. I knew this only because I felt the cold air rush into my warm, toasty world and I heard the door slam shut almost immediately after the cold air hit me. I watched this man and my father throw their arms around each other. It must be Johnny, I thought. It was the first time I saw my father show so much affection to any of my brothers. I can so clearly remember the way my father hugged his son that cold January evening. Moments like this seeped the truth into my heart—the truth that my father had the capacity to love deeply, which allowed us to tolerate his periodic harshness and cynicism. Seeing them hug like this told me that no matter what hurtful thing my dad said to Johnny about his choice to enlist, Johnny must have known that underneath it all was love and concern. I know now that I was right, not only from their embrace, but also from their exchange of letters which had begun while Johnny was in boot camp.

My father didn't have the perfect role model for a father, but it wasn't the worst situation. Pop, as we called our paternal grandfather, was kicked out of his own home as a young boy. My grandmother's family took him in. Nan, my Grandma's nickname, and Pop later married. I liked Pop. He used to call me Pocahontas because I had long, bone-straight, jet-black hair. Yet with a handful of freckles spattered across my pug nose and fair, Irish skin, this was a stretch. Either way, I liked how Pop differentiated me from the crowd of my siblings by calling me Pocahontas. I was an adult when I learned from my older sisters that Pop was an alcoholic. Once after having too much to drink, he ran over and killed the family dog, to whom my father had a deep attachment. He blamed my father for letting it run out under the car. There was no sympathy.

- - -

My brother Bill has the most to say about Pop. I interview Bill on April 26, 2009, over the speakerphone at my house in Michigan. He did not come in for any recent weddings and I was not able to entice him to take a flight out to Michigan, to vacation at my home in Grand Haven, even if I paid half. Bill, 53 now, is at his home in Loveland, Colorado. He was responsible and serious as a young boy, having had a paper route at the age of twelve. At nineteen Bill had a falling out with this grandfather over money Nan had given him to attend college. She did not tell Pop about this but he soon found out and was not happy. He let on his feelings to our parents one night, after his tongue had been greased with a few drinks, while the four of them were out to dinner. "...What bums Jim and Bill are. They should be working for their own money," Pop said. My parents co-signed on a $350 loan from the bank and had Billy give the money back.

"And when I paid them back I went down there, the basement of their house on Leavitt. He was sittin' in his office and he'd been drinkin' V.O., as always. I told him I paid him back and he was like, 'oh, well good,'" Bill tells me.

Due to lack of funds, Billy dropped out of college before his first semester was over and earned money through construction work to pay off the bank loan. Bill sounded very sad as he was retelling this memory. I wanted to hate Pop, although I had no memories of him being mean or drunk.

- - -

I never heard my father say one bad thing about his father. Actually, I don't remember him saying anything about Pop. My dad, on the other hand, didn't indulge in alcohol. He was a loyal father and husband. He was either at work, at home, out with my mother, or on a fishing trip with his buddies. He never wandered far from my mother or from us. Sometimes I wished he would though. I used to hate it when he would hover over me, watching me do something like buttering toast or putting the saddle on the horse and correct me. He would try to help, I guess, but I always felt like whatever I was doing was wrong.

Suddenly one of the raindrops gained speed and catapulted downward, gobbling up the others lying in its sporadic path just as Johnny got in the front seat. He turned around, said hello to us, reached back, and rubbed the top of Chris' fuzzy head. I don't remember the short ride back home, but I'm sure we sat in silent awe as Johnny and my father exchanged comments about his trip from California. They would have avoided any discussion about the Marines, boot camp, or Johnny's shipping orders as we headed the few blocks to home.

Our street was lined with mature oaks and maples, their lush, green canopy nonexistent at this time of year. Our sturdy brown-brick bungalow sat smack-dab in the middle of 90th in Oakley. The geometric designs of stained, leaded glass tastefully decorated each of the living room windows that spread across the front of our bungalow. All of this, I'm sure, provided Johnny a warm welcome home. I loved our house. With three full floors, it was comfortable and roomy enough for the fifteen of us—and Snowball.

Included in our household was Snowball, a Lab mix. She was all black except for the little white spot under her neck. Johnny had come up with her name in addition to her nickname of Cha-Cha-Goo. He had a knack for assigning names that stuck. He had assigned nicknames to all of us. Mariann's was Fairyann—no biggie. Margie was Pardge. Eileen was Bean. I was Peach because it was a fruit like Pear, which rhymed with Terr. Patti was Fatty—not a good one. Christopher, whom we normally called Chris, was Og-goo, which was very cute. Bonnie Marie was B.M, her initials. Snowball was Cha-Cha-Goo because when you say "you're such a good dog" really fast, it almost sounds like Cha-Cha-Goo (dog).

Although considered "Johnny's dog," it became apparent over the years that Snowball belonged to my mother. That was not my mother's design—no, this was Snowball's choice. That dog loved my mom, always lying quietly near her. Snowball loved Emma too. Emma was Grandpa's maid who worked at our house regularly, ironing and making peanut butter and jelly sandwiches. Snowball was loved by the neighborhood dogs as well and produced a handful of litters in her life-time. Bonnie was attached to one of Snowball's ugliest puppies with grey, smudged markings. Mom dubbed the puppy "Pretty-Ugly." Since Bonnie did not like her hair combed, nor grooming in general, we really didn't know if Mom was referring to Bonnie or the puppy she constantly dragged around.

Finally, we made it home and Dad pulled the car into the narrow, long driveway consisting of two tire-wide, concrete strips, with grass in between. During the summer months, my brothers kept that strip of grass trimmed short. My dad made sure of that. Our driveway ran side-by-side with the neighbor's. Over the twelve or thirteen years we lived on Oakley, the neighbors in that house changed once. The first people that lived there were an older sister and brother. I called the woman "Mrs. Mazel," although she wasn't married. I didn't know "Mrs." was for married women and "Miss" was for those still single ones. When my mom pointed this out to me it didn't make sense, since there was only "Mr." for a man.

Mr. Mazel was troubled, Mom told us compassionately on several occasions, and then said what a kind woman Miss Mazel was because she took good care of her brother. We never saw him. One day, I guess Mr. Mazel couldn't take living up in his room anymore and shot himself. My mom went over to help Miss Mazel clean up the mess. I was four. I remember watching my mother go inside that dark and scary house, worried that she might never come out. That was in 1963, the same year President Kennedy was shot and my sister Mimi was born.

As the twelfth child, Mimi brought an even dozen to our clan, evening out the girl to boy ratio to 6:6. She's never been called her birth name, Maribeth, by any of us, except occasionally by Mom and Dad when they were calling her for disciplinary reasons. To us she was always Mimi.

By 1970, Miss Mazel had moved away. Our new neighbors were very different. The father was Dr. Mackal, a University of Chicago professor studying the Loch Ness monster, supposedly in Scotland. He was once a judge on the Miss America pageant. His wife was the mother of two children from a previous marriage. She looked like the lady on M*A*S*H, the one they called Hot Lips. It was confusing that the kids had a different last name. There was a girl Dana, a year younger than me. Lyn and I sometimes played on their driveway with Dana, her brother, and my brother Joe or Mickey. They had a basketball net, so we played a game called PIG. Each time you missed, you got a letter from the word pig until it was spelled out and then you were the loser. Or we played four-square, where you bounced the ball to a square and the person in the square bounced it back. Dana's brother had long hair. He was tall and a lot older. I think he was in eighth grade in 1970. They both attended Morgan Park Academy. I didn't know where that school was, though I knew it wasn't Catholic.

Dad parked behind our second car, another Oldsmobile. We always had Oldsmobiles. My dad bought a new car from his good friend's dealership every two years, and his friend, Mr. Haggerty, got his teeth taken care of by my dad. I loved it when Dad came home with the new car. He'd take us out for a ride in it to Rainbow Cone, where we'd get ice cream. We had a single-car garage but neither of our cars were ever parked inside. The garage, made of the same brown brick and clay tile roof as our home, was reserved for the green metal trailer Dad hitched to the station wagon each June, after school got out. He loaded it with bags of our summer clothes and hauled it with us to our farm in Waupaca, Wisconsin. Dad also used this trailer for odd jobs and helping out friends when they needed to move large loads.

We all piled out of the car. Dad led with Johnny right behind, his Marine duffle bag slung over his shoulder and the three of us following. We walked through the front door and into the tiled foyer, stomping the snow off our boots before stepping onto the green shag carpet of our warm front room. Mom and the rest of the gang greeted us. Johnny gave Mom a big hug.

A banner had been strategically hung, taped to the cream-colored stucco wall and draped across the mirrored closet facing us as we all walked in. It read, "Welcome Home Soldier." A smartly drawn cartoon character in military uniform decorated the center of the banner made from white butcher's paper. This was the same paper Mom listed our chores on each Saturday morning and taped to the kitchen wall for us all to see. Johnny looked at the banner. His reaction to this artful greeting surprised us all.

- - -

"I do remember Patti had drawn this artwork thing and had put it on the mirror in the front hallway there. 'Welcome Home Soldier'—I dunno if you remember that. Then he goes, 'What's that? I ain't a soldier.'" Bill tells me and laughs. "Because he wanted to be known as a Marine."

- - -

Johnny was fresh out of boot camp and it was obvious that drilling pride into him had been part of the basic training. Patti had hung the banner thoughtfully, placing it where Johnny would see it when he walked through the front door. She kept a cheery face and said nothing in response to Johnny's comment. At the time, Patti was a third-year art major at Mount Mary College, the same school our mother attended. Patti, the oldest, was a Catholic parents' dream daughter. She arrived nine months after my parents were married, went on to college right after high school, completed in four years, dated lightly, and married a Catholic man in our country's bicentennial year, 1976.

We all moved under the archway shared by the living room and dining room. Once in the dining room Johnny set his duffel bag down and took off his coat and cap. Two-year-old Bonnie thought Johnny was Santa Claus, a clean-shaven one in green. She was convinced the bag he had just set down was filled with toys. He picked Bonnie up, just like Santa would have done. This frightened her a bit because she wasn't certain he was Santa. Yet, there were lots of positive emotions coming from the rest of the family so she knew it was a time of celebration.

We called our dining room the TV room. One side was lined with more of the tall, leaded-glass windows. I remember these windows well because Mom commissioned me to clean them. I took the job very seriously as tiny fingers were needed to get in between the leaded panes. A radiator situated below the windows served as a bench. We had no other furniture to sit on in that room. A wood hutch, made by my father, stood along one wall, displaying my mom's china and Waterford crystal. A pine table, also made by Dad, sat in the middle of the room, absent any chairs. Those were needed in the kitchen. Opposite the windows and radiator, a Zenith color television stood proudly on its four peg legs which nestled into the shag carpet. My brother Joe's twenty-gallon freshwater fish tank stood next to the TV. We were one of the first on our block to have a color television. My father kept that television in good working order with the help of his friend whom we called Mr. Fix-it. We sat on the floor to watch programs, usually right under the chairless dining room table.

We followed Johnny through the vortex of our house, a short hallway, and into the kitchen. This hallway usually swirled with activity because it contained our one phone and doors to the rest of our house, including the one to my bedroom that I shared with two younger sisters.

My brother Jim was not at home when Johnny arrived. He was at basketball practice. Jim was in his own world at sixteen, with high school, sports, and girls. Both Jim and Bill attended the all-boys Catholic high school of St. Rita, on 63rd and Claremont. Jim had not attempted to get into Ignatius, where my father had gone, because Johnny had not passed its entrance exam. When he took the entrance exam for Marist High School, also an all-boys Catholic school, where Johnny had gone, his results indicated he had to take summer school to be accepted. When Jim took the entrance exam for St. Rita he passed with no additional requirements. St. Rita was closer to home than Marist, an added benefit. In addition to these reasons to support choosing St. Rita over Marist, Jim did not want to have to fill his brother's cross-country shoes. He wanted to make his own legend. Jim and Johnny were close enough in age so that competition was a constant element in their relationship. Jim was on St. Rita's basketball, track and cross country teams. Johnny had been a top runner and captain of the Marist cross-country team. They both came with good looks, decent physiques, and their own set of female groupies to validate this. But Jim's five feet ten inches to Johnny's five feet eight inches gave him an advantage, for no reason other than Johnny had to look up if he was going to look his younger brother in the eyes.

- - -

"I had to be better than him. I had to out-achieve him," Jim tells me years later.

March 22, 2008 I drive up to Racine, Wisconsin, to interview my brother Jim. It is Easter weekend. At this point, it has taken four attempts to set up a date with Jim and I was beginning to wonder if this interview was ever going to take place. It is the first time I have been to this home of Jim's, where he has lived for a few years with his third wife, Joyce. The house is on Michigan Boulevard with the lake right across the street. The kitchen door faces east, looking out onto the beach and the vast, often churning waters of Lake Michigan. It is breathtaking. Jim jokes that it is a million-dollar view in a ten-dollar town.

When you walk into Jim and Joyce's home, there is an immediate sense of warmth. All 900 square feet of the one story brick, built in the late 1800's, are tidy and cozy. Photos cover the top half of their refrigerator and two built-in white, wooden bookcases. The case to the left holds photos of Mom and Dad, Johnny, an old family shot of a group of us kids and miscellaneous pictures of Guldans. The bookcase to the right holds photos of Joyce's family and her personal artifacts. The dining room walls neatly display matted and framed poems written by Jim.

Jim is a hard worker. He is taking night classes to get his undergraduate degree in business while working sixty-hour weeks for a seventy-five-year-old, whom Jim offishly refers to as a slave driver. Jim is gifted with the Irish charm and a boyish sense of humor. He is very generous. He would give a stranger the shirt off his back. He is as honest as the day is long yet often lacks the diplomacy—he says so himself—to communicate the truth in tactful terms.

When we finally sit down to talk, I am prepared to come away with little material, sensing Jim might not want to travel back to this time due to the multiple attempts at an interview. Yet, from the moment we begin I am grateful for my persistence, and the tape recorder because I cannot write fast enough. About ten minutes into the interview, with a beer in one hand, chased by a Manhattan held in the other, Jim reaches into his memories for the day he learned of Johnny's death. Jim shares his feelings as a sixteen-year-old, and the ensuing twenty years. As I write, I also feel: I am crying for this boy, for his father and for his mother. I don't let my tears distract me. Has he ever talked about this day, how he felt, with anyone? I am wondering as I write ferociously. I write what the tape recorder cannot capture. I document the impact of war, casualties of which the revered and brave journalists who posted themselves atop Saigon's Rex Hotel were not even aware.

- - -

When Jim got home that evening he joined us all in the kitchen, gathered around Johnny, who was still in his Marine uniform. Having been a long-distance runner, Johnny had always been pretty slim. Now he was stocky and solid as we looked at him that evening, listening to his stories about boot camp and the antics of the drill instructors. It was educational. For example, I learned that DI meant drill instructor. He told us how these instructors had hung privates from the Marine compound fence by their handcuffed wrists. He gave us an account of his own tête-à-tête with a DI. Johnny told us how he stood at attention in the sterile office of this DI, right in front of the man's desk, careful not to look at him. Johnny looked straight ahead, focusing on a seam of the stick-on, brown paneling that lined the one wall of the sterile military office. The crew-cut DI sat at his desk barking at

Johnny. Some very important papers on Johnny had been misplaced and this man was blaming Johnny. While Johnny stood at attention, taking this guy's abuse, the officer stood up and realized he had been sitting on the missing papers. Did Johnny actually snicker at that moment? I wondered as I listened with all of my attention as he told of this encounter. I couldn't imagine him not snickering. In either case, the Marine officer at the desk was certain Johnny had.

Johnny, just having gotten to boot camp at that point, immediately began to experience the "Marine" method of training—brutal. But this was to condition them not to react should the enemy do the same to them. This officer made Johnny stand at attention for hours. Was it two hours? Four? Six? Johnny must have needed water, to use the bathroom, no? Now, as a mother, I wonder if my mother thought about these things when she heard Johnny tell this story. As a mother, could I have listened to my son tell me about being subjected to this treatment? It would tell me they were preparing him for something harsh, that the worst was yet to come.

We stood around the kitchen for hours that night listening to Johnny talk about his training in San Diego and Camp Pendleton. The "fudge story" became the most well-known of Johnny's Marine Corps Recruit Depot (also known as MCRD) days. We knew not to send anything to him while he was in training, other than a standard white envelope properly addressed. Yet no one had told Aunt Annie Laurie of the severe mail restrictions the Marines had for their trainees. My mom, the oldest of five, had one sister, Annie Laurie. We never called her Aunt Annie Laurie. That would have been like saying aunt twice! Although, I never knew which name she wanted us to call her.

Annie Laurie had labored over her stove, cooking that fudge, forgoing the demands of her household of nine. Then she wrapped that fudge carefully in wax paper, packed it tightly into an empty shoebox, which she had to search for, traveled to the town post office between errands, and paid to mail that precious package. When it arrived at the MCRD in San Diego, it was not viewed as precious. Johnny was commanded to eat that whole box of chocolate fudge in front of his DI. In his next letter to my parents he wrote:

Annie Laurie sent me a shoe box of fudge. The D.I. made me eat the whole box in 20 min. Dad do not let anyone send me ANYTHING except for mail. I was sick for 2 days. Just tell Gramps to let her know.

Johnny could certainly take punishment.

- - -

In my interview with my brother Joe, he remembers the quarter-inch-thick wooden yardstick. This was Mom's weapon of choice. Joe speaks respectfully of her retribution with it. He describes one night when the boys were sitting at the dinner table with my mother, the yardstick nearby. Dad must have been away for her to be readily equipped like that. This was one of the few times Johnny antagonized his younger brothers with my mother in earshot. He said something profane, and in a moment Mom had reached over the table and whacked Johnny across the shoulders with that beastly yardstick.

"She must have hit him with all her might because that sucker snapped in half!" Joe says.

Johnny just sat there, Joe says, still hunched over, with his head down and his hands folded in his lap.

"He did not flinch. He did not say a word," Joe tells me.

- - -

Another lesson taught by the DIs of Marine training camp was swimming. Johnny told us how he learned by being thrown into the deep end of a pool and told to tread water for many minutes before he was allowed to swim to the edge. Johnny was not a strong swimmer. My mother tried to help with that when he was very young. During the summers in Wisconsin, we all took swimming lessons. It was then my mother discovered Johnny's fear of swimming. He was about seven. She was probably horrified listening to him talk about being thrown in water over his head with no one there to help him. But he obviously survived to tell the tale.

The one thing that stuck in my ten-year-old mind about that night in the kitchen was a statement Johnny made as he leaned against the kitchen counter.

"I'll never turn down another milkshake." Johnny told us.

A milkshake, which I could have any day, he yearned for. That statement opened my world to the suffering of others that have little, while I enjoyed so many simple delights. I laid in bed that night thinking about who was hungry right then. A serious question came to my mind: Why did God let me live in the house I lived in, and a farm with horses to ride, a pantry always full of food, ice cream in the refrigerator, while there were others that could not have milkshakes? I wanted to trust that God had this figured out. As a kid, I used to think a lot about God. Probably because my mom brought Him up regularly, as if He was another Grandpa that we never met. I talked to Him when I was alone, just like I caught my mother doing several times. God was an imaginary friend to me.

Listening to Johnny's boot camp stories was not what captivated Mickey's attention. The sight of Johnny in his fancy Marine uniform made him breathless. My brother Mickey's real name is Michael, but we never called him that. Mickey wanted to be like Johnny. He saw Johnny standing straight and strong in that uniform and thought Johnny's short hair was cool. He wanted to be like Johnny but not exactly like him, because he liked himself well enough. Mickey just wished he could be around him more.

- - -

When I interview Mickey in the fall of 2008, he is in town for our niece's wedding. He drove in from upstate New York, where he lives with his second wife and their two daughters. He has two other children from a previous marriage. Mickey is a dentist. He is the only one of us who followed in our father's footsteps. Mickey and I meet in the lobby of the Marriott Courtyard in Oakbrook Terrace the Friday night before the wedding. We find a quiet spot in the pool area so we can talk privately. Two years older than me, Mickey recalls how he felt when he saw Johnny in that uniform. Mickey tells me he yearned for the respect Johnny got when he stood in the kitchen that evening.

"I hardly ever saw him because he was always at Denise's." Mickey is referring to Johnny's visit home after boot camp.

- - -

Denise, Johnny's girlfriend, was away at school that January. This did not deter Johnny from spending a week with her. Johnny and Denise first met in the basement of our house on Oakley. The occasion was a dance sponsored by Academy of Our Lady (also known as Longwood or AOL) High School, the all-girls' catholic high school Patti and Mariann attended. Mariann and Denise were both involved with high school plays at Longwood. This is how they met and when their friendship began. Mariann had arranged for Johnny and Denise to meet at a pre-dance rendezvous she was hosting at our house. Johnny was to be Denise's date for the dance. It was love at first sight—for Johnny at least. Denise thought he was cute but there was one thing she didn't like.

- - -

"I remember he danced so weird," Denise says, scrunching her nose as we talk at a Chicago restaurant on Van Buren Street, in 2010. "He was real jerky, like he was boxing."

- - -

By the end of that evening, Denise had caved into Johnny's charm. The very next day, Johnny was alone while cleaning Dad's office. So he took the opportunity to use the phone. He first had to muster up the guts to call her. He was so nervous, yet he managed to ask her on a date and she accepted.

"I think I have a girl," Johnny thought as he hung up the phone. He confessed this to Denise two years later, on one of his tapes he recorded from a foxhole. Other dates followed. Within a few short months Denise was in love. Johnny's loyalty and dedication to her was what she wanted for the rest of her life. She gave him her high school ring.

During their high school years, Mariann and Johnny had the world in their palms. Life was good for them. Mariann and Johnny, only one school year apart, shared the same social circle. Mariann introduced Johnny to his beloved Denise and Johnny had introduced Mariann to her first love, Bob Greenfield. Sharing a common group of friends strengthened the already close relationship between Mariann and Johnny that had been developing since infancy.

Bob Greenfield was the "all-American" boyfriend you would imagine for Mariann. He was a broad-shouldered, crew-cut football player with straight white teeth and blue eyes. Mariann was a fair-haired, blue-eyed, pretty little Irish girl who took the world very seriously. Her heart was broken when that relationship didn't work out.

- - -

Mariann noted in a 1996 journal entry:

I'll never forget the first time I ever heard 'I love you' spoken to me. Bob Greenfield said those words to me when we were making out in his parents' car at the parking lot of the forest preserve. I walked around in a moony stupor for days. I couldn't believe that someone loved me. I was a drunk, filled with the liquor of love. I kept pinching myself and repeating the words over and over again in my head. Somebody loved me . . . ME!

I had one brief interview with my sister Mariann before she passed away in 2006. She was a writer and left many poems, short stories, and journals behind that her family was willing to share with me.

- - -

Mariann did not talk to anyone in our family, except Johnny. This was not because she didn't have anything to say—to the contrary. At the age of eighteen she was quietly opinionated, and most of those opinions centered on my parents. Despite this demeanor, Margie worshiped her. Margie once stole Mariann's favorite sweatshirt. Being a triplet who was always dressed like her identical sister, Margie thought that if she wore this trademark wardrobe item of Mariann's, maybe she would look like and act like Mariann. When Mariann discovered the heist, she was furious. No sympathy for the little sister.

- - -

"Mariann was in the National Honors Society. She was so smart. Mariann was valedictorian, class president, and homecoming queen in high school," Margie recalls. "Johnny teased everybody but her. Her eighth grade teachers chose her to crown the Blessed Virgin!"

Crowning the Blessed Virgin Mary was something Christ the King did each spring. One special eighth-grade girl who was most like Mary was chosen, by a popular vote, to do the crowning. In a church ceremony, as formal as a wedding, Mariann walked down the long center aisle, onto the altar, and placed a wreath on the statue of the Virgin Mary.

Like Mariann, Margie is quiet and soft spoken yet has very strong opinions on many topics. Only those closest to her are occasionally given an earful of those opinions. On Sunday, April 20, 2008, I interview my sister Margie. We meet at a Starbuck's in Orland Park, a few blocks from Margie's home. We enjoy the beautiful day and a cup of coffee as we sit al fresco. We will be heading on to our nephew's first communion right after the interview.

- - -

Johnny was not to be found around our house for the better part of these few weeks. He was usually out, catching up with friends. Although Denise was away at school, Johnny visited with her family, which included five of Denise's siblings and her parents. Mostly, Johnny spent time with his best friends Neal Beatty (a.k.a Beads) and Steve Pachol (a.k.a. Patch). Johnny built loyal friendships, such that the rest of us often embraced his friends as well. Beatty and Pachol were like part of our family. We never called them by their first names. In fact, I didn't even know their first names until I was an adult. Johnny met most of his friends through school, either in the classroom or on the track. One of those friends used to come to the house yodeling,

"Yo Johnny, Yo Johonny, Yo Johnny, Yoooooooo..."

My cousins, Anne and Jean, thought Johnny was like a movie star. To me he was just an older brother whom I didn't see very much. They wanted to sneak a peek at him, so I led them to him. We crept down the long second-floor attic hallway that ended at Johnny's bedroom. We stared at him studying a book or magazine. Anne thought he stopped reading and looked at us. We shot up and ran back down the long dark hallway, passing a small door leading into a scary attic.

We had three attics in our house. Each was a treasure trove of things to hide in and behind. They stored old clothes, boxes, and bookcases. The temperature in these attics was always uninviting. In winter, you'd freeze in there as if you were outside, and in summer you would choke from the humidity. They were spooky, like most attics. I had recurring dreams of ghosts locking me in these attics, never to be reunited with my family who lived right in the next rooms. I watched a lot of *The Twilight Zone* and monster movies.

Johnny had brought a few Christmas gifts for the youngest ones during his visit home that January. When he walked through the door one day, again with a sack over his shoulder, Bonnie was now certain he was Santa. He had a play kitchen set for her and a toy gun that shot plastic bullets for Chris.

- - -

"It was cool. I always liked it. But other than the gun, I just remember his bedroom upstairs, in the attic," my brother Chris says.

I interview Chris on October 26, 2008. He canceled the first two attempts at meeting within twenty-four hours before our scheduled time. I was certain there was something, other than Chris not being a master of his schedule, behind his cancellations.

My senses were right. I soon learned that bringing up old memories is not so easy for Chris, who was eight in 1970.

Chris and his family live in a new home in Tinley Park. It is beautiful. We chat in the kitchen before I begin the interview. I sit at the counter on a high stool against a black granite counter. Chris works at the range top facing me, preparing eggs and toast. He passes me a plateful of food, not accepting no. He is a most gracious host and a good cook, like our father.

After breakfast, Chris and I move to their cathedral-ceilinged living room. This is a bright and airy room with windows on two sides and a stone fireplace sandwiched between built-in bookshelves. I begin my interview with the simple question: "What do you remember about Johnny?" The long silence that follows tells me Chris has to search for the memories.

"Do you remember him calling you Ogoo and laying on the floor next to you, watching TV?" I prompt Chris.

"Yeah, that's right!" Chris says.

He is slightly more audible than his previous few words, and he continues.

"I can remember watchin' TV in the TV room. I'd be up early on a Saturday and he'd come down. Were you with us when he was doin' that?" Chris asks me.

"Yeah, I can remember watching TV and you'd be lying next to him like he was your protector."

Chris was three or four at the time. He was waif-like at that age and was clinically diagnosed as malnourished. We all just forgot to make sure he ate. His stomach became distended and the veins started to show in his head, through his ghostlike skin. For a short time, he had the nickname Ghostie.

- - -

When Johnny was a young boy, Uncle John, my mom's youngest brother, was off studying with the Christian Brothers in Minnesota. Uncle John completed his studies and returned to the Chicago area at the age of twenty-six. He began teaching at St. Francis High School, where he first learned of cross-country as a high school sport. It was at this time he became a big influence on Johnny, who was then an early teen. He planted the seed of cross-country in Johnny's mind. As a freshman Johnny stood no taller than 5 feet 4 inches. Uncle John observed that cross-country provided an opportunity for the smaller boys to compete and helped them develop self-esteem by allowing the boys to be recognized as individuals while at the same time contribute to a team. This sport involved three-mile-runs through woods and fields. Uncle John encouraged Johnny to join a cross-country team. He saw how Johnny's light physique would be an asset. It also challenged endurance and mental stamina, qualities from which Uncle John felt Johnny could benefit.

Uncle John's enthusiasm for cross-country spread to Johnny, as Johnny entered his first year at Marist High School. Uncle John suggested Johnny read the book, *The Loneliness of the Long Distance Runner*, by Alan Sillitoe. This book, along with his uncle's encouragement, instilled the love of running in Johnny.

As his competiveness developed during early high school years, it was important to Johnny to be part of a winning team— always. One evening Uncle John attended a St. Mel's vs. Marist basketball game hosted by Marist. Uncle John, being the athletic director of St. Mel's, had been invited to a pre-game dinner by the Marist athletic director and coaches, which he attended. The group at the pre-game event all knew of Johnny because of his track team performance and leadership. As the game went on, St. Mel's was stomping Marist. During halftime Uncle John went to the concession booths to say hello to Johnny, where he was working, yet he was nowhere to be found. Uncle John later asked my mom what had happened to Johnny.

"He was so embarrassed by Marist's performance he didn't want to see you," she replied.

Johnny did well in school and wanted to be the best at cross-country. Yet, Marist did not form a cross-country team until his senior year. So he competed in city meets, which Uncle John enrolled him in and attended. Johnny practiced and trained hard for cross-country. He had measured the block our farm was on by driving the station wagon around it. It was a twelve-mile hilly course littered with wild dogs. This did not stop him. He ran around that block with a sawed off baseball bat he had crafted from Dad's tools to defend himself against the pack dogs.

Occasionally, Mimi warmed up on the farm road alongside Johnny as he prepared for his long runs. She bent at the waste to touch her toes as he did, and then jogged in place, like Johnny. From the moment she was born, Mimi had a face for Gerber (modeling). In addition to her adorable looks, Mimi was a little actress. She was aware of the attention she got as she mimicked her big brother on the road and loved it. We all laughed as we watched, yet Johnny paid her no mind. He was too focused on what lay ahead of him.

Johnny ran track all four years at Marist High School. His senior year he was appointed team captain of their first cross-country team. Johnny racked up enough miles to be one of three boys on his team to make the 1,000-mile club. His coach told my parents he was a good captain and a comfortable leader. I think this was because of all of the practice he had bossing around my brothers. I attended one of his meets when I was about eight. I followed my parents amidst the crowd, watching the older boys stampede through the woods of 87th and Western. By the end of his senior year's season, Johnny was one of the top cross-country runners in the Chicago Catholic boys' high school division. His love for running inspired him to write the poem, "What Is a Runner," his senior year of high school.

WHAT IS A RUNNER?

He is one who is too small and scrawny to make
the football team and too uncoordinated to make
the baseball or basketball team.
This is a runner?

He is a reject from all other types of sports.
He is the one the football coach tells to put on
a little weight and come back next year. He is
The one that the basketball coach tells to grow
a little more and practice the free-throws then
come back next year.
This is a runner?

He is the one who is so dejected from being cut from
all the glory sports that he figures he might just
as well be a book-worm all his four years in high
school.
This is a runner?

He may be small, tall, fat, or skinny.
He may be smart, dumb, or a loner, but he is
not mediocre.
This is a runner?

He is the most foolish, patriotic, stupid, self-sacrificing, reliable, unpublicized, unglorified, painful, lonely, lungiest, and leggiest athlete there is in the school.
This is a runner?

He is the one who knows that there isn't any glory in running ten miles or more or pushing himself beyond the point of pain. That there are no nice little blonde or brunette cheerleaders to stand on the sidelines and cheer.
This is a runner?

He is the one who knows that he is out there all alone and that he cannot blame anybody else but himself if he does bad. He knows he can't blame or pawn off any excuse on somebody else like a guard, tackle, first baseman, or forward.
This is a runner?

He is the one who gets up half asleep at the crack of dawn to run 15 miles or more, come back to work all day, then run again at sunset. He lives, sleeps and dreams running. What type of fool is this?
This is a runner?

He is the one who says "no thanks" to a cigarette, or a drink of beer and whiskey. It is the runner who stays in on Friday night and gets nine hours of sleep before a meet instead of going out and

drinkin' with the guys. He is one who ignores all wisecracks, stones, beer cans, and sticks that are thrown at him as he runs down the street in his gym shorts. He ignores dog bites, swallowed mosquitoes and bugs, thorns, rain, snow, blazing heat, and a stone in the shoe to keep running.
Yes, this is a runner.

He is the benny who finds out that he is slow when he thought he was as fast as Jim Ryun. He is one who discovers he doesn't look too good in shorts and has knobby knees. He is a boy who sticks with it and runs 12 months out of the year to make himself better and faster.
This has got to be a runner.

He is one sad boy when he discovers that all his practicing seems as though it is and was in vain because he still isn't the fastest one on the team.
This must be a runner.

He is a senior who finds out that four years of hard, grueling, and monotonous training has paid off. That all the times he pushed a little harder and a little faster to come across the finish first, to ache so much that he falls to the ground gasping for air, has paid off tremendously and that he is now the fastest one on the team.
This is truly a MAN.

By John Guldan

Grandpa didn't miss any of Johnny's high school cross-country meets at the Dan Ryan woods. My mother's father was the traditional grandpa—kind and patient, always with a LifeSavers® roll of candy in his pocket, ready to hand out. Johnny and Grandpa had a close relationship, as I learned from my aunts and uncles. Grandpa trusted only Johnny to clean and install his storm windows every fall and replace them with screens in the spring.

At various times throughout Johnny's high school years Jimmy had shared a second-floor bedroom with him. Once a week, Jim lay on Johnny's bed and quizzed him on his Latin spelling tests.

"Don't mix up the order," Johnny scolded.

"Well they're not going to give you the words in the exact order so you have to be prepared," Jim quipped back.

Johnny had a very serious side to him, whereas Jim was a joker. Not that Johnny didn't joke around, but the joking just wasn't incessant. By his senior year, Johnny was 5 feet 8 inches and carried all 68 of those inches as if he were six feet tall. Jimmy coveted his big brother's leadership. His circle of friends thought Jim was great, but to command the respect that Johnny did from his peers was a feat Jim had not mastered.

Johnny was not only a leader but also a teacher. He showed Jimmy how to defend himself against someone coming at him with a knife. This involved the choreography of three or four moves flowing together in a discipline they called "Tie Qwon Doe"—that's how I spelled it. Knowing this form of self-defense could be quite useful if one ventured too far outside the boundaries of Beverly. Johnny also taught my brothers the basics of boxing. Johnny was a Golden Gloves boxer at some point in high school. He use to practice at the Golden Gloves gym in

Chicago. It was there he met Cassius Clay (later known as Muhammad Ali). Johnny looked up to Mr. Clay, who represented himself as a passive, nonviolent man. Although Mr. Clay used the reason of religious contradiction to keep himself out of jail for refusing to fight in Vietnam, Johnny continued to hold out respect for Clay.

Occasionally, a few fellow boxers came over and boxed with Johnny in our basement. Dad had mounted a boxing bag to the basement ceiling so Johnny could practice. Johnny would roll his gloved fists against it in a speedy, rhythmic motion. I'd stare at the two—his hands, the bag—waiting for him to lose pace with it. He never did. This routine always ended with him grabbing that little bag with both hands and stopping it in mid-motion. Every time I tried this, while standing on a chair, the bag hit me in the face. I'd watch him jump rope. That same rhythmic motion flowed between Johnny and the rope that flowed between Johnny and the punching bag.

- - -

Uncle Mike remembers Johnny coming to De La Salle High School's locker room after a few football games.

"Something was special about that," he says.

Uncle Mike, one of my mother's brothers, joined the United States Army Reserve Officers' Training Corps (ROTC) while at Marquette University. He graduated in the mid-fifties. After college he served six months full time in the Army and then completed his reserve time, all during a period of peace. While in the reserves, Uncle Mike taught history and English and coached football at De La Salle High School. After several years of teaching, Uncle Mike went to work at Grandpa's firm, Bansley & Kiener. At this time he also attended night school at DePaul and earned his CPA. While attending DePaul, he played rugby and softball. A fellow rugby player introduced him to Aunt Diane, from St. Ignatius parish on the north side of Chicago, now referred to as Rogers Park. Aunt Diane and Uncle Mike married and had four children.

Uncle Mike and Aunt Diane had been married for forty-three years with six grandchildren when I interview them. They have lived in Evanston, Illinois, all of those years, most of them in the home they are in today, a large, brick bungalow on a narrow tree-lined street, a couple of blocks from Northwestern University's Dyke Stadium. Before he got married and had a family of his own, Uncle Mike spent a lot of time with Patti, Johnny, and Mariann. I ask Uncle Mike if he remembers Johnny as a young boy.

"Absolutely. He was my oldest nephew!" he replies.

Uncle Mike went to the beach, amusement park, and zoo with Patti, Johnny, and Mariann. He recounts his experience with them at River View, a popular Chicago-area theme park. They ranged from about nine to eleven years old at that time. Mariann and Patti were together in a car of the roller coaster while Uncle Mike and Johnny rode in another car.

"Johnny was so scared," he laughs, "he was on the floor of the roller coaster and he says to me, 'I'll never go on another ride with you again Uncle Mike—never. I don't know why you take me!'" Johnny was about ten years old. Uncle Mike tells me this and finishes, "he was a lot of fun to be with. Good memories of that,"

I learn that Johnny Gallagher, Annie Laurie's oldest child and my mom's godson, occasionally joined Uncle Mike and the three oldest. Mom was first-born in the Bansley family. Her sister, Annie Laurie, two and a half years younger, was second oldest, then came Uncle Jim, followed by Mike and then John.

"Jimmy was the first boy in the Bansley family in quite a few decades. He's been a celebration ever since," Uncle Mike says.

We both have a good laugh. Over the years, I have admired how Uncle Mike could traverse the serious to the light-hearted view of a situation in one breath. He was the symbol of stoicism when he stood at the altar's pulpit the day his son, Michael, was put to rest. Uncle Mike, with his booming voice, told us about the courage and beauty of young Michael's life. I was amazed he could deliver that oration without falling apart. Neither Uncle Mike nor Aunt Diane talk much about their Michael's death, or his life, other than that day on the altar.

"I had fun. They were very well behaved kids. I had absolutely no trouble managing them at all. I mean they were fun to be with, the three of them," Uncle Mike says.

- - -

Johnny's relationship with his uncles began as a toddler, when he spent a lot of time with both of our grandparents. Nan and Pop, my dad's parents, lived a few blocks south of my mother's parents. I had thought that Grandpa Guldan acquired his nickname, "Pop," from his ritual of bringing us popsicles on Sundays. Yet, it was during Dad's service in Korea, when two-year-old Johnny was always looking for his daddy. He called the mailman, "Daddy." When arriving for a visit to my grandparents during Dad's absence, Johnny ran up and jumped into Grandpa Guldan's arms, screeching, "Poppy!"

Three years into her marriage, Mom found herself in California with two toddlers and a baby on the way. Dad was stationed at Fort Ord on the Monterey Bay from 1951 to 1952 and then was shipped to Okinawa for a year to serve as an army dentist in the Korean War. He had attended Notre Dame and

Loyola before he was accepted to Northwestern, where he earned a dental science degree (DDS) prior to the service. Mom was an army wife, taking care of her children alone, pregnant and in a strange place, once Dad was shipped an ocean away. Even then, at less than five years old, Patti was old enough to help.

My mother was very close to her parents and missed them dearly when she moved across the country. She was heavily dependent on them in the first ten years of her marriage. Mom adored her father and it was clear that she was the apple of his eye from the baby journals and photo albums he had kept. When she was very young, Grandpa occasionally traveled to New York on business. It seemed to him that each time he went, someone he knew died. This made him superstitious about traveling far from home, and so he seldom did. Grandma was much more of a traveler. She flew out to California and packed Mom up when it was getting close to the date for my mother to deliver Mariann, her third child. Grandma, my mom, Patti and Johnny all flew back to Chicago, without my father. He had several months left on his Korean War tour and it was agreed that Mom would deliver back home, where her parents and younger brother John lived. Uncle John was ten years younger than my mother, who affectionately referred to him as "the baby." He was a junior in high school when Mom, Patti, and Johnny returned from California to live with him and her parents. Mariann was born a few months later.

After Dad's service, they all settled back in Beverly in a one-story brick home built by Pop. This modest little house was but a few blocks away from both of their parents. Mom and Dad spent the next six years of their marriage in this home and added six more children to their crew of three. Right before I was to arrive, they moved to our bungalow on Oakley, a short walk from their first home.

With ten children under the age of eleven, my mother was devastated when Grandma suffered a debilitating stroke in 1961. I was two when this occurred, so I knew my mother's mother as only in a wheelchair or lying in her hospital bed. I never heard her voice. Grandpa set her up with round-the-clock care, put her bed in the dining room and built a ramp out the back door of their home, on Leavitt Street. Their red-brick green-shuttered home was across from the playground of the public elementary school and one block from our church and school, Christ the King.

My mother got along with everyone, even the people she didn't like, although you could count them on one hand. Her mother-in-law would have been one of those few. Nan went to church every day, prayed the rosary, and blessed herself with the holy water she kept in her bedroom. She had one of those holy water vessels hanging on the wall. The kind you dipped your finger in at church.

My father had one sister, Alice, who was a few years older. They seemed close. They were always friendly toward each other. I was close with my cousins from that side, although we didn't see them as often as my Bansley cousins. They lived in the neighboring parish of Saint Walters, still within the Chicago boundaries. We visited them about once a month. On holidays and birthdays we saw them at Nan and Pop's house. Nan gave us baths when we slept overnight. She scrubbed so hard behind my ears it hurt. But her bathtub was really cool. It was midnight-blue and so were the tiles surrounding it. Nan and Pop's house was like a museum. I was careful not to touch anything. I never liked to sit on their couch because the plastic coverings stuck to the back of my legs. Nan paid Joe and me to clean for her. I dusted the few spots where I could find any dust and the few specks of dust came floating back down on top of the furniture. When I said I was done, she inspected my job and asked me if I had dusted.

"I did. Honest I did," I told her and then showed her how the few dust specks fell back on the dresser after I wiped it.

It wasn't all bad though. Nan played fun board games with us, the kind where you learned things. I enjoyed the challenge and soon mastered the one that taught spelling. My brother Joe didn't like them so much. He struggled and Nan had a lot of patience waiting for him to finish spelling e-l-e-p-h-a-n-t or v-i-o-l-i-n. I could tell he didn't really want to play, but he was a good sport and usually played anyway.

Joe, fifteen months older than me, was sometimes mistaken as my twin while we were growing up. Even though he jabbed a jump rope handle down my throat when we were about four and five, causing me to almost choke to death, we were close. He had to repeat third grade, so after that we were in the same grade.

I did not know my older brothers so well. Occasionally I had a spat with Jim or Bill, but I usually stayed away from them. I hardly ever saw Johnny; only when he'd watch TV with us or when I'd go to his room to bring him his glasses or tell him something my mother wanted.

- - -

"I didn't really know him until we got married, and he was in our wedding," Aunt Diane says.

"He was in our wedding," Uncle Mike says, almost in unison with his wife.

"Johnny, Patti, and Mariann were all in our wedding," Uncle Mike adds.

I was five years old when Aunt Diane and Uncle Mike married in 1964. I remember their wedding day. We had

McDonald's for dinner. There were bags full of hamburgers and fries. I remember what a treat it was and wished there were more family weddings.

"He didn't have anything to eat. He was getting very faint. He was fourteen and smart enough to go across the street to a little grocery," Uncle Mike says, while still thinking about Johnny at his wedding.

"He left the altar and went across the street to Anderson's Bakery," Aunt Diane interjects as she chuckles. This was her hometown. She knew the stores.

". . . and got a little chocolate milk and a donut or a Twinkie," Uncle Mike adds.

"I don't know what stage the mass was in at that point," Aunt Diane says.

It was a noon mass and most of the wedding party had not eaten anything since early that morning. Uncle Mike and Aunt Diane hadn't noticed Johnny's absence at the altar. They were preoccupied with the ceremony and with each other. In fact, no one at the altar noticed that he wasn't there.

"We only found out later," Uncle Mike says, recalling that he learned Johnny had almost fainted.

- - -

Johnny did faint once, but not at a wedding; it was at a baptismal service at Christ the King church. Aunt Barbara and Uncle Jim's seventh child, Johnny, was being baptized. My brother Johnny was to fill in for the godfather, who couldn't make it due to heavy snow. When Johnny began to feel faint he made a dash for some fresh air. On his way he crashed into a solid glass door and fell to the ground, unconscious.

In 1970, Uncle Jim and Aunt Barbara had had eight of their eventual twelve children. Their oldest daughters, Jean and Anne, were like sisters to me. Anne and I attended kindergarten together. All three of us went to Christ the King (also known as CK) school and wore the same uniform every day until fifth grade. That is when I transferred to the public school while Jean and Anne remained at CK. On weekends we took turn sleeping at each other's homes. Jean and Anne liked the better choice of breakfast cereals at my house, although they were afraid of my father. I liked staying at their house because it was fun and crazy with lots of younger kids. Though it was always great fun, after a weekend at the Bansley's house, I did like going back to the comfort of my own home.

When I stayed at my cousins', Aunt Barbara often had an art project for us. I liked my Aunt Barbara. She taught me how to sew. She held organized sewing lessons at her house for Jean, Anne, and I. I didn't like the time Aunt Barbara cut our hair—very short. I almost fainted trying to sit still, for what felt like hours, while she snipped and snipped some more. Aunt Barbara let me go on the Girl Scouts camping trip one year even though I was not a troop member—she was the Girl Scout leader and could decide who came and who didn't. However, the next year she explained to me that it wasn't fair if I went camping again without attending their weekly meetings and activities like all the other girls. And so I did not go camping with the Girl Scouts again.

My mother appreciated Aunt Barbara's help but I think she was intimidated by her. Maybe it was just that Mom didn't know how to take the five-foot-seven, opinionated, slightly eccentric women's lib person Aunt Barbara was. These two women, mothers of twelve and thirteen children, spent a lot of time helping each other through motherhood and marriage over the years. One summer Aunt Barbara stayed at our farm, watching seventeen kids while my mom was back in Chicago recovering from a miscarriage. Johnny was about eleven years old then. One day Aunt Barbara was driving on the winding country roads with Johnny in the passenger seat beside her. She turned a blind corner and came upon two cows in the middle of the road, one on top of the other. She screamed. Johnny laughed.

"Oh, Aunt Barbara, haven't you ever seen two cows mating?" Johnny asked.

It was a first for her. She was horrified.

During this same period at the farm Johnny worked with Uncle Jim to get a lantern lit during a blackout—the electricity was very temperamental at that old farmhouse. Johnny and Uncle Jim had set the lantern on the hood of the station wagon, right outside. There they were able to catch the moon's rays to provide some light by which to work. They must have worked on that thing for about twenty minutes when finally, they got it started. As they lifted their heads from the lantern and cheered their brilliant efforts, they noticed that the lights were on in the farmhouse. Uncle Jim yelled to Aunt Barbara, "How long the lights been on?"

"Oh, 'bout fifteen minutes," she replied.

It is those additional fifteen minutes he shared with Johnny that Uncle Jim remembers today.

In the fall of 1968, Johnny left home for Ohio. Defiance College had offered him a cross-country scholarship, which cinched his decision on colleges. He also liked the name—Defiance. With the security blanket of college to protect him, there was little to no chance of being drafted and going to Vietnam. However, Johnny was restless during his first year of college. He wrote home and repeatedly told my parents how unhappy he was there. He lasted only half of his freshman year at

Defiance. For the second half he transferred to Bogan, now known as Daley College, a community college he commuted to from home. He ran on Bogan's track team that spring and had plans to run on their cross-country team the following fall. But Dad was unhappy with Johnny's choice to come back home. He put pressure on Johnny to make plans for his future. So Johnny began making plans.

Stirrings

"We baby boomers grew up in the aftermath of the 'Good War' and in the fifties we really believed in America. . . . Then along comes Vietnam and every ideal was totally destroyed. I think that shock threw an entire generation into moral abyss and I don't think we've crawled out of it yet."

—Christian G. Appy, *Patriots*,
Fred Branfman interview,
American humanitarian in Laos 1967-1971

During his first days at Bogan Junior College, early 1969, Johnny began to drop the idea of joining the Marines to those around him. Denise had a few weeks left of her senior year in high school when Johnny told her he didn't feel right being in college when guys his age were over in Vietnam getting killed. My brother Jimmy noticed this shift in Johnny when Johnny moved back home after leaving Defiance. They shared a room again and, because of that, I guess, some private moments, too. Jimmy lay in bed one evening, falling asleep to the radio. Johnny walked into their room as a newscast reported that some Chicago-area boys had been killed in combat. He turned up the volume and listened intently. Another evening that spring, Johnny walked by the TV while Jimmy was watching a news flash of war footage. Johnny stopped and stared as he watched the report on young men his age dying for our country.

Johnny's choice to join the Marines was the beginning of much discussion, argument, and distress within the walls of the home I loved.

"Go to school instead and become an officer. Why do you want to join the Marines? They get the dirty work," my father told Johnny. I guess this only made Johnny more determined to prove his way was right.

My mother chose few battles with my father. It was just too much work to argue with him. One battle she did choose came late one summer night at our farm.

"If anything happens to him I will never forgive you," my mother said.

The walls were thin and there were open vents in the floors. Patti clearly heard my mother's angry voice as she lay in bed trying to fall asleep after a fun Saturday night with friends at the casino in Waupaca. It was one of the few times Patti had heard Mom so angry. Mom rarely disagreed with our father, but that night he could not appease her, no matter how hard he tried to convince her that Johnny would be fine.

If anything happens to him I will never forgive you— became a permanent fixture in our family home. Like the dining room table in the middle of our TV room, it didn't seem to fit, yet our acceptance of it came with our silence as we positioned ourselves around it and under it. Eileen, Margie, and Billy all heard our mother say this to our father on another occasion that summer. Johnny heard it too. He was standing right there.

"I'll never forgive you if anything happens to him in Vietnam."

This time my father didn't respond. Johnny didn't either.

- - -

Aunt Diane tells me that Johnny wanted to go back to school but my father put the "kibosh" on those plans.

"That's what we heard. That may not be very—" Uncle Mike begins to say.

" . . . So what he did was join the Marines instead of going back to school," Aunt Diane finishes over Uncle Mike's words.

"That's where your controversy with your mom and your dad supposedly was," Uncle Mike says. He calls this "my controversy," because my questions are targeted on this issue.

"I know your mom was very, very upset about that," Aunt Diane continues.

"Yes, she was very upset about that," Uncle Mike quietly adds.

"And she supposedly said -"

Aunt Diane does not complete the sentence as I interrupt, "Yes, I know what Mom said."

"'He better come home alive, John, or I'll never forgive you.' Now that's what we heard," Aunt Diane says.

When speaking with Margie about this "controversy," I learn that she too was aware of my mother's notorious words.

"I thought she was goofy," Margie says, recalling that she thought Mom was being overly dramatic and pessimistic. Although I was not aware of this argument between my parents, years later when I was informed of it by my older sisters, I, like Margie, was confused as to why my mother would have ever blamed my father. After all, it was Johnny's decision to join the Marines—my father had been dead set against it. Thirty years later, my sister Margie explains.

"It was the oldest-son-syndrome," Margie says.

"Johnny had this thing about proving something to Dad, when he was probably trying to prove it to himself," I say.

"Like he was a man or something," Margie adds.

The two of us—women—were trying to figure out this male father-son thing. We couldn't.

- - -

I watched a made-for-TV movie sometime around 2010. It showed an older couple, probably in their sixties, whose son had died, but not recently. The woman's words were brief and terse, attaching an air of resentment to the dialogue she exchanged with the man. She made a few remarks that clearly indicated she blamed her husband for their son's war-related death. She said their son would not have joined if the father hadn't pressured him. Their dead son's name was Johnny. Were we a textbook family? A cliché?

Even with the underlying battle about Johnny's choice, my parents were affectionate with each other. Many mornings I watched my dad come into the kitchen and give my mom a big bear hug as she stood over the stove, in her bathrobe, stirring his oatmeal. Before I was old enough to remember, Dad used to come home for dinner and then go back to work. By the time I was ten, he no longer kept late hours, but still did not eat dinner with us many evenings. Mom didn't serve the meal until Dad got home, which was usually 7:00 P.M. I was starving by then. The table was usually crowded with all of us seated around it eating dinner, except Dad. He ate in his bedroom on a TV table, watching television. While emotion ranged the gambit on a daily basis with my father, my mother was the stabilizing factor of the household. Without her patience and consistency, it would have been a much different set of dynamics within the four walls of our home.

Balance was a constant struggle—for both my family and our country. My parents and their generation were loyal followers of our country's leaders. Their loyalty was admirable yet involved a trust that was not deserved. Following this period of obedience came the crazy, rebellious, and sometimes violent seventies.

- - -

"Martin Luther King was killed in April of '68, Bobby Kennedy in June, the democratic convention in August, which was a total mess. All that just added to the upheaval of this anti-Vietnam War," Uncle Mike states.

I am trying to understand the meaning of this reference since it was actually the year before Johnny went into the Marines.

"As a young man he was really in the throws of—" Aunt Diane begins.

"Yeah, he was really goin' against the tide," Uncle Mike says.

"Peace and love and hippies and all kinds of stuff goin' on, so," Aunt Diane says.

"It was the age of Aquarius," Uncle Mike adds.

I was grateful for the lesson my aunt and uncle were giving me. I realize that when I was growing up, teenagers spoke out. They didn't fall into step like my parents' generation. Six of my siblings were teenagers at that time. My parents had their work cut out for them.

"I don't know how accurate this is: Ricky DeWolf coached Johnny at Christ the King or was involved with Johnny at Christ the King, somehow," Uncle Mike says. "And Rick had been over there [Vietnam] and injured and came back and coached. Again, I don't know how accurate it is but Rick, supposedly, had a great influence on Johnny goin' there. Because Rick, not to glorify him, said 'there's a lot of kids over there, and they're really, really subject to an awful lot of terror and hunger and exposure.'"

"Oh, little children?" I ask.

"Yup," Uncle Mike continues. "Rick supposedly said now that, um, 'I really felt like I was helpin' these kids, to get to a better life.'"

"I just always thought it was," Aunt Diane interrupts, "because I remember Eileen saying, 'If he'd gone back to school this wouldn't have happened.' But we can 'If' our lives away, ya know."

- - -

At the time, Johnny was working a summer job in Chicago and went to Grandpa's office at Bansley & Kiener at lunch to tell him he had enlisted. Johnny had spent the previous summer working for Grandpa and enjoyed it but when the opportunity to work at the Board of Trade came it was too exciting to pass up. Uncle Mike had been discussing work and family with Grandpa when Johnny walked in. They were expecting him. After a brief, warm greeting Johnny got right to the point.

"I'm joining the Marines."

Upon hearing this, Uncle Mike was flooded with conflicting feelings. He was proud to have a nephew serve our country, yet was consumed with anxiety over the possibility of losing his nephew coupled with the concern as to what horrors this gentle boy would face. Uncle Mike knew Johnny would be dealing with events much more frightening than the Bobs at River View.

Uncle John was surprised and saddened to hear Johnny had enlisted. Uncle John, in his early thirties at the time, was disappointed that his influence on Johnny did not prevent this choice. He had spoken to Johnny about the war and made it clear that he strongly opposed it. Uncle Mike and Grandpa weren't as strongly opposed to the war as Uncle John, yet they tried to guide Johnny away from Vietnam just the same. Johnny told them he didn't like school and was getting hassled by Dad. Based on the

Vietnam War's draft system, his high draft number and enrollment in college would have guaranteed that he'd be bypassed in the draft.

- - -

"There was enough in society that was saying, 'Hey, this war makes no sense,'" Uncle John tells me. "You [referring to me during the interview] met those people there [in Vietnam]. They're not a war-like people."

He was right. I had traveled all the way to Vietnam in 2007 to learn the Vietnamese were not aggressive people. Yet this man, my Uncle John, knew that back in 1969 without having set foot outside of the Midwest. After college, he had taught at all boys high schools as a De LaSalle French Christian Brother. My 2008 interview with my mom's youngest brother was a lesson in history.

- - -

Prior to 1960, fighting in a war was considered an honorable thing. World War I and II, the Korean War, the Civil War—these events are associated with such glory. Hollywood capitalized on the romance of war with the 1960's show Combat! and the actor Audie Murphy, a famous World War II veteran-turned-actor. Margie saw that this actor was one of Johnny's heroes and she was sure that what Johnny saw on television played a part in his decision.

The truth of what happened in these glorious wars wasn't talked about amongst the general public until World War II combat was exposed in Tom Hanks' Saving Private Ryan and Ken Burns' war documentaries. These movies allowed a lot of World War II veterans to come forward and show their tears and emotional scars as a result of what they experienced. Ken Burns' 2007 television series on World War II showed interviews of the veterans fifty years after they fought. These men were visibly saddened as they spoke of the things they saw and the friends they lost.

There were only a few young boys in our neighborhood who had been drafted or enlisted prior to Johnny's enlisting. Joe Heeney was one of them. Johnny looked up to Joe. He became a close friend and confidant when Johnny began considering the service. Like Johnny, Joe had chosen the Marines. Joe Heeney's family lived nearby in a solid-built brick two-flat. Joe's mom rented out one of the flats. This added income, along with the Heeney Funeral Home they ran, helped Mrs. Heeney, widowed at the prime of her life, keep her two growing boys fed. Mrs. Heeney was alone with her youngest son, Mike, when Joe Heeney went off to Vietnam. Families with single parent heads were rare in our neighborhood in the early 1970s. There was no support system except for a few caring neighbors, like my mother. Mom called Mrs. Heeney from time to time, to see if she needed anything or just to say hello.

Women have always been good at supporting each other. My mother and her sister Annie Laurie were two and a half years apart. When Annie Laurie lived on Green Street in Beverly, she and my mom talked on the phone every day. Yet, in 1967 Annie Laurie and Uncle Jack moved to a suburb outside of Detroit, reducing their phone calls to once a week due to the high long distance charges. Annie Laurie was no longer in close touch with what was going on with her sister's children. So the subject of Johnny going into the service was never discussed in their brief weekly calls. Suddenly Johnny was in the Marines! Annie Laurie didn't know Johnny had actually made this decision. She thought he stood in a line with all the other young men that had been drafted or enlisted, and they were chosen randomly for the various divisions. Army, Navy, Marines—someone pointed and decided with a glance. Johnny was tossed—"Marine."

One thing Annie Laurie did know was that there were an awful lot of issues between my father and Johnny during this time. She was also well aware of the threat my mother made. My mother never mentioned the possibility of divorce to her sister, yet years later confessed to me that she had considered it. Women in those days did not talk about such things. Not even to their sisters.

Theories

War is a drug. . . . It can give us what we long for in life. It can give us purpose, meaning, a reason for living. And war is an enticing elixir. It gives us resolve, a cause. It allows us to be noble.

—Chris Hedges,
War Is a Force That Gives Us Meaning

There were a handful of theories as to what would have made Johnny drop out of school to fight in a war. I believed Johnny was a master boxer and kung fu artist, so who else was better equipped to go overseas and clear the villains out of that country. Johnny showed us some self-defense moves. He gave Joe, Mick, and I a paperback instructional booklet with illustrations of figures in karate outfits. I stared at the drawings of the little people on the pages in their white garb and mimicked the movements until I could do it in one flowing action. Then I practiced on my younger brother or sister.

- - -

When my sister Eileen thinks about the summer of '69, she remembers that Dad was not happy with Johnny's decision to join the Marines. Eileen's earliest memory of Johnny is his role as a bumblebee in a dance recital. Mom made him take tap when he was five or six. Although Eileen couldn't have been more than three years old, she remembers how Johnny hated this. These feelings were apparent from the pout on his little face as he posed in that bumblebee suit for a photo.

"He had lipstick on!" Eileen says.

"I can't believe Dad let Mom do that! Maybe this was Johnny's deep-rooted reason for joining the Marines. He had to prove his manhood after being forced to take tap and dress as a bumblebee . . . with lipstick on!" I say.

We both laugh.

Eileen and I meet at the restaurant in the Nordstrom's department store at Oak Brook mall for our interview. When I arrive, I cannot find her in the restaurant so I begin searching the store. I find her buying bathing suits and other summer garments for her daughters. Eileen's giving is bottomless. I wish I could be more like her.

Eileen is petite. She stands 5 feet 1 inch tall and weighs about 105 pounds soaking wet. She keeps herself well styled and has always looked younger than I, although I am five years her junior. She meets me for this interview after a manicure appointment, wearing a pair of dark stretch-jeans and a black silk T-shirt. Her jeans are accented with a two-inch black leather belt showing off a big blue turquoise stone in the middle of the buckle. I have often been her dance partner at weddings and nights out, doing the country-style swing. She is always fun to be with.

- - -

Dad tried, in Dad's way, to talk Johnny out of joining the Marines. He even called on the help of some friends and neighbors, Dick Barry being one of them. The Barrys lived on the corner in a sprawling, white-brick ranch. My mother often visited Mrs. Barry. Dick was five years older than Johnny and had begun serving a tour in Vietnam by the time Johnny decided to enlist. Dick had joined the Air Force a year out of high school, after spending a year working with the family business. At that time, Vietnam was not yet recognized as a war; it was referred to as a "conflict" by President Johnson.

At the age of 20, on December 10, 1965, Dick Barry began the first of the four years he had committed to the U.S. Air Force.

After training at the Lackland base, in Delaware, Dick was then assigned to Chaplain Services and sent on to Amarillo, Texas, for specialty training. Dover, Delaware, was his first assignment as a chaplain's assistant. Dover, although such a small town that the only public transportation in and out was a bus, was one of the two main U.S. bases that ran a military mortuary. The other was on the West Coast, at Travis Air Force base. Part of Dick's job at Dover was office work, while another responsibility of chaplain services was to inventory the retuning young men in the mortuary, where their bodies were prepared to be shipped home to their families. Dick learned the Marines made up the majority of the bodies coming back. Once he went to a returned serviceman's family to deliver the news—he requested never to have to do that again.

After two years of stateside service at the Dover, Delaware, Air Force Base, Dick volunteered to be sent over to Vietnam. In December 1968, Richard Barry headed to South Vietnam. He was 23 years old. His trip there began with a flight across the country to Washington State. After a week of paperwork in Washington, he traveled in a commercial airliner filled with men from all branches of the service, all heading to Vietnam. The seats were about eighteen inches wide, eight across, each one occupied, all the way to the back of the plane. Dick did not know a soul on that aircraft accompanying him to the other side of the world. Yet, oddly, he was looking forward to it. He was also a little nervous and excited. Fifteen hours later and one stop for fuel, Dick's flight landed. All passengers went off in different directions based on their orders. Dick reported to a serviceman at a desk that told him where to go to catch a ride to Pleiku. Dick arrived at Pleiku, where the after effects of the TET offensive were still apparent. Observing sand bags burst open, Dick realized that "this could be dangerous."

Soon after Dick arrived for duty in Southeast Asia, he received a letter from my oldest sister. Although there was a four-year age difference, they were on friendly terms. Taking advantage of this friendship, my father insisted Patti write to Dick, asking him to write to Johnny about what he might have to expect if he joined the Marines. Dick immediately did so, providing big-brother advice, telling Johnny, "Get into anything but the Marines. It may look glorious but it's not. Do something else." My father hoped that if Johnny could get the perspective of the Air Force versus the Marines, he might not join the Marines. Like Dick had learned, Dad knew the reputation of the Marines—they were the ones who cleaned up, the ones who were given the most dangerous jobs. Any other military unit was safer for his son than the Marines. So my father hoped that whatever Dick Barry had to say would tear away at Johnny's idealistic vision of a Marine in Vietnam.

It seemed Dick's letter did make an impact on Johnny, temporarily. Johnny wrote back, passionately telling Dick of his strong desire to serve our country and letting Dick know he had decided to join the Army. That was in February 1969. Yet, early in the summer of that same year, Johnny had decided to enlist in the Marines after all.

- - -

In the fall of 2012, I sit with Dick Barry and his wife, Cathy, in the kitchen of their suburban ranch home in a peaceful, wooded suburb southwest of Chicago. When asked why he signed up, Dick replies, "Vietnam was hot at the time and all my friends were being drafted. I was young and everyone was getting their stereo equipment over there by going to Hong Kong . . . [I] didn't want to go into the Army or Marines . . . [I] didn't want to be in the thick of the things. I wanted to have a nice bed to sleep in every night. When I got to Dover, because it was the only air force base on the East Coast accepting all the bodies that were coming back, then I got to see it was pretty serious. A lot of things you didn't hear . . ."

- - -

My father was a well-educated man, having attended St. Ignatius, a private college prep high school, and Northwestern University for undergrad work and dental school. He went into dentistry to placate his mother's wishes. Nan, my grandmother, did not want her son to be a plumber, like his father. She felt a tradesman job was beneath them and definitely would not have approved of farming for her son either.

Although he earned a living as a dentist, farming was my father's first love, aside from my mother of course. As soon as my father could, he bought a 137-acre farm in the middle of Wisconsin, which he dubbed "Guldan's Tooth Acres" and painted that on our mailbox. He continued to practice dentistry full time, while the farm remained his hobby. We had cattle, of the Hereford variety, three horses, and a Shetland pony named Snuffy. There were also sheep, chickens, rabbits, and cats at one time or another over the course of about twenty years. There were three main buildings and four smaller ones, one of which was an outhouse. The Victorian-style wood-frame house, red garage, and barn were the three largest buildings. There was a chicken coop, a milk shed, and small sheep shed across the road. The farm was without electricity and plumbing when my father purchased it. With the help of his father and some friends, he soon upgraded it to include these luxuries.

Guldan's Tooth Acres had a variety of terrain. There were rolling hills, wooded fields, flat, grassy pastures and a river. The expansiveness and beauty of the farm land made it mystical and at times wonderfully exciting to explore. There seemed always to be a new piece of a forest or field to probe. The parts of land that were farmed changed their makeup week by week, from growing period to harvest time. We ran through them, hid in them, and rode our horses all over them.

At the beginning of each summer, my dad attached the green metal trailer to the hitch on the station wagon, packed it full, covered it with a tarp, and moved us all to the farm. We'd depart at four a.m. on a Saturday in mid-June, right after school got out. We'd sleep in our clothes the night before so my parents could load us right into the car. I was always so excited about going to the farm that I could hardly sleep. Not all my siblings shared this sentiment. My brother Bill hated going to the farm each summer. He was not able to join the Beverly little league team and felt he missed a great deal.

The five-hour trips to the farm were not easy; we were all squished in our station wagon, Snowball included. Getting all of us in and out of the car at stops was a huge ordeal. If we didn't take our bathroom break when Dad stopped for gas, he would not stop if we needed to go later. I was the one who always needed another bathroom stop. My dad dubbed me "Tiny Tang Terr." One time when I really couldn't hold it, my sisters laid out a blanket in the back seat for me to pee in. I sure hope they threw that blanket away.

- - -

Joe recalls one of these long drives to the farm where Dad got so frustrated at Mom he pounded on the steering wheel.

"I swear to God that steering wheel was gonna bust right off," Joe says.

According to Joe; this "steering-wheel" argument was centered on finances. To my amazement, I do not remember this episode, although it was probably pretty frightening to think the steering wheel might break off the car you are riding in at seventy miles an hour. Maybe it's part of God's plan for each of us to remember unique events throughout our lives, and these memories are part of what shapes us into who we are.

- - -

Horses and cattle ran through our farm, but so did the Tomorrow River, a clear, flowing stream of fresh water. We swam, rafted, caught tad poles, and fished in it. Snowball knew where we were headed as soon as we put on our swimsuits. When we opened that porch door to head out, Snowball did what she rarely did otherwise—she left our mother's side and came down to the river to swim with us. Each season trout fisherman knocked on our door and asked to fish in the river on our property. Often, when we played in the river, swimming or floating down its current while stretched across inner tubes, fisherman in their rubber wading trousers, pole in hand, walked alongside us. Typically, we floated by them without a word, for we knew not to disturb their fish.

The river attracted the fishermen in the summer and the wooded acreage on the farm drew the deer hunters in the fall. During hunting season, we wore bright orange or red colors to help the hunters distinguish us from the deer. There were many opportunities for accidents on the farm yet our days there passed with few injuries. In the summer of 1968, Mimi was badly bitten by a dog we knew. We were at the home of close friends who lived near our farm. We were all gathering to take a group photo when their dog, unprovoked, attacked Mimi. The dog had been a part of this family for many years, but our neighbor did not hesitate to lay the dog down the following day. My father and his friend worked things out so that Mimi's medical bills could be shared between them. Mimi went to her first day of kindergarten that year with bandages on her face.

The long days of summer in the sixties and early seventies were a performance of well-choreographed plans. We were the actors and my parents the directors as they maneuvered us kids, ensuring we were all supervised appropriately. Half the family stayed with Mom at the farm during the week while the older girls stayed with my dad in Chicago. Jim and Bill provided some brawn for my mother when any heavy lifting or strength was needed to fix things around the farm that couldn't wait until Dad returned. They were both learning to drive, so my mom would let them drive into town for errands or fetch milk down at the neighbors' dairy farm, while she supervised in the passenger seat. I often think about how my mom felt when my dad left her alone on the 137-acre turn-of-the-century farm with eight or so children. He left her for three to four days every week. There was not a neighbor for a quarter mile in any direction, and only one party-line phone that was usually occupied by the voices of strangers. Sometimes this was quite fun for us kids. Not so for Mom. She did not love the farm.

During his weekends in Wisconsin, Dad worked hard; the boys did too. They farmed the land, fed the cattle, and repaired fences. The fields of alfalfa were harvested for hay, which then had to be stored in our barn to feed the cows and horses throughout the winter. Cows were eventually sold for meat or butchered for our own table. We bought a new cow or bull occasionally, even a new horse. I once watched Dad write a large check on the hood of our car for a thoroughbred. He bought it to breed but it never got pregnant. In addition to running the farm, Dad also had time for socializing with the neighbors. He'd invite them over to our place, exchange tools with them, and ask them for tips on farming. He probably even provided dental advice from time to time. One neighbor housed and milked our one dairy cow. We had free milk and Dad made cream, butter, buttermilk, and ice cream. It was delicious.

My father's Aunt Nora and Uncle Bill oversaw our farm when we were not there. They lived at the farm all year round, staying in their trailer home in the summer while we were all there and in the house during the winter. A small patch of fir trees separated Aunt Nora and Uncle Bill's little home from the farmhouse, providing privacy for them. I enjoyed the short walk through the tall pines to get to their little home. Aunt Nora and Uncle Bill were my godparents. I played canasta with Aunt Nora, and sometimes won. We snacked on beer sausage and Ritz, while Aunt Nora and Uncle Bill drank Point beer. Occasionally, I was invited to sleepover, squeezing into the small bed with large Aunt Nora, at one end of the trailer, and listening to Uncle Bill snore in his bed at the other end of the trailer. I felt special all summer long.

The same fir trees that separated the house from their trailer provided a roof during the hot summer days when Aunt Nora tutored us kids. She gave us workbooks, coloring books, pencils, and crayons. Most weekdays, Aunt Nora had our attention while we sat at the oblong metal fold up table under the fir trees. She saw to it that we maintained some structure and mental training during those long summer months. It also brought some sense of peace to my mother that we all could be accounted for during these few hours each day while she hung laundry, prepared meals, ran errands, and kept baby Bonnie content with Space Food Sticks and Tang.

In midsummer, Dad squeezed in a two-week vacation. Otherwise he arrived back at the farm each Friday evening. Sometimes he'd arrive before it got dark. In that case, we'd badger Mom to know exactly when she thought he'd arrive and walk down to the fork in the road to wait for Dad's car in the distance. Like clockwork he came. We chased after the car the short distance to the farm driveway, excited to see Dad and whichever sister was with him. On Tuesday mornings, Dad and one of my sisters would leave before everyone else woke and head back to the city to attend to his patients. This was our summer routine.

Occasionally, my father invited one of his patients or friends up to the farm. The guests would usually arrive with little warning to my mother. The summer of 1969, Johnny drove to the farm with the Vincents. By this time, Johnny had dropped the bomb that he had signed up for the Marines. The Vincents, close friends of my parents, attempted to dissuade Johnny from joining. Mr. Vincent, an FBI agent at the time, was well versed in civilian combat, yet knew the combat Johnny was heading toward was quite different. I had been playing in the yard while Mrs. Vincent sat on the nearby picnic table with Johnny. My father—woodworking being one of his hobbies—had made this picnic table. It was large enough to hold all twelve of us. Mrs. Vincent, a strong woman by appearance and demeanor, sat straddling the bench, facing Johnny who sat on the same bench a few feet away. As I headed towards them to see what was going on, it was apparent to me that I did not want to be included in their conversation. Something was up. Mrs. Vincent spoke seriously to Johnny, leaning toward him, her eyes reaching out as if trying to take hold of his face to look at her. Although Johnny did not look at her, he did not look uncomfortable with the conversation either. He was nodding, his head of thick dark brown hair bent slightly down. It seemed like he was listening closely to her.

"I won't ask you the question I'm sure you're sick of answering, 'Why are you enlisting?' I'm guessing you probably don't even know."

Johnny chuckled at Mrs. Vincent's directness—that's what he liked about her.

"Do you know what's going on over there, John?" He still wasn't looking at Mrs. Vincent.

"I've gotten letters from Joe Heeney and Tim Hansen. They're over there," Johnny replied.

"Do you think they'd give you the straight scoop? Do you think they'd write to you about it?"

Mrs. Vincent asked these questions knowing Johnny wasn't about to answer. She hoped he would think the whole process through. Johnny, still looking off, shrugged, the white t-shirt moving with his lean shoulders.

"I don't know," Johnny answered.

"My husband carries a gun. The first time he had to use it, he was a changed man."

Mrs. Vincent opened her arms wide and leaned over to Johnny. They hugged. "God bless ya," Mrs. Vincent said with watery eyes. She hugged him as if he was her own son. I stood and watched them from several feet away.

Adult stuff, I thought.

George Evans was a medic in the air force hospital at Cam Ranh Bay during the Vietnam War. It is not for his experience in Vietnam that I mention Mr. Evans but for his sense of something amiss among the World War II veterans he grew up around. I learned of Mr. Evans from one of the interviews in Christian Appy's book Patriots. Each Memorial Day celebrated during George Evans' childhood, George, his veteran father, and his father's veteran friends would decorate the grave of each soldier in a Pittsburgh cemetery with a small American flag. Some of them would tell George stories about the war and the soldier whose grave they attended if one of the WWII vets had known that particular one. Although the vets spoke of glorious heroes and events, George, even as a young boy, could tell there was a sadness, a void that hung in the air around their patriotism. If things were so great, why were they hanging out in bars telling the same old stories? George asked himself. This contradiction of messages about the war George received from these veterans developed an existence within him and continued beyond the years of hanging with these vets. George was lured in to the romance of the military and patriotism from an early age. He was not able to get that out of his system until he went to Vietnam in 1969 and experienced, first hand, what he sensed of war as a young boy—that contradiction of messages, the unspoken things. It was the same unspoken things Mrs. Vincent tried to warn Johnny about; the un-pleasantries of war no one mentions.

Johnny had talked little to Jim about why he chose to go to Vietnam. From Jim's perspective, Johnny had everything going for him. Johnny, working as a runner at the board of trade the summer he enlisted, communicated his restlessness to his younger brother Jim. "It's something I have to do." At sixteen, Jim was old enough to recognize that Johnny's high draft number and college deferment would have kept him out of the service, if Johnny wanted it so. Why would someone intentionally put himself in harm's way, Jim wondered.

"I want to do something for my country," Johnny told Jim before leaving for boot camp.

Still, this choice did not make sense to Jimmy. Since there was enough turmoil in our family, he did not advertise his feelings and doubt. He kept quiet in order to keep a balance in the family, a balance within himself. We believe we must engage in war in order for our society to survive, yet it tears at the basic structure of a society—family. This is a balance our government must keep.

That summer, before Johnny headed off to boot camp, my uncles made a special effort to spend time with him. Uncle Jim asked Johnny to help him put up a swing set in his backyard at 9323 Longwood Drive. Johnny worked all day, tirelessly, with Uncle Jim, assembling the swings, the slide, and then setting the poles into the fresh concrete. They didn't have any heavy talk about going off to war. They kept it light as they worked on that swing set. Uncle Jim shared with Johnny lighthearted stories of his Parris Island adventures, while in the service, and as a sailor in the Coast Guard.

My sister Patti questioned that war the summer of '69 as she was lying across the queen bed in the back room off the kitchen, flipping through the pages of a Life magazine. This bedroom had a long radiator running under a row of windows that looked out onto the backyard. Patti had become engrossed in this June copy of Life. There were hundreds of pictures of young servicemen in their dress blues, greens, and grays. Most were their boot camp graduation photos; each serious, determined and youthful. Some were photos of them out in the fields of Vietnam with guns in their hands. Patti studied these photos of Americans who had died in Vietnam within a single week. There was an astounding number of them. Page after page. As she was studying each dead person and his age, written in the caption under their photo, Johnny walked into the room. Patti rolled over and sat up on the bed. The spacious room allowed distance to hang between them. Patti picked up the magazine, open to a page of the photos. She showed Johnny and softly exclaimed, as much to herself as to Johnny, "You could be one of them!"

Johnny looked but did not respond. Patti began to realize that Johnny might not return home.

Boot Camp

I felt that my parents regarded me as an irresponsible boy who still needed their guidance. I wanted to prove them wrong.

—Philip Caputo, *A Rumor of War*

The day before Johnny was to fly out to the Marine camp in San Diego in August 1969, he and Denise took a walk together around Denise's short block and ended up on the curb at 106th and Maplewood. They walked slowly around that block, holding hands and talking a bit. When they reached Maplewood, they sat down on the corner and cried as they said their goodbyes. They weren't crying because they knew what Johnny was heading into. They didn't know what Johnny was heading into. They were crying simply because they would be apart, far away from each other, for a long time. Johnny proposed to Denise right there, ring and all. He asked her to marry him when he got back. This would not be the first time he proposed.

"Tell me not to go and I won't," Johnny said to Denise.

She would not. Although she wanted him to stay with all her heart, Denise knew he had something to do before they could begin their life together. She gave the ring back. She didn't refuse it on the grounds that she didn't want to marry him. Oh, she did want to marry him, and told him she would. She couldn't keep a ring and look at it each day on her finger and be confined to a desperate hope from its sight alone. Johnny had to go to Vietnam and fight. He had to be a Marine and Denise had to go on living her life.

"Hold on to it until you return," Denise told him.

She took his hand, pulled it up close to her face, placed the ring in it, and closed his fingers tightly around it. She placed her lips on his knuckles with one long, soft kiss. She then wrapped his arms around her waist and hers around his. They stood there, eternity passed around them while the sun's rays soaked them with warmth.

In August 1969, Johnny quietly headed off to boot camp. There was no going-away party, no brothers and sisters waving goodbye, and dog chasing after the car as it pulled away. We were all at the farm, most of us unaware of the fact he had left. My parents were very aware. Dad had driven Johnny back to Chicago after his last visit to the farm. When Johnny left, there was barely a goodbye between the two of them. Johnny attempted one. He went in to see my father, who was in his bedroom reading, with the television on, glasses perched at the end of his nose.

"If you join the Marines, I'll disown you," my father said to Johnny.

"All you had to do was say, 'don't go'," Johnny said.

He turned around, uttering these words as he walked out of the room. Johnny, sensing Dad's guilt, rubbed it in like a brush to a burn when he left that day. He thought he was outsmarting "the ol' man," as Johnny would refer to him in his boot camp letters to Denise. After this encounter, he proudly proclaimed in a letter to Denise how he left my dad nursing his wound. This was the reaction of a young boy, wanting something from his father that he couldn't get—reassurance. This came later, in that train depot parking lot, with a big, welcoming hug.

Johnny was a proud little boy who wanted so much to please, especially his father. Yet, when Johnny was about ten years old, he had done something that my father thought needed punishment. It was summer and our whole family was at the farm. At that time we had sheep, which were kept in a field across the road from the farmhouse. In that field was a little lean-to wooden shed with a dirt floor. It had one pane-less window adjacent to its small, door-less doorway. On the day my father was upset with Johnny, he ordered Johnny to go out and sit in this shed. My sister Margie was so upset to see her big brother sent out to this dirty place all by himself that she went and sat with him to keep him company.

"You've got to break his spirit," my father once said to me in reference to my son Kevin. This was after the three-year-old had reached across the counter and grabbed one of my father's nitroglycerin tablets that had spilled out of its bottle as my dad was opening it. Kevin popped it in his mouth and swallowed it before we could blink an eye. My dad believed that breaking a child's spirit was a parent's responsibility and the breaking in of a horse as an analogy; the horse's spirit has to be broken to some degree in order to calm it down enough to be trained, to be controlled by the rider on its back—the rider having the best interest of the horse in mind, of course. By breaking a child's spirit, a parent can then control the child, like the rider controls the broken horse, for the child's benefit and protection.

Now, with two adult children, I have experienced the paradox of parenthood, which is that fine balance between trying to control your child's choices and painfully watching him struggle.

Johnny arrived at the Marine Corps Recruit Depot-MCRD in San Diego and was assigned to the 3rd Battalion 1st Marines. His letter writing began soon after. Johnny wrote to my parents, Denise, and a couple of friends. He kept Mom and Dad informed through his letters, as to his life, although he had less than an hour each night to do so after a day starting at five a.m. He may have left home physically, but his heart was still connected.

Dear Dad,

This will be short & as you can see by the writing that lights are out. I want to tell you what happened today...

In this letter, Johnny proudly told Dad how his drill instructor (DI) had him run around a track with his army boots and M14 because he did not learn a drill quick enough. The DI finally stopped him and could not believe Johnny was not breathing hard. Johnny was amused to see that all of his disciplined cross-country training was beneficial in the Marines and shared that with Dad.

Throughout his boot camp days, Johnny often wrote about the antics of his DIs. DIs were not the most patient of humans. In fact, at times they did not appear human at all, as we all learned when he returned home after boot camp. My mother had to leave her nineteen-year-old son in the hands of the USMC. I think she was in constant prayer.

I read an article in Guidepost magazine written by a mother whose teenage son had joined the Marines. She described how she cried uncontrollably after she received the phone call from him after he had arrived at boot camp. She could hear the fear in the nineteen-year-old boy's voice as he tried to be brave while telling her he had gotten there. She went online to reach out to others who might understand what she was going through. There was an immediate response, which gave her a sense of support and comfort, something my mother did not have when her son went off to be trained for war. My mother did not even know enough to reach out. It's not the way things were done in 1970. Mom dealt with her nineteen-year-old son in severe conditions on his own, all on her own. A letter to my father telling him about his training added to her worry:

I am in close combat now & it is an accepted fact that I am being trained to kill & kill fast without hesitation. The physical stuff isn't bad...

A friend of my parents had a daughter, Gail, who was about Johnny's age. Johnny and Gail had been friendly with each other while in high school and I'm sure it didn't hurt that she was an attractive girl. Gail and Johnny kept in touch through letters. She must not have been aware he had left for boot camp and sent a letter to the farm. Unfortunately for her, one of her letters arrived in the "Guldan Acres" mailbox while my sister Mariann and Denise happened to be visiting the farm. Mariann collected the mail that day and noticed the letter to Johnny. I walked into the small linoleum-floored kitchen to find Mariann and Denise huddled over a pot of boiling water. They were munching on wild rhubarb they had picked along the barnyard corral's four-rail fence. The corral was used to herd the cows, one at a time, into a metal device that trapped their heads. It held them tight at the shoulders while the vet or my father performed any needed procedure or branding. Denise had a piece of rhubarb in one hand and an envelope in the other. She was holding this envelope over the steam billowing from the boiling water in the old metal pot on the gas stove. Something did not seem right.

"Whaddya doin'?" I asked.

"Steaming open a letter," Denise replied.

Mariann wasn't giving up any information. I continued asking questions, which Denise continued to answer. She was straightforward and frank. Denise and Mariann were steaming open a letter addressed to my brother Johnny, from another girl.

Denise and Mariann did not even try to assure me that what they were doing was right. There was no doubt it was. I got the sense that if any part of the circumstance were different, their actions would have crossed over the line of "right" into "wrong." Besides, I liked Denise. She had a devilish, fun-loving side to her and treated us younger kids like equals. I suppose a friendship sparked between Mariann and her because they both had an element of mischievous rebellion to them—a Butch Cassidy and the Sundance Kid kind of thing.

Mariann and Denise both assured me they would put the letter back the way it was. Denise explained that was why they were steaming it open, to prevent damage to the envelope. I wondered how they were clever enough to know to steam the glue on the envelope in order to reseal it without a trace. Had they done this sort of thing before? I walked out of our dank, farmhouse kitchen that day with an education and left behind a bit of my girlhood innocence.

Johnny went off to boot camp and the churning days of the 1969 summer came to an end. Denise went off to her first year at a small Catholic college in Ottumwa, Iowa. Ottumwa Heights College was a liberal arts women's college. The Sisters of Humility of Mary operated the school. Denise's father helped her search for a school. He had not gone to college and her mother did not finish high school. They were so proud and excited for their daughter to attend college. Johnny was also proud of Denise, telling her so in his letters. Unfortunately, Denise was not one hundred percent committed to college. She was drifting. She found herself at this small private college far from home only because her father had done most of the work to get her there. From the beginning of the semester, Denise's grades suffered terribly.

Life changed for many that had been close to Johnny that fall when he left for boot camp. Bill missed him immediately. He had excitedly cheered his big brother on at a track meet just a season earlier.

- - -

"It was in late spring. . . . Johnny had a meet in DeKalb, Illinois. It was just Mom and me; we drove up there to watch his meet. And, uh, like I said I think that mighta been in late April, early May. Of course, before school got out. But I rode up there with Mom to watch him race. . . . And then that summer is when he joined the Marines. It was summer of '69. It had to been late July when he joined. That's when Mom said to him [Dad], 'I'll never forgive you if anything ever happens to him,'" Bill recalls.

Bill's memories are detailed and vivid. Five years younger than Johnny, Bill speaks of him as if he was here recently.

- - -

Football was not a sport Johnny had participated in yet it was a sport in which Jimmy excelled at a young age. He had been a star running back for Christ the King, yet my father did not approve of the boys playing football. He was afraid they would get hurt. And Dad was right after all. Jimmy's eighth-grade opponents aimed at his knees, causing permanent damage. As a result, my parents did not allow Jim or Bill to play high school football that fall. Despite Dad's discouragement of football, he did attend St. Rita's homecoming game. My father had arranged to have Jimmy ride into the homecoming game on one of Uncle Ray's quarter horses.

I was engrossed in the nervousness of my first days at a new school that fall. My father had decided that he no longer wanted his children going to Christ the King. My emotions back then were mixed about this change and to this day, I don't know what his reasons were. I had been the only one left attending CK and now I was to go to the public school across the street. I had liked the association of a higher quality school that was attached to Christ the King. I would miss that prestige and challenge of French and phonics the nuns taught me. Yet I looked forward to sharing a class with my brother Joe, who was now in the same fifth grade classroom with me at Kate Starr Kellogg. I was also happy about not wearing a skirt to school every day. My brothers Joe, Mickey, Chris, as well as my sister Mimi, were already attending Kellogg. The older kids continued to attend their Catholic high schools.

Since Dad grew up with the Catholic Church and schools, removing his children from this institution was a big statement. It was another step toward breaking away from the Catholic Church. Most of us went to mass regularly each Sunday along with Mom. Dad didn't attend. I think it had to do with the Vatican II changes. He liked the old way of doing things. As a young girl, I witnessed his struggle with the Church. He disagreed with many of their decisions published in the newspapers and Catholic publications. I knew this because he would tell my mother, with the paper in his hand, flinging it around. His glasses would be hanging on the edge of his nose so he could read a few sentences to my mother and then go on loudly about how ridiculous they were. It seemed he wanted so much to believe in our church, yet it continually disappointed him.

Denise was learning about the relationship between Johnny and Dad. She saw how Johnny tried to be better than my father. He even wanted to compete with Dad at the number of children he had and told Denise that he wanted more than thirteen children. Denise's eyeballs about popped out of their sockets when she heard that. Johnny never talked back to Dad.

Instead, he let his frustration out in his letters to Denise and his close friends Beady and Pachol.

> *One thing is that the D.I.s are like my old man so I'm not too afraid,...*

Johnny wrote to Pachol, September 21, 1969.

In the little time his boot camp schedule allowed he was able to write Denise daily, home weekly, and often enough to his close friends Beady and Pachol to maintain ties. In this same September letter to his buddy Pachol, Johnny shares his feelings about boot camp.

> *Dear Patch,*
>
> *I'm writing this short cause the fu—ers here don't't even give ya time to SHIT. Did ya ever try & shit in 30 sec. & then get dragged off while the turd was still in your ass? Well I have & now I can both shit & piss in 30 sec.*
> *Patch don't tell anyone else but Beads that this place sucks so much I feel like deserting. Don't tell anybody cause everyone else thinks I like it. It is hot as hell & I just love running 3 miles with combat boots & pack on. Patch I can do it in 18 min. with all that crap on.*
> *Ya know what makes me laugh? Thinkin' of you & Beads at Pop's while I am playing fu-k-fu-k with the D.I. in the 100° sun. The sand is great around here it has a funny taste I'm beginning to enjoy it.*

Johnny made it through boot camp without attempting to desert. As the rigors and life of boot camp went on, some time in late October of 1969, Johnny admitted to my sister Patti that he missed home:

I miss everyone & want to get home quick, but I can't rush it or something may happen...I get a few letters from Dad every now & then & they make me feel real good. I never thought I could miss them folks as much. I write to them every Sun. along with Dee...

Johnny missed Denise most of all. If the Marine Corps had put a limit on the amount of mail a recruit could receive I am certain Johnny would have been punished for that as well, because Denise wrote him every day that fall. He wrote back almost as frequently. If not writing to Denise, he wrote about her, gushing to Patti in this letter about the difficulty his love for Denise brought him:

I Love her so much, but when I think of her I start fallin' apart and I can't afford that in this hell-hole.

The Marine Corps sent all the recruits to a movie. It was mandatory. When Johnny realized this movie was telling them not to think about their family or loved ones, Johnny walked out. The next letter Johnny wrote to Denise, he asked her to send him her school ring. He was going to prove to the Marine authority that keeping thoughts of his loved one would help him survive in Vietnam. With the ring on his finger, he would keep his love for Denise literally within his grasp, regardless of what the Marine Corps told him.

In this letter, Patti is reminded that her brother's date for Vietnam drew nearer:

I sure hope Timmy is alright cause I'm going to be joining him in about 4 months.

Patti and Johnny were both friends of Timmy Hansen, one of six boys from a farmer's family that lived on the other side of the block from our farm. In the middle of Wisconsin, the other side of the block was about a six-mile drive. Timmy, also a Marine, saw real combat and later returned home. I had heard he became a preacher or maybe I just imagined that since I remembered him as being so kind to us younger kids.

In October, Johnny admitted to the fear Patti had asked him about several months before while looking at all the pictures of the young men in Life magazine:

So around January I'll be in Viet Nam, I'm scared a little, but I am much more proud and that makes up for it . . .

. . . Pat, I feel so god damn responsible now. I'm not a kid anymore, I am a man and I feel awful damn weird taking on the responsibility of defending my country. Denise used to be the most important thing on earth, but now something is much more important and that is my duty . . .

A Marine yearbook was sent home to my parents when Johnny graduated but none of us ever saw it.

- - -

"It is sad that Mom and Dad never went to Johnny's boot camp graduation," says my sister Eileen.

Eileen and her husband, Pat, attended their son, John's, graduation from MCRD in San Diego forty years after our brother Johnny graduated. Eileen, named after my mother, not only shared her name but the distresses of watching a child go off to boot camp and then to war. Eileen tells me how moving the ceremony was. It was a defining moment for their son and Eileen and Pat wanted to be a part of it.

". . . and there Johnny graduated from boot camp and none of us went, Dad, nobody. Yeah. Ya know, It just shows ya how things were different. But I'm sure, ya know, Mom and Dad had a lot of other things too. They had, ha, twelve other kids. Ha," Bill says when I bring up this same topic with him in 2009.

- - -

Denise did not attend Johnny's graduation ceremony from boot camp either, but she saw him when he came home in January.

January 1970

"But the funny thing about it, Terri, is you'll see it in any kid that joins the military and goes to boot camp, when they come back out it's like they matured ten years. I remember seein' that in Johnny."

—Jim Guldan, *2008 interview*

In the brief time he was around during this pre-Vietnam visit home that January, Johnny gave some advice to his younger brothers:

"Don't join the Marines unless there's a war. They'll teach you to survive but unless there's a war don't join 'em."

Mickey heard him say this and took it to heart until he was old enough to make such a decision. Johnny had taught Mickey many things, including how to shoot a rifle while in the back fields of the farm. One summer day he walked down the lane to the river, behind Johnny, and put his hands up in the air to measure the height of his big brother. He was amazed that Johnny was taller than even his hands when he held them up as high as he could reach.

- - -

Mickey and I both laugh as he recalls memories of Johnny like playing on the green shag carpeting in the dining room of our Beverly house. Mickey, Billy, Jimmy, and Joe would lie on top of Johnny and he would fling each one of them across the room, catapulting them with the strength of his arms and legs. They took turns, crawling back for more after each toss. They played kneel down football on that same green shag carpeting and got yelled at by Dad, Mickey states, fondly. We both erupt into a fit of laughter as we talk about this years later. Occasionally, their football games would result in a broken pane of glass in one of the French doors between the dining room and the living room.

- - -

During this time at home, Johnny showed Jimmy combat moves in the basement. What to do when someone is coming at you with a knife was defensive training Jimmy picked up, courtesy of the MCRD-Marine Corps Recruit Depot. This training could prove useful while living on the south side of Chicago.

My parents would have preferred Johnny being around the house more during those few weeks in January. After one week home, Johnny borrowed a friend's car and drove five hours west to visit Denise. She took a train to meet him in Mt. Pleasant, Iowa, an hour east of campus. Denise was so excited to see Johnny waiting for her as she got off the train, decked out in his dress blues, she ran up to him so fast, despite her suffering from a toothache, that she knocked his white cap right off his head as she flung her arms around him. That pretty white cap went flying. He squeezed her tight in his newly muscular arms. They laughed. The next four wonderful days were theirs alone.

Even then, Denise did not have a clue as to the severity of the war they were about to enter. Denise did not know that the chances of coming back from 'Nam not maimed were slight, if one came back at all. And Johnny was unaware of the hell an American teenager was transported to when dropped off in Vietnam for duty. Johnny had bought a small diamond ring for Denise while in boot camp, yet when he talked to her over the phone and asked her for the second time to marry him, she refused once again. She didn't think it was a good idea just yet, so he sold it back. Denise was Johnny's love and Johnny hers.

In addition to his visit to Iowa during his January leave home, Johnny spent time with his close friends Beatty and Pachol. There were moments Patti and Mariann had with him and moments with Bill and Jim. There were moments he was nearby my mother. It was then there was sadness in her eyes, a slant of her head, the pained look on her face some of us saw in that flickering instant when she reached out and touched him as he passed by her.

Billy overheard a late-night conversation between Johnny and Mariann. Bill, in ninth grade at the time, was in bed in the second-floor bedroom he shared with Jimmy. Bill and Jimmy slept in a bunk bed, and there was a twin bed for Johnny. Bill had just drifted off to sleep when Johnny and Mariann came into the bedroom.

"Aren't you afraid you'll get killed?" Mariann asked.

"Nope. If I do, I do. But I ain't afraid," Johnny replied.

Another night that January, in that same bedroom Jim and Bill shared with their big brother, the same room where Jim quizzed Johnny on spelling words, as they lay in their beds, lights out, waiting for sleep to overtake them, a heaviness was in the air.

"Are you afraid of dying?" Jim asked.

"I hope you don't have to go," Johnny returned.

Jim didn't feel this was an odd response. He made it clear to Johnny that he was not keen on the war. Jim would have to be drafted and then dragged over to Vietnam, he thought.

Johnny's brief three-week visit home that January was followed by a few more weeks of training back in California.

February 3

I got fitted for my bullet-proof flak jacket today. I will wear it every day in Nam, it weighs 20lbs.
—John A. Guldan, *February 3, 1970,*
to Denise

After the completion of specialized training, being shipped to Vietnam was Johnny's next step. Other than his Marine boot camp stories, Johnny had not yet spoken of his fears or concerns about combat and war and the expectation of killing that goes along with those two things. It was his letters home that told us bits and pieces of his feelings while he was in the midst of a world I hope I'll never know.

Our neighbor, Mrs. Barry, was getting her son back from Vietnam just as Johnny was being shipped out. Although they had exchanged letters, lived down the block from each other, and attended the same school and church, Dick and Johnny had never met. While he was in the Air Force, Dick Barry's flying was constrained to helicopters, as a passenger, not as a pilot. As a chaplain's assistant in Vietnam, Dick Barry accompanied the chaplain to orphanages and leprosy colonies, with the understanding at that time that touching a leper could make you a leper. Chaplains weren't supposed to carry guns, so it was Dick's job to go out with the chaplain and to defend him.

- - -

"I was acting more as a body guard for the chaplain than I was an ambassador of Christ at the time," Dick Barry tells me with a chuckle when I interview him and his wife, Cathy, in the kitchen of their suburban home, southwest of Chicago.

- - -

Pleiku, although a small Air Force base with only choppers and Cessnas flying in and out, was right in the thick of things. The U.S. Air Force base there was shelled constantly by .122 millimeter rockets from the North Vietnamese, who had little accuracy with their weaponry. A stray bullet once downed the helicopter Dick and the chaplain were in. They were on their way to nearby bases to offer spiritual support. Fortunately for them, they were soon picked up by another helicopter. The Cessna planes at Pleiku did reconnaissance, informing jet pilots where ground troops needed help. Dick's one-year tour in 'Nam had been extended by two months due to the difficulty the Air Force was having in finding his replacement. On February 4, 1970, Dick Barry returned home, discharged after four years and two months of service. He was aware of the negative attitude many Americans had toward Vietnam veterans by then, yet was never subjected to any disrespect.

February 8

Take it from me Denise, I know this. I am going to leave
these United Sates of America, I am going to step off
her shores to defend her so that she will survive.

—John A. Guldan, *February 8, 1970,*
to Denise

We had just come off a warm spell for Chicago, and now
the temperatures were back to their usual frigid lows, but us kids
didn't mind. I was feeling very patriotic and proud of my brother,
knowing he was protecting our country.

He wrote another letter to Denise, later that day:

I miss you Princess so I decided to make a prayer I will say
every night until I am with you again:

AS I KNEEL BY MY FOX HOLE EACH NIGHT,
AT THE CLOSE OF A WEARY DAY,
I BURY MY FACE IN MY TREMBLING HANDS AND
TEARS FALL AS I PRAY.
DEAR GOD, UNWORTHY THOUGH I AM, I BEG ONE
THING OF THEE
LEST SHE I LOVE FORGETS SOMETIMES, PLEASE
HELP HER REMEMBER ME.
DEAR GOD SHE IS ONLY HUMAN AND SO WHEN THE
DAY IS DONE, SHE MAY BE LONELY AS I AM NOW
AND TURN TO ANOTHER ONE.
I CAN NO LONGER GO TO HER AND HELP HER TO
UNDERSTAND MY DUTY TO COUNTRY, SO HELP HER
KEEP ME IN HER HEART, 'TIL THE DAY WE MEET
AGAIN

AND THOUGH THIS NIGHT IN VIET NAM
WE MUST BE FAR APART, I LOVE HER
AND MISS HER GOD, WITH ALL MY
LONESOME HEART.

I don't know why Johnny wrote this in all capital letters. Maybe he wanted each word to stand out because each one was so very important. Or maybe he wanted each word to be clear and easy to read so that Denise could read it every night, knowing Johnny was doing the same.

Johnny's letters to Denise reminded me of the romantic way Dad wrote to Mom eighteen years earlier, while away, serving in the Korean War. And Mom wrote back to Dad almost every day, just like Denise responded to Johnny. The difference was that Dad and Mom were married and had two children. Following is one such letter, written January 8, 1952. Like Dad did in this letter, Johnny also included the date in the upper right corner of his letters. In this letter Dad had written about the Christmas gifts he had sent the kids. There was a doll that wet for Patti, which she didn't like, and an electric train for Johnny. Mostly Dad wrote about how much he missed Mom and his family.

Tue 8 Jan 52

My Darling -

Your letters have been coming through fine. I get one every day, and some days when letters from other people arrive I get 2 or 3...

It will really be a novelty to be with my family for Christmas, and kiss the New Year in once again with my cute little wife. One of the kicks to having kids and a wife is to be with them on such occasions. So far my batting average has been pretty low. I've just got to be with you next Christmas. In fact I've got to be with you a lot sooner than that. I don't care where we go when I get back—just as long as I'm with you and the kids. Gosh will that be wonderful. I can picture everything so plainly—it's almost like being there—but what a let down when I come to.

I keep feeling sorry for myself. I'm glad to hear, or read about, you doing the same thing. That means you must miss me almost as much as I miss you. I wonder what it would be like to be over here, and not to be married to you. Somehow, I don't think I'd mind at all. I miss you and love you so much that it takes up my whole capacity to do so. If I didn't love you —who'd fill in the vacuum. I suppose I'd miss my folks - as I do now, but that's sure not the same as missing you. Being away from you is like being in a coma. Physically I'm here, mentally I'm about ½ here, and spiritually I'm right at your side. That's not a lot of baloney either. I've just got to get back with you quickly. Please hurry those letters.

... Well I'm going to crawl into my little bed, and visit my little— oops—I mean growing, family.

I love you takson (Okinawan for too much)

John

And just like Dad taught Mom a bit of the local language in this letter, Johnny would come to teach Denise Vietnamese terms.

February 9

When I was very young I had dreams about the girl I would ask to be my wife and the mother of my children. I reached for the stars and captured a universe of happiness, beauty & Love.

—John A. Guldan, February 9, 1970,
to Denise

Johnny and Denise had known each other for three years by this time. The writing flourished on both sides.

...Denise you can't begin to realize what you make me feel like when you say that you will wait for me forever.

Johnny prepared for his year away.

February 15

Dear Pat & Marianne,
Well here I am in my fightin' jungles. I thought you might want a picture of a Marine,... I am in Okinawa now & am waiting for my unit to be flown to Nam. I gotta go, I'll get my address to you as quick as I get one.

—John A. Guldan, February 15, 1970,
to sisters

Mariann was adamant, with most people, about spelling her name with no e at the end. With her brother John, she seemed to have looked past this.

In late February, Johnny was considered ready for combat, but before he left, he called Mariann and Patti at school to say good-bye. Mariann was a freshman and Patti a junior at Mount Mary College in Milwaukee. This would be the only school year they shared at Mount Mary. In 1970, the dorms did not have private phones in the rooms, and cell phones were yet to come. Mariann had not been around when Johnny called, so it was just Patti, who held that hallway phone close to her ear for what seemed a surreal conversation with her brother. It was a brief and cordial good-bye. The next day Johnny shipped out to Vietnam.

Patti and Mariann's relationship with Johnny over the next five months was maintained through letters. He wrote separate letters to each and letters addressed to both. In every one, he talked about his undying love for Denise and his plans for their future together. While waiting in Okinawa, he confessed how much he missed her:

> *...I never, ever thought I could be so very much in love with a girl until I realized that I cannot live without Denise. War tends to do that to a trooper. I'm gonna marry her when I get back, I gotta cool it though cause I have to get settled in school & a job. Oh yeah there's one other thing, she has to love me more than anything in the world (it would help).*
>
> *Love,*
> *John*

I often wondered what that flight was like for Johnny. What commercial airlines did he take, and did he land in a neutral city, like Taipei, on the way to Vietnam, and then was he transported by a military helicopter into his Da Nang base? While I was researching this book, my sisters shared with me letters they had kept for many years. I learned that while en route to Vietnam, Johnny landed in Okinawa and stayed there for a few weeks—in the very same place where my father was stationed during his service in the Korean War.

Dad had told me a few things about his time in Okinawa and the morning routine of all the servicemen. After I'd heard the same story a few times, one scene formed in my mind. I saw my father, dressed in army fatigues, waiting in line for the latrine on a beautiful, tropical island. The soldier exiting the port-a-potty hands the day's newspaper to the next man in line as he enters the small office. This happens as smoothly as the passing of the baton between world-class relay runners. This simple routine was an element of war: the camaraderie of soldiers. I imagine Johnny did the same on Okinawa.

March 2

> The goofy stewardesses who flew over with us were cryin' when we got off. Man, it makes us G.I.'s feel good, it also makes us sad...
>
> —John A. Guldan, *March 2, 1970,*
> *to Denise*

Did he know what those tears were about as he looked down at Denise's school ring on his pinky finger?

I once spoke to a woman who was a stewardess during the Vietnam years. She said she used make an extra effort to be nice to these young guys who were on their way to Vietnam. She knew that some of those she talked to would not be returning home.

...I can hear shelling in the distance. It is all so very real now Denise. I am no longer afraid for some reason...

With this reality abruptly settling in, Johnny believed, or hoped momentarily, that he wouldn't really have to do what his orders said. He wrote to Mom and Dad, explaining how he was "not in Kansas anymore."

Dear Ma & Pa,   *2 Mar. 70*

I'm in Da Nang right now & am awaiting orders to get to my unit. I don't even think I'll be going into villages as my original orders said.... I can hear big guns in the distance & jets are flyin' over all the time...

I don't have too much to say except that it is all awful real and it's a funny feeling. The people are real small & their stomachs are bloated from the bad water. The women work like mules so don't ever complain about work. I gotta go right now, so I'll talk to you later.

Love,
John

His first letter to Denise after he arrived in Vietnam was a short one. Johnny closes with:

...this thought that came to me: for those who have fought & died for it, the taste of true freedom will never be experienced by the protected.

I LOVE   *all my Heart,*
YOU DENISE   *John*

Early March

Well here I am in Viet Nam on a lonely hill known as hill 55...

—John A. Guldan, *Early March, 1970,*
to sisters, Patti and Mariann

Hill 55 was to become his place of refuge. A hill I would visit one day.

One of the first people he met on Hill 55 was his new sergeant. He recognized Johnny immediately as he greeted him with a firm handshake and welcomed him to Vietnam. This was the same D.I. that made him eat the fudge in boot camp. Johnny never imagined he'd be happy to see him again.

Johnny wrote to Mom and Dad as soon as he was able. He knew Mom was waiting for his address and anxious to hear from him.

Dear Ma & Pa,
Here is my address, I don't think it should change:
PFC GULDAN JOHN A. 2570886 USMC
MIKE CO. 3rd Bn 1st MARINES
FPO SAN FRANCISCO, CALIF. 96602

There might be some changes in it later, but for the time being this address is good enough. I'm goin' to some village, I don't know the name of it yet. Right now I'm on HILL 55...

Located just southwest of Da Nang, this hill was referred to by the U.S. Marine Corps as Hill 55 because it was fifty-five meters above sea level. Although another hill nearby was also fifty-five meters above sea level, Johnny's Hill 55 became distinguished enough to Johnny and his family and friends back home.

Johnny shared with Patti and Mariann the suffering of friends, fear, and vulnerability he had already experienced:

A man in my company was killed today & another lost his eyes. They are very brave men... They are the most valiant men I have ever known.

Some things he wrote to Patti and Mariann he didn't want Mom to know about. These things were just beginning to touch upon what war was about.

Here is the story, but don't tell Ma cause she'll worry. Myself & 30 other Marines are on this hill 55 in the Arizona territory near Dodge city (it isn't a resort for Marines, ask one if ya know one, ask Timmy). We have been shelled every night & it's hell bein' scared shit.

- - -

"He was always afraid of the dark and he had a nickname—Gooch? I don't know where the hell that came from," Uncle Mike tells me.

We guessed it must've been Grandpa that gave Johnny that nickname.

- - -

We are suppose to hold this piece of dirt... All the rest of the Marines were pulled to another location. So it is very hairy & the shit is gonna hit the fan tonite. I am never tired anymore. I am separated from all my buddies I went through training with. They all got stationed in a very bad area, worse than the one I am in.

His letters to Patti and Mariann mentioned non-combat things too.

...I was to work with statistics & Logistics. As you know I turned it down. I don't know why but I did probably cause I came to the Marines to fight for my country, not to sit at a desk while my buddies are getting' shot. Don't tell Dad...

He jokingly (I think) threatened his sisters not to leak any of this to Dad. They received his letters at school, thank goodness. If they had been home, they might have been tempted to tell Mom and Dad.

Johnny was dropped in the middle of a free-fire zone, putting him in imminent danger without the proper equipment. He felt defenseless. More angry than frightened, he wrote Mom and Dad about this military SNAFU (Situation Normal All Fucked Up). What were my parents feeling when they read this?

I was in a combat zone for 1 week before these assholes issued me a rifle & I still haven't got a helmet, flak jacket or pack. That's the Marine Corp way.

This comment was the beginning of my father shipping Johnny everything from gun and rifle cleaning equipment to binoculars. I'm surprised Dad didn't send Johnny a dictionary for not adding the 's' to 'Corp'. My mother took care of the food and toiletries they sent in care packages. It was as if he went off to college. Yet they all knew this was not the kind of education a young man should get.

Before Johnny left for Vietnam, he and Denise had agreed that it was all right for her to see other guys as long as she had only one date with any one boy. He confides in his sisters about how crazy this makes him, desperate for their female guidance:

Why did she go with him 3 times, ...
She told that boy I was in the Army! When he asked about me & when I asked her why she quit goin' out with him she said he was gettin' too handsy (you know). Pat & Marianne why would she want to show some of the affection for another if she loves me. Now she cries terribly whenever I leave, but Pat & Mare she cries at movies also. Marianne you know her, I can't live without her, ... Pat & Mare I would marry her no matter what even if she was a damn whore I would still ask her to marry me cause she would make a wonderful wife & mother for my kids. Tell me what you think you two. I can't afford to be mixed up here, it could mean my lousy life ...

In this same letter to his sister, Johnny switches gear-

I am going into Dentistry when I get out, don't tell Dad that either. I have decided I want to, it feels good to know. Gotta go time to watch for CHARLES again ...

Johnny's struggle to win Dad's approval was another battle he fought even if only on a piece of paper.

Your Brother in
Green,
John

P.S. For those who have died for it

The sweet taste of freedom will
Never be experienced by the protected.

THINK ABOUT IT!

God I Love Denise!

Maybe ya ought to send this letter to her, I could never tell
her what I just told you two sisters of mine.

Mariann did not keep up with the frequency of her letters to Johnny, and he noticed. She now had college, new girlfriends, and a new love in her life. Midway through Mariann's second semester, she and a couple of college girlfriends attended a fraternity party at nearby Marquette University. Mariann and her two girlfriends needed a ride home from the party that night. An engineering student named Bruce DaCosta willingly obliged. Mariann, eighteen, and Bruce, twenty-two, began dating after that.

Johnny stayed on Hill 55 for three or four days at a time after being out in the bush for up to thirty days. Hill 55 was a respite, yet still rough in the eyes of the "office pogues" back on Freedom Hill. Da Nang was referred to as Freedom Hill, Johnny explained. There, he and his platoon mates refilled their supplies at the PX. At Freedom Hill he saw beautiful Red Cross girls and wondered what they were doing in a place like that.

Although his location did not change, Johnny's address did change, almost immediately. He was assigned to work with the 5th Marines as a combined unit platoon (CUP) designated to work with the ARVNs (South Vietnamese Army) and the South Vietnamese people. He sent the updated address home and kept writing. He wrote to Patti and Mariann, Jim and Bill, Margie and Eileen. He wrote to our aunts and uncles, grandparents, friends, and even friends of my parents and sisters. He had my sisters writing to his platoon mates as well.

Seventeen days after Johnny arrived in Da Nang, Tom Wernig joined the Hill 55 platoon. Tom and Johnny hit it off right away. Tom had grown up in Boston and was also from a large family, which drew them close. When Tom experienced his first night watch, it was clear to Johnny that Tom was pretty scared after he went through an entire case of flares in his first half-hour on duty. Johnny stayed beside him, talking him calmly through the entire night.

Johnny tried to calm my parents as well:

...The way brass is talkin' I might not be here for 12 months I hope...

Johnny was told a year, maybe ten months, possibly even six months, and he would be back home. With this news, I began to plan a block party to celebrate his homecoming. I had to be prepared for a fall party in case he did get home in six months. We had never had a block party at 90th and Oakley, yet my cousins had a block party on 93rd and Longwood every year. Johnny coming back from the war was the perfect reason to have our first neighborhood party. He was saving our country— everyone should celebrate. I was psyched. I planned to knock on each of the neighbor's doors and inform them of this event. I did not get very far in my execution when my excitement about the whole thing was squelched. I told my mother about my plans for the block party. She looked away from me with a terribly sad expression on her face as she said, "I don't know, let's wait and see."

My mother did not think it was a good idea to plan such a party until we knew that Johnny would be home. I got very upset with her.

"Stop thinking like that!" I said to my mother.

I didn't know what she was thinking. But what could possibly happen that we would not celebrate? My Mom had always enjoyed a party. Did she not want to have one because she didn't know when he'd be home? Even if he came home later than expected, we should plan to celebrate. The concept that Johnny might not make it home at all was attempting to enter my consciousness, yet I would not allow any thought of that to permeate my reality. He would be returning triumphantly, I persisted.

"Don't you have faith in Johnny?" I asked.

It had nothing to do with faith in Johnny. She knew that. I did not. She had an idea of the horror and the danger Johnny faced every day. I did not.

Out of stubbornness, I continued to try and plan a block party and ran into the next obstacle—our neighbors. My parents did not talk about politics. But if they did, they would vote for someone who was Catholic, was against abortion, believed in war, and liked big business where everyone works hard for their money. Our neighbors, on the other hand, were different. The father was a professor, divorced, and his son had long hair. When I told them about the block party I was planning, the older boy with the long hair said they wouldn't come. I did not understand that at all. At ten years old, I didn't know about political parties like Democrats and Republicans and how they competed against each other to get their person to be president. All that mattered was that my brother was in a foreign land, willing to give his life so my neighbors could live a free, posh life. How could they not appreciate that? This boy called my brother a baby killer. He was mean and conceited. I was angry and frustrated. Angry in defense of my brother and frustrated because I didn't understand. There was so much I didn't understand. I jumped on his back and started pounding on this boy three feet taller than me. I hated him. He didn't hit me back. He just held his head down so I could not reach it. I slid down off his back after a few blows.

"You're a jerk!" I said.

He was silent. I marched across our driveway, in through the back porch, into my house. I told my mother what he said. I did not get an explanation. I wanted her to hate him too, but she didn't.

As I look back and think about the opposing attitudes my neighbor and I had in 1970, the mirror of our parents' attitudes reflecting in each of us is now obvious. The two of us represented the two opposing political perspectives in the United States at that time. One supported the war, standing behind President Nixon without question, while the other opposed the war, questioning everything our leaders were doing. For my neighbor and I, the beliefs of our elders were what we knew. It was our security. Now, as a woman of fifty-three, my opinion is completely different. I oppose the war. I would support a draft dodger. And my neighbor might now be pro-war!

Johnny wrote about ambushes and ARVNs, teaching his letter recipients about a whole new world. An ambush squad consisted of fourteen to sixteen Marines. CAP and CAG referred to combined action platoon (also known as Combined Action Program) and combined action group, respectively. The following is the CAP mission statement, taken from the CAP Marine website.

The Combined Action program involves special units made up of both US Marines and Popular Force [PF] personnel. The Combined Action concept was conceived to provide a sufficient force to occupy and control areas uncovered by the forward movement of the US and ARVN units and to assist in Revolutionary Development efforts within these areas. The primary mission of Combined Action organization is local defense. In this connection, the Popular Force members of the Combined Action unit contribute to the combined effort by their knowledge of the local area, people, customs, government, and Viet Cong activities. Marines contribute to the combined effort by training the PF and increasing the PF's combat effectiveness in artillery, air strikes, or reinforcements if required. Marine personnel are assigned to these units on a semi-permanent basis to permit sustained operations in a certain area and continued association with a particular group of people. The program is coordinated at all levels by Marine commanders and local Vietnamese officials.

The ARVN were supposed to fight alongside the Marines, yet when they encountered enemy fire, they either didn't shoot or they laid their guns down and ran the other way. In an early March letter to Patti, Johnny was dismayed by the ARVN reaction to defending their own land:

We have a regiment of South Vietnamese soldiers, but every time we get hit they run. I had one holdin' onto me in a foxhole when I was tryin' to shoot. I feel sorry for these people, they are so helpless...

These were the very people they were supposed to be teaching to defend themselves. It was a confusing situation. Yet, the South Vietnamese soldiers exemplified a microscopic view of the larger, political picture. No one wanted to be there. Everyone lacked commitment except the North Vietnamese.

- - -

Today, Uncle Mike has strong opinions about what was going on between the world politicians and the Vietnam War.

"That's the thing about Ho Chi Minh. Our nationalists, in the mid-forties—if you read, I think you'll find that our state department, right after World War II, was very heavily inundated or involved with the communists. And, ya know, the treaties that were written at that time were all favoring dear mother Russia and China. I mean Mao Tse-tung was backed up into the corner of Manchuria by, what's his name, by Chiang Kai-shek. And they pulled the plug on Chiang Kai-shek, all of his arms and munitions. Mao Tse-tung—what the hell was he? He generated a godless society of Communism. But, ya know, that was the main theory is all, 'The Domino Theory,' in the sixties. But getting back to Johnson; it just appeared that what really frustrated him was that he couldn't sit across the table with Ho Chi Minh and negotiate with him."

"They felt Johnson could have stopped it at a certain point. He didn't want to get out of it because of his ego, partially, and being the president—'He can do this. He can get it done. He can win. We can get out of there. We can finish our job. When at a certain point it just shoulda' been done," Aunt Diane says.

"Kennedy was also involved," Uncle Mike adds.

"Yeah, but he didn't agree with Johnson, yet politically, he was very careful," I say.

- - -

Uncle Mike became very well-read on many aspects of the war that lured his nephew away. Still, it was hard for him to understand. There was a lack of disclosure and transparency of politicians' actions. This led to mistrust from the American people. Political tension brewed across the nation. Riots and protests were daily news. Popular magazines reported events in Vietnam and the politics behind it that were not favorable to the U.S. People around the nation came home from work and watched it on their television sets, right in their living rooms. It became known as the "living room war." The reality, or what appeared real, was televised every night. For the first time, our country was not united. And my parents had their son fighting on foreign soil, in hostile territory, for a country that was not fully supporting him. There was that crack of doubt that we were not the strongest country, an invincible country.

This "Living Room War" took place in almost everyone's home—television, radio, newspapers, or magazines made sure of that. What message did that send to a ten-year-old?

- - -

"I remember the black and white all the time," my cousin Anne tells me.

She is referring to the war footage. I ask if that news frightened her then. It did somewhat. It was ominous, eerie, like the beginning of *The Wizard of Oz* in black and white. Anne has only one other memory related to the Vietnam War aside from Johnny's death: "My Mom and Dad were always watching the news."

- - -

In spring 1970, my cousin Anne and I took tap lessons together. I ditched so often that when it was time for the recital, I had to stand in the back row and watch her. I was amazed that she knew what to do. When did she learn that? I thought as I watched her kick out the tap movements in unison with the other girls on stage.

Mid-March

Dear Ma & Dad,
Right now I'm in a village called BIC BAH we are living right with the people. If you saw these children, it would make you cry. These people are in pretty bad shape, the infants not only have big scars from bullets & napalm, but the malnutrition is terrible. I don't know what is worse war or hunger, in this place they are partners. Kids Chris's age smoke cigars and swear like old men. I give the kids as much chow as I can, but it still isn't enough.

—John A. Guldan, *March, 1970,*
to my parents

Through March and April, Johnny's correspondence with my parents was constant. He described the war to my father as if he was discovering a new land, with foreign natives and all:

...You wouldn't believe this war, in the Southern part of NAM it is guerrilla fighting & a lot of booby traps and the part between Da Nang & Phu Bai it is a mixture of guerrilla & NVA warfare so I must be lucky I get them both. North of PHU BAI up to the DMZ you would think it was KOREA or even WWII cause, dad, these NVA are dug in & they are seasoned fighters. They also have tanks & jets & choppers

up NORTH. Most of the NVA I have run into are CHINESE
troops & they aren't small like the VC they are a little
bigger than me. We run into them when they come out of
the mountains to take rice from the villes & that's where
we nail them. But these kids & women are the ones I don't
trust cause most of them are V.C. & informers. I gotta go,
take it easy.

Love,
John

The VC he refers to are the Viet Cong, the co-viet fighters
in the North Vietnamese Army (NVA). In this letter Johnny did not
sign off asking about home and speculating when he would be
there again—that was rare. My parents probably sensed
something must have been going on for him to end this letter so
quickly. My mother would have.

Johnny wrote and wrote. He must have averaged three
letters a day to keep up with all of the people he corresponded
with back home. In return, he sometimes received three or four
letters a day. One of his platoon mates snapped a picture of him
reclining on Hill 55 with four or five letters strewn over his lap and
one in his hand and a big smile on his face. Hearing from home
was his celebration of the holiday traditions that did not exist in
Southeast Asia:

What are ya gonna do on Easter? Denise said she is gonna
come over to visit Ma, over the holidays. If she brings her
room-mate, look out she hates war mongers like myself...

Early on, Johnny saw how critical it was to be alert and on
your guard. He noticed how some of the other Marines who may

have been there longer than him had developed a laissez-faire attitude.

The Marines here are very careless cause many don't care any more, I hope to God I never get like that cause ya can get hurt bad if you get loose. I got to go on patrol.

Love,

John

On March 17, 1970, Patti turned twenty-one. She planned a birthday night out with a few of her schoolmates at Mount Mary. When she got back to her dorm after her last class that day and picked up her mail, there was a letter from Johnny. He had not forgotten her birthday:

I would send ya something for a present, but there isn't much out here except hunger, suffering and death, I know you wouldn't want that stuff. I don't know how God could make a place like this.... Happy birthday

As a young woman of 21, Patti carried a great burden—the truth Johnny exposed to her in his letters was harsh and bleak. She handled it the same way she handled Johnny's criticism of her Welcome Home sign—calmly. No matter the seriousness or the undulating moods throughout his letters, he did not send any of them off without lightening up the mood:

Say hi to Marianne & you two have fun this summer cause I'll be thinking of what I am missing. Gotta go I can't sit too long in one place. Happy birthday.

Your Bro in

P.S. A circle is perfect   Green,

and the world isn't   John

a circle.

I was about two years old when my sister Patti saved my life. She doesn't remember this, yet I remember it clearly. She sat me on the bridge and went upstream. I could see her and her friends jumping and splashing in the water, not far away. I became curious and bored, I suppose, and climbed down from the bridge. The next instant I remember I was hanging in the water, gripping tightly to a wooden plank while the water rushed past me, pulling me under the dark underbelly of the bridge. I remember feeling like I should not have done that. Patti came as fast as he could to reach me, stepping carefully on top of the large rocks under the rushing current. The water was waist deep on her. She grabbed me just as my fingers were going to slip off the plank.

March 29

It sure doesn't feel like Easter here. Last Sat. nite we ran a kill team and the V.C. fixed it so we shot a 13 yr. old girl, God that pissed me off.
—John A. Guldan, *Easter 1970,*
to Mariann

Spring break was over by the time this letter arrived at Mount Mary. Mariann sat in her dorm room and read. She felt nauseous when she learned of the death of the young girl. Had Johnny killed her?

At home, we had no idea. Mom had an Easter basket hidden for each of us, filled with Fannie May chocolates and candy necklaces. I didn't believe in the Easter Bunny any more and that was okay. We colored a dozen eggs in our kitchen, and then Margie and Eileen hid them all over, even in our backyard. It was a whole lot of fun finding them. We girls had to polish our patent leather shoes, rubbing Vaseline on them with a tissue before wearing them to Easter mass. It was one of the few times I didn't mind wearing a dress. After mass, we went over to Grandma and Grandpa's for a huge breakfast of scrambled eggs and sausage, and more Easter egg hunts.

Patti wasn't with us for Easter. She had gone off to Puerto Rico with a college friend. She was adventurous. I wanted to be like her when I grew up and go to Mount Mary College. Johnny caught up with Mariann in this Easter letter. He had learned from others' letters that Mariann's relationship with Bruce caused some stormy waters at home:

> What's this guys name who you're goin' out with? I got a heck of alot of buddies with me here from New York & they are all great men so he can't be all bad. If you want to go to New York, go do [what] you want even if the folks don't dig it, but do it diplomaticly and get 'em on your side.

Johnny wanted to know about the guy his favorite sister was seeing. He not only mentioned Bruce in his letters to Mariann, but also to Denise, Patti, his friend Beatty, and my parents.

He signs off this letter to Mariann:

> Listen kid, if ya see Denise tell her I Love her, but if she has her room-mate with her look out cause she dislikes me tell her that she is BUKU DINCI DAW pronounced (BOOKOO

DINKY DOW) which means very crazy. Have fun this summer Marianne and tell me if you're still going to Eastern next year, I might join you when I get through with this job. My summer won't be the same as the past without Denise.

Love,
John

By the end of this short letter, Mariann laughed about "Buku Dinci Daw" and envied the love Johnny had for Denise.

Early April

Tell me what Easter was like, I want to dream I was with you like last Easter.

—John A. Guldan, *early April 1970,*
to Denise

Although Johnny yearned for home, he did not want to come back unless he could come back whole.

Pray for me, for us Denise I want to get back to you so badly, that is all I want, but I want to get back in one piece, otherwise I'm not comin' back. I saw a man blown in half & he lived, I'm never gonna let that happen, I am not gonna come back half a man. I will never do that. I Love you,

Princess. Take care of yourself, I want you, your life, your heart.

All My Soul

&

Heart,

John

P.S. BE MY WIFE?

All of the letter writing sustained sanity, not only for Johnny, but also for Denise, and my older sisters and brothers, and especially for my father. My mom did not write much, other than a simple note she included with her packages. Letters hurt too much. Sending Johnny what she believed to be essentials sustained a certain level of sanity for Mom. She sent t-shirts, cookies, toothbrushes, dried soup, razors, and more. He appreciated all of what he received. Johnny put everything Mom sent to use, although some things were not used for their intended purpose.

Dear Jim & Bill,

Thanks a lot for the letters, I appreciated them very much. Tell Mom, thanks for the package, but there were a few things I didn't use for the purpose she sent them. I can't wear white tee-shirts cause they show up too good, I have to wear green. I don't wear skivey drawers because of heat rash & jungle rot. I gave the shirts to the kids and used the skivvies as a rag for my rifle. Everything else I use except for the tooth-brush, I use that for my rifle also...

In this same letter he tells my brothers about his new best friend:

...It's hard to keep that M16 clean, but it is a great weapon and has saved my life 4 times already (don't tell Ma)...

While not on watch or in the midst of a firefight, Johnny maintained his "big brother" status and provided brotherly advice on many topics:

...Have you 2 guys got any girl-friends yet? I hope ya do cause when I get back I'm getting' a 1971 Nova SS with all the good stuff in it if you guys wanna use it, ya can, but let me tell you two, your broads had best be mighty fine or forget it...

Billy arrived home from school and tore open this letter from Johnny, reading it intensely before handing it to Jimmy, who read through it quickly and set it down. The girls were calling our house and interested in Jim, but I'm not so sure he was that interested yet, nor was he interested in the other topics in his big brother's letter. Billy read it multiple times before tucking it safely away. Jim did not hear much said about the Vietnam War by family, friends, or otherwise. At the time, he didn't care much about it other than that his brother was involved in it. He did know some things from Johnny's firsthand account in his letters - he knew that Johnny was a radio operator and still remembers that today.

As it stands now I am the squad radio-man during the day & automatic rifleman at night on ambushes, so tell Timmy I'm doing about the same he did, but I gotta carry the radio on my back with the 20 ft. antenna in the air.

As Jim read this, one April day in 1970, he would not allow his imagination to fill in what might happen when carrying a twenty-foot antenna in hostile territory.

April 9

We have moved to a village called DUC-KY there are suppose to be a heck of a lot of VC here, even the kids. I found that the kids were selling popsicles with bamboo shavings in them when I bought one just to investigate their ware. After I bought it they ran so seeing as it wasn't a time bomb or a frag, I set it down & dissected it with my bayonet. Sure enough, there was so much there it would have tore 2 men's stomachs out. I guess the men will have to give up ice cream for Lent they never had here.

—John A. Guldan, *April 9, 1970,*
to my parents

On the other side of the world, Jimmy, the new oldest brother in the house, also had a way with children. He entertained us younger kids with his ventriloquism act, making his arm muscles talk to each other. With both hands on top of his head and his elbows bowed out to either side, he'd pretend his biceps were having a conversation. He turned his head from right to left as each bicep spoke, flexed the muscle on the arm he was looking at, in sync with what he was saying without his lips moving, as if the bicep was talking. He was good at this for a teenager. Not only did he do a good job of keeping his lips still, the conversation between his biceps, which he thought up on the fly, was so entertaining we forgot to pay attention to see if he moved his mouth.

He also pretended to speak Chinese. He broke into this nonsense speak to divert someone's attention from something he had done or to stop one of the younger kids from crying. Between his inflections and intonations accompanying the strange words he threw together, he had me to the point where I thought he might have known some Chinese. Did they teach that at St. Rita, along with Latin, I wondered, not daring to ask Jim because he never gave a straight answer.

Johnny's boot camp letters to Denise had been filled with complaints about my parents. Yet after a few months as a Marine in the bush of Vietnam and his twentieth birthday approaching, this harshness seemed to soften.

...When are you people goin' to the farm for the summer? I need not say how much I want to be back so I could go, thought you would never hear me say that did you? Well, I say & do a lot of things now I never use to...

Johnny was a big help with all of the jobs that needed to be done around the farm. The fact that he had suffered from hay fever did not lessen the work my father demanded of him. Johnny wore a mask while loading the bales of hay on the wagon out in the fields as they rolled out of the baler and then when stacking them in the barn.

If the month of March had not indoctrinated Johnny into the world of war, April surely did.

...We are now in the Spring offensive like you said Dad. We have made a village in the Arizona territory a free-fire zone, that is cut down anything that moves. We have lost so many Marines there it is sickening. More than half the

ones who I went through training have gotten it one way or the other...

Johnny mentions Duck-Ky again, calling it "a bad place." The Arizona territory was an area South of Da Nang, filled with hamlets and tunnels. It spanned about a five-mile radius and was also referred to as Dodge City.

... we are a CUP unit (combined unit Platoon) work with ARVN's & the people the V.C. hate us cause we keep them from eating or getting rice.

I think Johnny was worried that the VC would be even more brutal for taking their rice.

... Maybe I'll get lucky and they'll pull us all out before my tour is up. We got a new Capt. Luckily. I have to close now, I wish I was home.

Love,
John

April 13

Friday's child is loving and giving

—A. E. Bray, *Monday's Child:*
Traditions of Devonshire

Mom never told us her age, but we knew her birthday was April 13. Grandma said it was good she wasn't born on the 30th, joking that the date of her birth, the 13th, had something to do with the fact that she had 13 children. Grandma was superstitious. I think Mom didn't like to have birthdays. She was good about celebrating ours though. I really wanted to know how old she was that year, so when she wasn't around I snuck in her purse and stole a peek at her driver's license. 1970 minus 1927, I calculated: Three years to 1930 plus forty more came out to forty-three. I sure did not want to tell her that she was that old.

Mid-April

*...Ya know Darling, fear makes a guy mature awful fast
& everyone here seems as old as my Dad.*
—John A. Guldan, *April 1970,*
to Denise

With fear came little sleep. Johnny explained to Denise that he didn't need much sleep, that he could go all day on just two hours. Along with fear, lack of sleep, and the VC, the day's heat had to be battled:

I've never sweated so much in all my life. I wear your ring on my little finger and every time I sweat it starts to slide off my little finger and I gotta watch out it doesn't slide off that easy. But some day it might slide off if I keep losing weight. I'm not a skinny dude but this FREAKING heat!

He sat on that Hill 55 and produced letter after letter. Each one different, with a tone all its own.

April 15

Thanks Dad, for the advice on how to set up security & stuff, but I already know what to do here & I'm learnin' life saving techniques every day. . . . I am the only one who knows how to set charges of C-4 where it does the most damage, and the only one who knows more about demolition & mines than anyone here cause my fire team leader, who rotated taught me everything, his MOS [military occupational specialty] was demolitions.

—John A. Guldan, *April 15, 1970,*
to my parents

Johnny's platoon mates had nicknamed him "Prof," short for professor, as soon as they met him. This was because of his one year of college and his black horn-rimmed glasses with thick lenses. He never mentioned this nickname in any of his letters to my parents. Yet he did tell my parents that because of his education and his ability to learn new techniques, he was provided training and asked to lead a special team that searched out and decommissioned land mines.

...you would be surprised to see how many men don't see what's happening here. You can tell by lookin' at their boots if they are torn & ripped they are grunts if they're shined they're M.P.'s or office pogues. When we get to go to the PX everybody looks at us funny.

Johnny treaded through leech-infested rivers and rain-saturated rice paddies. He slept in his ripped up boots, which increased his chance for lesions, known as jungle rot. Feet were a crucial part of combat. If a grunt had problems with his feet, it could mean life or death. Johnny attributed his healthy feet to the powder he put on them regularly.

The boy in him wanted to remain in the world he was from, the world he knew well and wanted to get back to:

I wish Dad would give me a hair cut, it's curling in the back again.

Johnny's hair grew profusely over there in the heat and humidity. He complained about it often. He sent photos home and we saw how his curly hair had grown since the crew cut he had had in January. He tried to shave when he could, otherwise bugs got in his mustache. The hair on his head, his face, his chest, and his legs itched him constantly. He looked like a Beatle, he said, with his long hair. Then he changed his mind and said no, he looked like a Monkee and that he preferred The Monkees over The Beatles. I did too. Mickey, the drummer, was my favorite.

Through his correspondence with my parents, Johnny let them know what he needed. My father placed an item or two in a package my mom put together. Johnny knew what had come from Dad and what was from Mom. He knew Mom had sent him the shaver.

That shaver is great, it even works great without shaving cream.

My grandparents, sisters, and friends sent Johnny packages as well, filled with good things to eat and daily necessities.

More than one month after arriving in 'Nam, he was still hopeful that he would be sent home soon.

Billy wrote me a letter and it was cool. I can't wait to get back to those guys & mess with them again. How is Beatty & Patch? I wrote to Patch once & never got an answer, he must have a girl or something. How is Bonnie? I'll bet I won't even recognize her when I get back. Well, I'll have to sign off it's getting dark. Say "hello" to everyone, and I hope you're right about getting' pulled out, Dad.

Love,
John

The North Vietnamese were not the only enemy a soldier had to contend with in Vietnam. There was drug abuse. In Christian Appy's "Patriots," he cites a 1974 study conducted by the White House office for Drug Abuse Prevention, which determined that thirty-four percent of U.S. troops commonly used heroin during the peak of the Vietnam U.S. military drug abuse epidemic in the early 1970s. How dependable was an M-16-carrying Marine alongside a comrade coming down from his last heroin fix? It was not long after Johnny arrived on Hill 55 that he discovered this sad truth. In an April 15 letter to Patti, he writes:

...All that stuff Timmy was sayin' about pot is all true & I could tell you stories that would make your head spin, as a matter of fact my squad has 21 men 11 of which are on

herbs 24 hrs. a day. It is very easy to get & smoke, even my squad leader smokes it. They even do it at night when it's the most dangerous, so the 10 of us who don't smoke watch out for those who do. I have seen 3 men have flash-backs and start shooting at us instead of the enemy. You see it is foolish to do it, but some men let fear take hold of them too much and they want to escape reality of what's goin' on here. Ya can't keep them from what they want to do they are men and have their own mind. I don't really want to talk about that stuff it's pretty ticklish in a place like this.

- - -

"Just from what I knew what he was doing over there, ya know, he really was in harm's way . . . day in and day out," Uncle Mike recalls.

"Yeah, right, with his own people, let alone the enemy," I say.

April 17

I may be glorifying Johnny but I really felt, and I think he felt, that he was goin' over there to do some good. I think a lot of kids went over there with the same concept.

—Mike Bansley, *2008 interview*

When Johnny was going on raids in Vietnamese villages and jungles, we were celebrating Easter and Mother's Day and getting psyched for school to end. Johnny, on the other hand, had become a warrior, fallen away from his parents' teachings and family traditions. By this time, he had written about ambushes and killer teams.

Bill was amazed by Johnny's detailed account of his team's nocturnal mission as he read about it that April of 1970. He was fourteen. His big brother could do no wrong. Jim and Bill were the privileged ones to be burdened with this truth of combat. They exchanged several letters with Johnny. Jimmy tossed out his letters from Johnny after he read them. Bill did not. Johnny shared some of the horrors of war, including the feeling of the kill, in his letters to his brothers, preceding or ending these narratives with "Don't tell ma."

Bill saved all his letters from Johnny and hangs on to them like I clung to my passport while living in the Middle East. He knew exactly where they were after almost forty years and would not give up the originals to me like others had. Reading these letters, I learned of the gruesome details of the "killer teams." When first reading through Johnny's letters, I had overlooked this term. In an April letter, when he first brings it up, I thought it was just another term Johnny had devised for ambush. I happened to be reading an interview of Charles Cooper II, a battalion commander in Vietnam in 1970, in the book Patriots. I read this at the same time I came across the term "killer team" in Johnny's letters. These teams put camouflage paint on their faces and did other professional things to set up an effective ambush. The goal of the "Killer" ambush team was specific. They were sent to kill, to up the body count that defined victory for us. A ploy developed as a result— fabricated reports of combat and NVA kills, referred to as "sandbagging." Troops would hide in a remote location and report back that they were engaged in a firefight that resulted in a reported number of NVA deaths. Eventually these fabricated deaths rolled up into the body tolls we heard each evening in our very own living rooms. Once Cooper's teams had reported twenty of the enemy with five VC killed and a confiscated weapon. Since there were only five U.S. soldiers against twenty, with no American casualties and the serial number of the weapon retrieved previously confiscated by another "Killer" Team, an intelligence officer was sent to the ambush site to investigate. He found nothing. But in the nearby village, he found twenty bodies, all women and children.

The following letter is difficult for me to read forty-three years later, a sister who barely knew her brother. Johnny left little to the imagination in his April 17 letter to his younger brothers.

...This is what happened last night, don't tell Mom. I went on a killer team last night and...

...we raided a VC meeting place in a village called DUC-KY. We snuck up and heard them talking & playin' a stupid radio. We all had tracers in our M16, we kicked open the door & started cuttin' the gooners to bits. Some ran out and tried to get away in the village, we broke into 2 man teams & started searchin' the hooches. My buddy & me went into one part of the ville with about 12 huts our job

was to search & kill any suspected V.C. male or female, don't ask questions. My buddy, Red Eagle just had 20 grenades & I had 410 rounds for my black beauty M16. We kicked in each door, he threw a frag I waited for them to run out & cut em' down. That M16 is the most deadly weapon there is...

... one gooner ran out shootin, I let him have 2 rounds in the belly and his head cracked wide open. We had to search a few tunnels, but mostly we threw gas & I just waited for them to sky out. After it was all over 20 vc were counted dead, none wounded, one Marine got scratched a little. I wasn't scared while I was fighting but Christ I almost threw up when it was all over. We went back to that ville today & found 3 booby traps, one M14 rifle with scope, one dead mama san (lady), who turned out to be a squad leader for a VC mortar team (she was fine as hell) and 3 tons of rice that was to be given to the NVA for food. I guess we struck it rich. Anyway I'm glad its over and the Capt said we are to get a 3 day vacation, but Its probably just talk. Oh yeah these South Viets soldiers who are suppose to be helpin' us aren't worth a shit. They run. See ya Bill it's dark

Your Bro, John

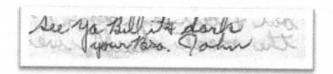

The incident Lt. Cooper spoke of happened in the year 1970. I wondered: Had Johnny been on this "killer team"? This was what he was telling us about. Participating on a killer team was not a normal thing to do for the first nineteen and a half years of Johnny's life. He writes about it as if to make it normal. He did what he felt he had to do to get back home to us.

- - -

My interview with Bill took place after I had read one of the letters he sent me from Johnny.

"I'm glad I got that one to ya, because you can see what he wrote us compared to what he wrote other people. When you get these other letters, ya know. You'll probably ... I don't know. They're just pretty cool actually . . ." Bill tells me, referring to the letters from Johnny that he still holds and treasures. I didn't question Bill any more on this because I was too numb after reading it. I was 50. Bill had been only fourteen.

"What's it been? Yeah, well, thirty-nine years, that it still upsets me. The easiest way for me, like everything else . . . Ya try not to think about it." Bill's voice is shaky. "That's the easiest way to get through it. But that way it still always hangs on ya," I say.

"Every time you'd read about these other families . . ." Bill begins and starts to cry a bit.

"With the Iraq War you mean?" I ask.

"Yeah. It just brings it all back," he says. Bill is still crying.

"It does. Everyone in those families goes through what we've gone through," I say.

"Yeah! Ya go, 'Jesus, I feel sorry for that family,'" Bill says.

April 20

I had a 3 day vacation at a place called Stack Arms at China Beach. Guess what, that is where Joe Heeney is stationed and I missed meeting him by about 3 hrs, cause just as I was leaving I got a note that a L/cpl Heeney was looking for me so I missed him but I have been writing to him.

—John A. Guldan, *April 20, 1970,*
to my father

Johnny wrote of one three-day R&R he took on China Beach, only a few miles from Hill 55. It was sad to learn our neighbor Joe Heeney and Johnny never met up. Joe and Johnny had been close friends since grade school. Joe took a trip to our farm once with just my dad and Johnny and a couple of sheep in the back of our station wagon. Joe had arrived in Vietnam September 17, 1969; almost six months before Johnny. Joe was stationed by Da Nang as well, at the Marble Mountain Marine base located right off China Beach, in a village called Bihn-Ky. Although they were only a few miles apart, Johnny and Joe had to stay in touch through letters. It was through their letters that they had arranged to meet up on China Beach during a short R&R Johnny had planned. Joe Heeney snuck past MPs (military police) to get to China Beach to meet up with Johnny. Joe searched for hours, entering every hooch, with the hopes of finding Johnny. They remained connected only through their letters.

Although difficult for Johnny or any other Marine to take R&R because it meant leaving buddies behind, many took in-country R&R at the Marble Mountain base. This base was adjacent to the beautiful China Beach, where I stood thirty-seven years later hoping to hear Johnny's voice in the roaring waves.

In this letter Johnny brings up the enigma of the ARVN again. He is usually frustrated with them but seems to have a bit of empathy.

> ...They [ARVN] don't want to learn anything & they don't want help, they just want us to stop stomping through their rice paddies and to quit teasing their water buffaloes...

No matter the mood throughout the letter, he seemed to always sign off on a tender note. This was his link to sanity.

> Tell Mom happy birthday & I'm sorry I forgot. I won't forget Mother's Day, but what can I send? I hope your knee gets better too.
>
> Love,
>
> John

April 22

> ...From the profound statement by Nixon it looks like I'll be here the full 12 months, oh well I only have 9 months & 20 days left to this day. I might finish a year at Bogan or I might go to Eastern with Marianne, or I might just go to work as a plumber or something right away. I will have to see when I get there ...

—John A. Guldan, *April 22, 1970,*
to my mother

Johnny looked for a fundamental good to get through those remaining days and he found that within the children. He saw that the Vietnamese are people just like any other people he knew. He saw that when he gave the children his c-ration candy. The way they flocked around him reminded him of his own siblings and cousins. For the most part, they helped each other. The kids helped interpret and the Marines bought ice from them (carefully inspecting it, of course). They didn't care that it was made with rice paddy water. It made things cold. Between leading his platoon mates and befriending the children in the area villages, he felt he had fathered a large family before the age of twenty. He wrote of a time when he helped a child with a head injury. He told my parents about the children's features, the beauty of their skin and their innocence.

Johnny was very taken by the Vietnamese children and wrote to my parents about his desires to be a pediatrician in an April letter to my mother:

> *...I got some new kids their names are Tui (means autumn) GUP (means Richard) SAME (means what it says) TONY (yeah Tony) and FANG (yeah he's got lousey teeth). They are all very smart & are aged 6 to 12, there is one little girl who looks like Mimi. I've been trying to break the ice with, her name is CUA (means sunset). I am teaching them English & they are teaching me Vietnamese. It's comin' along real well,...*

The Corpsman had received a camera from home that Johnny borrowed. Johnny sent a picture home of him and a

Marine buddy with three or four of the young boys gathered around and hamming it up for the photo. He named each of the little boys on the back of the photo. They were cute and looked at home, out there among the sandbag bunkers and machine guns.

The kids liked Johnny because he didn't do "boom-boom to the mama sans," they told him. Johnny let them know about his mama san back home and showed them her picture. Denise had light, crystal blue eyes that jumped out in the photograph. When the kids saw this, they called her "water eyes" and thought she was boo-koo de plume (beautiful). They called her Mama San Waki. Waki means world, Johnny explained in his tape to Denise. America was the world to these children—a mystical land of plenty. Yet when Johnny invited them back to "the world" with him, he was surprised to hear that they wanted to stay in Vietnam.

April 28

War, by its nature, can arouse a psychopathic violence in men of seemingly normal impulses.
—Philip Caputo, *A Rumor of War*

I am thankful Johnny had the sense to write out his feelings, the courage to let Denise know what he was involved in despite the risk that he'd lose her love and respect. He somehow knew this was the right thing to do in order to survive emotionally, to live within his skin. Denise, on the other hand, became another victim of war as she was exposed to these horrific details as a young woman of eighteen.

Dear Angel,

...I have to tell someone and I want to tell you because I Love you. On the night of the 27th of April, just after I got through writing my last letter we got hit and hit bad. You see Denise they hit us from the villager's huts so we had to fire back, they used the civilians as shields and a lot of people were hurt. It is their own fault because the people knew the VC were going to attack us that night, they should have told us but they didn't. As a result many Marines were pissed off, so we were ordered to stage a zippo raid on the ville (burn it down). All night people cried and screamed and the burning flesh of pigs & water bulls could be smelled far into the next morning. If all that wasn't enough, it has been raining for the past 5 days straight...I haven't had a dry piece of clothing on for 5 days. I stink like shit, I sleep on an old grave filled with ants and worms! I can't set a tent up cause the V.C. can mortar it. Sweet-heart listen, I am not feeling sorry for myself, I'm not saying I'm a martyr I'm not getting hyper-patriotic like I did before. I have just come to a conclusion while sitting in the rain, my Love. Denise, I am a fool, all of us here are complete, ignorant fools, and do you know why Angel, because this is why: at home when it rains my buddies, all they have to do is roll up the windows, go into their houses, go over to their girls, and keep dry & have fun at the same time. I have to stay wet, stand in the rain and freeze when the wind blows, there is no way I can shed the rain. Now Denise you have to admit only a complete, stupid, ignorant fool doesn't have the common sense to

come in out of the rain. *That statement wasn't made to be funny so don't laugh. Only a god damn fool gives up an easy life for a harder one. Yes Darling, I goofed I am a fool in joining the Marine Corp, I am a fool, we are all fools to be risking our lives for people we don't like, to be dieing, to be sweating to be shedding tears for these people here who don't even want us here. Denise, if these people wanted us here they would help us find the VC and inform us when they are gonna attack, Baby. We have built houses for them, we have given them more food than they have ever had before, we bandage them up when they bleed, we show them how to keep clean, we sweat for them, we bleed for them, we live in filth for them, we even die for these ungrateful assholes. Darling I didn't know how good I had it back there, to be able to be near you when I wished, to be clean, to be able to sleep without fear, and to be able to have fun with you, until I gave it up...*

Please forgive me if I let out an occasional gripe or bitch once or twice, sweet-heart. I have to do it once or twice or it will build up inside and I'll burst. Please bear with me Denise cause even killing doesn't release the bitter feelings I have for these people. It all seems so very worthless, Nixon should pull us out, we don't belong here. Besides I'm tired of this war business, I want to go home to you, now. I want to feel your tenderness again, there isn't any beauty or softness in Viet Nam.

All My Heart,

John

P.S. This has been inside me for quite a while Denise, I blew my mind & wrote heavy. Please don't be mad if it sounds like my old complaining letters I use to write.

I
LOVE
YOU
DARLING

I will write a book when this is all over, about the worthless war.

Denise didn't confine herself to the conservative opinions of the period. She considered herself a hippie in the seventies. She could not bring herself to watch the nightly news about the war, its body count and politics. She was aware how Nixon kept these young men in the battle zone while back at home he gave the youth more responsibility as well, by lowering the voting age from twenty-one to eighteen.

The platoon's Corpsman, a medical Marine in the field, was on R&R the terrible night of April 27. Johnny was acting Corpsman that night. The following day he described to my parents how he helped a Vietnamese girl with a broken arm, omitting the detail he had provided Denise:

...one chief was so appreciative for setting his daughter's fractured leg he offered her to me for the night. Thanks but no thanks was my reply.

In this same letter, Johnny's struggle between what he felt in his heart versus the rules of engagement is honestly noted while he was acting as the Corpsman:

...we got hit by a zapper force of VC. We had no injuries, but they did and according to all humane laws of the

Geneva Convention I'm suppose to care for the enemy wounded. Well I tried, but some how my mind went blank.

In these early months, Johnny lived in a world with events very few people at home could even begin to imagine. "Fraggings" were mutinous acts of troops tossing grenades in close proximity of their commanding officers. In 1969, there were 126 reported fraggings, and in 1970 there were 271. These numbers are only the reported ones. Johnny nonchalantly mentions one such incident in his letter to "Dad and Ma":

...We got a new Capt., the last one mysteriously caught a grenade in Division Rear. I guess the troops didn't like him too well.

Johnny had only been in country for two months at this point and was already a seasoned "bush Marine," careless about the act of fragging. Karl Marlantes provides a detailed account of a fragging in his book Matterhorn. Marlantes writes that the loyalty of a Marine to his commanding officer was breaking down during this period. The reason for the war was in question, the reason for burning villages, the reason the daily body count was more important than the lives of those bodies wore away at Johnny's belief that he was there for a greater good.

About this time, a paradox began to manifest within Johnny's letters. The voice of a man emerges from this nineteen-year-old boy. This April 28 letter to my parents continues:

As I was standing there in the rain soaking to the bone last night I realized a very ironical & almost hysterically funny fact while on watch. I am a fool, ... Yeah we are all fools over here, but we all asked for it, nobody made us come...

Habits learned over many years do not fall away quickly. So it is with a touch of sarcasm that Johnny reverts back to in the next few sentences as he asks Dad about his life as a younger man:

By the way Dad, you never really told me what your job was in the service. I know you were a Dentist but how did you get your commission? I'll bet you skated pretty much, didn't you?"SIR, CAPT. SIR"

Although he did not have to take part in combat, as part of the Army's Dental Corps during the Korean War, Dad saw enough to know what was wrong with war. He did not have to experience it firsthand to get a glimpse of the horrors a young man faced on foreign soil among native enemies.

When my father spoke to me about the Korean War, he spoke of the rations, the food divvied up and once identifying the remains of a soldier from his dental work. Dad owned guns and was a regular hunter, yet I never saw him kill a deer. He'd skeet shoot in the back hills of the farm, yet I never saw him aim at a bird, always the clay pigeons. He went pheasant hunting but I never heard him talking about or showing a dead one. He invited many friends and acquaintances to come and hunt on our property, though I never saw him kill anything other than the fish he caught. How difficult it must have been to know your son was experiencing killing far beyond taking the life of a fish.

Late April

The measures of a unit's performance in Vietnam were not the distances it had advanced or the number of victories it had won, but the number of enemy soldiers

*it had killed (the body count) and the proportion
between that number and the number of its own dead
(the kill ratio) . . . I was death's bookkeeper.*
                                    —Philip Caputo, *A Rumor of War*

W e carried on as normal throughout the spring of 1970 while the television continually reported the body count. The tally of the dead on each side was used as an indicator, by the United States, as to who was winning. The body counts were reported on the news like basketball scores during the NBA playoffs.

I was oblivious to any of this. My daily life consisted of rushing home after school to watch Dark Shadows with my friend Lyn. We even created our own Dark Shadows club. Our nice big color TV usually was not on during the 6 p.m. news because Mom was preparing dinner, Dad was still at work, and us kids were either playing or doing homework. After dinner, I watched shows like *Rowan and Martin's Laugh-In* or *The Dick Van Dyke Show*.

- - -

"I remember more about John F. Kennedy dying [1963] from on the news than I do about the Vietnam War," Mickey tells me during our 2008 interview.

Mickey was only six years old when John F. Kennedy died and twelve years old when the Vietnam War was being televised, yet he remembers Kennedy's death and not the Vietnam War.

"That war was brought home every day to you, on TV," Uncle Mike says as we sit at his kitchen table on a November day in 2008. He watched it regularly and is amazed when watching the replay of these scenes on documentaries today. Uncle Mike explains the difference in perception when watching the film reels then and watching them now. Due to the anti-war sentiment during the Vietnam War, when you watched any live footage, you got the feeling the media was exposing only the scenes that would fuel that anti-war attitude.

"There were always numbers. Always. Numbers, on how many killed, wounded. Our side and theirs, ya know. Every night, I remember; '4 Americans killed today in combat, 37 of the enemy were killed,'" Bill mimics the newscaster's words as he recalls those telecasts.

I did not see the war on television. Oddly, I felt envious of Bill's memory of these broadcasts.

- - -

Dad informed Johnny of what was going on at home in his letters, and Johnny wrote back about life in South Vietnam. Is it a nineteen-year-old boy enduring sleepless nights in the dirt, watching others nearby blown in half, yet remaining alive, fighting beside friends with their eyes blown out and consoling others as they're dying, praying, "God, please don't let them die"? No, it is a man, writing about defending his life and his fellow Marines. However, some of the events weren't easy for my father to read.

Patti was home from school for a weekend to help Dad at the office. She walked into my father's room to ask what time they'd be leaving for the office. He was reading one of Johnny's letters as he sat on the edge of the bed with the television on. She recognized it right away—its small size with the military envelope sitting on the bed next to my father. She asked if she could read it after he was done. His reading glasses were resting at the end of his nose as he looked up at her.

"No, he makes it sound terrible. I don't want you to read about some of the stuff he says is going on."

Patti was actually receiving more detail than what Johnny wrote to Dad. Neither one of them knew this. She didn't want to think what could be worse than what she had already read. She turned around and walked out, forgetting the reason she had come in there.

Johnny quickly learned of my father's discomfort with the information he was sharing. A boy, nineteen years old, in a foreign place, trying to reach out to his parents and having them shut him out must have added to the loneliness Johnny felt over in the jungles of Vietnam.

Dear Ma & Pa,

Not much happening here, anyway I don't think you would like to hear about this war anyway except that it is a terrible place to be. Ask Mr. Mahoney if when he was in the Corp, if he was a grunt. If he was ask him what it really was like cause Mom & Dad a person who says he's been in Viet Nam doesn't necessarily mean he is in a war zone. Right now Joe Heeney & I are the only ones who will really know what's going on in this place.

Teenage developmental years, the angst years, is a time of development and change. Change in the body. Change in desires. Change in hopes and dreams. At nineteen years old, Johnny was at a point in his life when war was seen as an opportunity to become a man. His idealism of "doing the right thing" had lured him to the Vietnam War. It was Johnny's chance to be a hero for his country, for his friends and family, especially his father. Yet in his letters, as early as April and May, he wrote that now that he was there, he saw the "evil" of it all.

I don't know what truth there is in us pulling out by July, but I hope to Christ we do pull out. I have never been so damn scared in my life, but it's funny cause as soon as the shots are fired something snaps into gear. It's like a bad

dream, the buddies I went through training with are almost home. They were only here 5 days and that was that. There are 5 men I went through training with that are left with me. God must have plans for me or something cause I'm awful lucky...
Please send a tooth-brush & razor blades & razor cause my stuff was stolen.

His eyes were now opened to the privileges he had been blessed with his whole, young life:

I'll tell you what though Mom & Dad, I know now, oh yes, I know now, the very, very high price the soldiers & Marines had to pay to keep that country you're living in free. These people over here are starving, they are almost animal...
if I, if this man, if this Marine ever complains about school, about a job, about any little petty thing. I will personally beat myself about the head & shoulders. I thought school was hard, what a laugh. I'll tell ya what I'm gonna go to night school & I'm gonna work during the day & Dad I'm gonna learn & earn. I am sick of the stupidity I have seen & watched my friends pay these brass asses their lives for their low common ignorance. I hate brass with a passion, if I don't get busted before I get out it will be a miracle...

Each day the dead Americans would be listed alongside the dead Viet Cong. Johnny referred to these in his letters. He was incensed by how his commanding officer cared more about the dead VC reported than the buddies he lost that day. Johnny is sickened by it all. He writes to my father:

...Any type of leader who is more concerned about how many enemy were killed instead of how many of my

friends, my buddies who risk their lives, gave their lives for me for him for this rotten country, were wounded or need emergency treatment ought to be shot. I got bitched out & almost busted for tellin' that capt. on the radio to stick the enemy up his ass & to get a chopper to me quick cause two of my friends, who I love like brothers were blinded. Dad I'm tellin' you this is madness here, they just don't care about us, our lives. It hurts to see my friends hurt I want to cry but I'm too mad...

What could my dad possibly have felt when reading this? My mother? I was only aware of the injuries my brothers were encountering at home; like the ones they sustained when riding their bicycles. We only had two bikes to share among us. Dad didn't allow any more because he was afraid that the more often we rode bikes, the greater the chance we would get hurt on them. His premonition was right-on that spring. We suffered two mishaps on our two bicycles. The first one came when Joe was hit by a driver without brakes as he followed Jimmy early one morning. Jimmy was out jogging while Joe rode close behind him. They crossed an intersection while the light was red and a driver with faulty brakes came plowing through. He hit the bike. Miraculously, Joe was unscathed. Although an ambulance did show up, Joe did not even go to the hospital.

The other bike incident involved my eight-year-old brother Chris. Margie and Eileen were riding Chris and I to Grandma and Grandpa's house. I was on the seat of the bike Margie was riding and Chris was on the handlebars of the bike Eileen was riding. We were headed south down Leavitt, being chased by boys on their bikes. Chris' legs were dangling on each side of the front wheel when Eileen turned quickly into Grandpa's driveway, thinking we were home free. But as she turned, Chris' right foot got caught in the spokes and tangled in between them. The bike stopped suddenly and would not go any further. Margie stopped quickly right behind them and I held on to her tightly. Chris whimpered. It was then Eileen realized what made the bike stop and she quickly planted her feet on the ground as they both began to tip to the side with the bike.

"Oh no!" Eileen shouted.

The boys who had been chasing us immediately came to help. They worked for many minutes, removing Chris' shoe before they could free his little ankle from the spokes. His foot was black and blue. It turned out that it was broken. Little Chris laid on my parents' king-size bed with his foot elevated on an ice pack for a day before Mom convinced Dad to bring him to the hospital. He was a casualty of the spring bug that was biting the young boys' hearts who had been chasing after my sisters Margie and Eileen. Margie and Eileen took good care of Chris while he was laid up with his leg in a cast. With his sparkling, baby blue eyes, outlined in black and accented with lush, dark lashes, Margie and Eileen applied mascara to see how long they actually were and envied them.

At the same time Johnny lived on in a world with nothing to envy:

...Dad, if you ever hear of Jim or Bill wanting to join don't let them, don't ever let them. I'm sick of military & war, I'm sick of it but I asked for it didn't I? I'll tell you now I don't want people to owe me a thing, nobody asked me to do this. I gotta go, oh yeah send me Gail Wallaces address & send me a pen. Nobody will ever know what hell is till they've been here in a grunts boots. George Blough knows, he paid just like my friends did.

Love,
John

- - -

"The type of work he did in Vietnam was the type of work I never imagined him doing. But then again you don't know what the training and discipline did for him, in that respect," Uncle Mike says to me while we sit in his kitchen in 2008, talking about Johnny.

- - -

Through Johnny's letters, Uncle Mike learned of the firefights, ambushes, perimeter patrol, and reconnaissance missions in which Johnny was involved. He could not imagine his nephew capable of doing such things. It was a far cry from the fun-filled, innocent days they had spent together when Johnny was a young boy. Uncle Mike sensed that the world Johnny was getting accustomed to was almost impossible to bear. It was about this time, two months into his tour, Johnny got into a bad funk. He wanted to go home so bad he was going to shoot his foot off. His buddy Tom talked him out of it. Later, Tom found himself in the same funk. Johnny talked him out of it.

As Johnny was getting to know his platoon mates that spring, we were working together with our platoon back on the farm to clean up after winter. We had gone to the farm for the week of spring break. Mick, Joe, and I were tasked with the chore to bury a calf that had not made it through the winter. The lifeless body of the little brown and white calf with its matted coat laid frozen on the grassy drive that wound behind our garage. My brothers tied a rope around its spindly front legs so that we could drag it out to the back fields, where we would bury it. Joe began walking forward with the rope over his shoulder, his back to the calf. The calf's body was still frozen to the ground. Joe tugged and tugged. Mick and I had been standing alongside the innocent-looking calf, when suddenly, to our horror, its legs ripped apart from its body. Joe just kept walking, with the legs dangling from the rope behind him. Although Joe didn't look back, I think he knew what had happened and was trying to make us laugh. And that he did. Mickey and I looked at each other and burst out laughing. It was so bizarre that it struck us as funny. The dead little calf had been such a sad sight that to laugh was a relief.

May 1

Boy this moving to Mundelein came up all of a sudden. Is the block taking over that fast? It sure will be awful funny when I get back and go to a different house.

—John A. Guldan, *May 1, 1970,*
to my parents

Dad was considering moving to Mundelein, a suburb fifty miles north of our Beverly home. And just as Dad was sensitive to the things Johnny wrote in his letters, Johnny was sensitive to change happening within the family, and "White Flight" was threatening change in ours. White flight was a term used in the United States starting in the 1960s and carrying on into the '70s. The reason these families moved stemmed from fear and anxiety about increasing minority populations. Our little community of Beverly, ninety-nine percent white in 1970, was greatly affected by integration. Attempts to achieve effective desegregation by means of forced busing in some areas led to many families relocating.

My classmates and I felt the direct impact of integration at Kellogg. This was most apparent on the playground as we watched the first black students standing alone during recess. I went up to one lone girl and offered a friendly hello when an older black boy came screeching toward us. She ran and he chased after her with a leather belt he had removed from around his waist. This young girl seemed terrified as she sprinted past me and a few of my classmates. We all watched in horror. The young girl eventually settled down and moments later was hanging around the older boy with the belt, who we found out was her brother. I wondered if my discomfort with the scene I had just witnessed was because I didn't understand. Were people so different outside of Beverly and the sheltered circle in which I had lived? Mom and Dad gave us a safe home surrounded by good people, and no matter where we lived, it was a home to which Johnny yearned to come back:

It looks like I won't be home this summer though, so have fun, I'll be thinkin' about everybody. Gosh I wish I could be there, but that's life in the military I guess. Tell Bill thanks for writing and I'll try and write back soon.

Johnny doesn't say, 'I am thankful to my parents I have God, when there is nothing else to count on.' Yet through his action of continuing to write to all his family and loved ones, specifically, my father, tells me it is their beliefs he chose to keep close.

I'm sorry, but I censor a lot to keep ma from worrying so you'll just have to take my shorties, I'll tell ya what though

I am writing a book about this when I get out and it's gonna be a good one.

Love,

John

I hadn't known Johnny wanted to write about his Vietnam experience until I read his letters for the first time in 2011.

May 2

Look Pat my letters aren't long and they don't mean much. I have my reasons why I don't write much and one reason is that I hate relating to someone back in the world what I see and experience here.

—John A. Guldan, *May 2, 1970,*
to Patti

Johnny was being paid 14 cents an hour and received his first paycheck of $465 after five months as a Marine. He wanted to know what Patti's plans were for the summer, where she was going to work. He longed to have another summer working at Grandpa's office in downtown Chicago. Included with this light-hearted content, Johnny also explains to Patti that he does not write about the death and suffering in his letters to Mom and Dad. Yet, that was the truth of his job and he needed to speak it to someone.

...I'm sick of this hell-hole, I miss Denise so much I can't sleep at night and the enemy aren't gettin' any friendlier. Dad get's mad cause my letters aren't long enough. I really don't give a shit cause I told him once what really happens here, but he said it couldn't be that bad. So I decided not to tell him anything that happens, ...I'm fine physically my morale along with every Marine's here is very low. The VC have started a May & June offensive and it isn't a pic-nic so that's it. If you see Denise tell her I Love her.

Love,

John

Other than My Lai, a 1968 mass killing of Vietnamese women and children by American soldiers, the general public did not hear or read about the life of a young American boy in South Vietnam. Patti, as a girl of twenty-one, did. She learned about her younger brother living among leeches, with centipede fever, stolen toiletries, friends maimed and killed, and sleepless nights of "gook" torment through his letters. The impact of these words, written by a single soul in a battlefield, was felt a thousand miles away. This war became her war too.

When I read his letters now, I see how they may have acted like tentacles of an ocean squid reaching out and zapping its prey—Denise, Mariann, and Patti's young lives. Maybe in the future, science will be able to measure the total impact war has on the human mind and the human spirit by taking into account these invisible tentacles.

On Saturday, May 2nd, in Beverly, us younger kids were dealing with moments we considered rough in a world of our own. It started out as a normal Saturday with most of us doing our chores while the youngest kept themselves entertained. Mimi was carrying a pair of scissors pointed straight out when Bonnie ran around the corner right into them. Immediately there was blood all over, somewhere in the area of her eye. Margie and Eileen had to deal with this trauma since Mom was at the grocery store. Margie ran down the block to Mrs. Barry.

"Bonnie ran into the scissors and it cut her eye. She might be blind," cried Margie.

Mrs. Barry didn't ask questions. She dropped what she was doing and ran back to our house with Margie. When they walked into the living room, they saw Bonnie lying down on the couch with Eileen at her side, bloody towel in hand. The scissors had just nicked the side of Bonnie's nose. Bonnie would be fine. We were all relieved, especially Mrs. Barry, who stayed with us until Mom got home.

May 4

The rich weren't fighting that war. It was the kids from the neighborhood where Daley grew up.
                              —John Bansley, *2008 interview*

Richard J. Daley Senior was our mayor and had been for fifteen years. He came from a working-class neighborhood on the South side of Chicago where many young men were drafted because they could not afford to go to college. Mayor Daley had a big job on his hands to try and keep peace within our city this year.

On May 4, 1970, shootings took place on the Kent State University campus in Ohio. Police shot and killed four students during student protests. By then, protests had been raging for two years around our country. This brewing started to become obvious to us in Chicagoland with the 1968 Democratic Convention. Uncle John, although he opposed the Vietnam War, calmed his conservative father when he told him he was attending the convention strictly for historical reasons. This was true. He had no intention of participating in a demonstration. Uncle John and his fellow Christian Brothers were excited to be part of history as they stationed themselves in front of the Conrad Hilton. The police were revved up. Daley had given them orders to control the crowd at all costs. He wanted no violence. However, this "no-violence" command did not apply to the actions of the police. Uncle John witnessed a young woman being hit on the head by a policeman's baton. Uncle John then walked south, back toward the Conrad Hilton, with his Christian Brothers. They approached a group of policemen on the corner of Michigan who instructed them not to proceed any further south. The police officers directed Uncle John's group east, toward the lake. Moments after they began heading east, the police suddenly began to chase them. The Christian Brothers all took flight among the crowd, yet sticking close together. A girl, running alongside Uncle John, tripped. He reached out and grabbed her while his friend across from him did the same. As they both picked her up, a policeman who had been chasing them came running up from the rear and hit this girl on her back with his baton. Fortunately, she was not badly hurt.

Chicago was celebrating its fiftieth anniversary that month. It had grown to a beautiful city despite the hard times and continued to endure the issues of the time. War and abortion were the headlines on the Chicago Tribune this day.

May 6

Here is a picture of the village kids of Bic Bah from left to right: Larry, Tony, Gup, Pwong, and Dino my squad leader. You are looking at the future of this war torn land. By the time they get to be 18 yrs old this country will be won by them, my squad took up a collection to send the kids to school in Da Nang.

—John A. Guldan, May 6, 1970,

to my parents

Johnny took photos to show my parents the Vietnamese children. Dad had just taken up photography as a hobby. Maybe Johnny had influenced him with the photos he sent home. Dad made us sit still to take our photos and then shut all the light out of the kitchen while he developed them. Johnny described the features of the little girls like a painter might describe an exotic flower.

Don't lose that picture I want to see it when I get home. I can never get a picture of the little girls, they always run away. I guess it's cause of us Marines and the reputation we have. They are the cutest little girls I have ever seen, they have deep, rich slanted eyes. Some day I'm gonna get a candid shot of the little girls and I'll send you it.

Having been to Vietnam myself and visiting orphanages there, I understand what Johnny meant. Their beauty was not just in their flawless, olive-bronzed skin and their spry little bodies. They had old spirits peeking through their brown, almond-shaped eyes, yet were quick to giggle at the slightest playfulness.

By the time my parents had received this letter, Mother's Day had come and gone. My brother Jimmy had gotten my mom a tiara with diamonds on it. I thought it was the best gift even though he told me they weren't real diamonds. I picked my mom a bouquet of dandelions. I didn't know they were weeds until I gave them to her—my brother Jim told me. My mother put them in a vase of water. I thought they were pretty. I didn't care if they were weeds.

I'll tell you what I want for my birthday. A pair of good binoculars with a case...
That's it take care. I miss you all.

Love,
John

When most young men in the United States turned twenty, they might ask for the latest Neil Young album or extra money to take their girl out. Not my big brother. After receiving this letter, Dad went out and bought the best pair of binoculars he could find. Johnny had them by the middle of May.

May 10

You say Ma worries when I write my letters, well the only way to prevent that is to stop writing...
                                    —John A. Guldan, *May 10, 1970,*

to Mariann

Jim, our postman, was a welcome sight to us kids. He always gave us a stick of chewing gum and a ride on his mail cart, which carried two big, brown leather sacks, full of letters and small packages. He was always friendly and never tired of us asking him for a stick of gum. I imagine the feeling Jim-the-postman gave mom, each day he arrived, wasn't quite so enjoyable.

May13

Dear Dad,
I got a letter from you today, it said that my grammar, penmanship and spelling are getting better and that I might amount to something after all. Well I'm not really concerned with how my English composition is progressing if I was worried about it I would write some prose to you...

—John A. Guldan, *May 13, 1970,*
to my father

Yes, this was really my dad, correcting Johnny's penmanship while he was amidst gunfire, bombs, and booby-traps. Throughout April and May, Johnny wrote several letters a week to my parents. Some were addressed to both of them, some only to my mother, and some only to my father. The occasional banter in letters to my dad showed that the contentious relationship between them continued, in spite of the life-threatening situation Johnny was in. It was all in keeping things normal. The struggle for Johnny to share the truth of death, suffering, and fear with my father continued:

> *From your past letters I have come to the conclusion that it would be better not to let you people know what really goes on here where I am at so that you won't worry. Since I won't write what is going on my letters will be much shorter and probably won't make much sense to you, but what can I say. I guess all I can put down is that I am O.K., it's 130°, I haven't lost any weight yet, the V.C. are active and they aren't playing games here. That's it, that is all. I can take care of myself if I couldn't I wouldn't have gotten this far.*

> *Don't worry about me.*

Johnny closes this same letter asking for binoculars (help) again and a yearning:

> *...If ya want to send me something for my birthday send me binoculars. I could use them alot here. Thanks for the picture, it does bring back memories. I only wish I had more time to sit and think back. Say hi to all, I miss them.*
> > *Love,*
> > *John*

Dad had sent Johnny a picture of the prettiest part of the farm-the river. During the summer, we fished off the bridge with bamboo poles and long sturdy sticks, Huck Finn style. One of the many hooks or lures from our father's tackle clung to the end of each kite-string line as the current tugged at it, threatening to carry it away. Of course, we took only the lures Dad said we could use. Mimi was too young to fish with us. She stood by and watched. On one occasion Mimi got caught in the back with Joe's hook. She screamed and jumped about so much it was impossible to get that hook out without causing more damage. Joe, feeling responsible, immediately rushed to Mimi and worked carefully to release the hook's grip from her back while Mick and I held her.

May 14

We have a new orphan kid here and you'll never guess what his name is? Don't tell Ma or Dad, it's "BUG-FUCK"! Yeah he looks like an ant & we had to pump his stomach cause he drank a bottle of insect repellent. He's cute as heck even cuter than the other kids I sent in the flick.

—John A. Guldan, *May 14, 1970,*
to Mariann

The Vietnamese traditionally have strong family units and village communities. To have war tear apart this tradition must have been a pain that went to the core of their souls.

A few weeks before receiving this letter, Mariann had worked hard at putting a package together for Johnny while she was away at school, with little money.

...thanks for the package the whole squad devoured it. I got one from Mom the same day, thank her also. We had quite a feast...

At the same time he had received this package from my sister Mariann, he got a rifle cleaning kit from my fourteen-year-old brother Bill. Johnny sends his appreciation for that as well in this letter.

May 15

Right now it is 131° and I just came off patrol, we found 4, 50lb box mines buried in the trail we were walking on... This place sucks ya sweat your balls off in the day, it rains for 5 hours & then the God damn mosquitoes attack you. So I don't get too much sleep, but fuck it I don't trust anybody. I might never wake up if I sleep. Joe Heeney is here, I have written him a lot, he is a truck driver. Excuse me, a jet was just shot down we have to get out there. Well, I'm back and there's no trace of the pilots.

—John A. Guldan, *May 15, 1970,*
to friend Tim

As his time progressed out in the bush of South Vietnam, Johnny wrote about going out on ambushes like it was a nightly routine. He had seen plenty of action by this time. He tried to focus on his friendships, what was good in his life, what he knew was normal and safe. He kept trying to survive.

I've been here 3 months and that's enough for me I'm ready to go home, this war shit is getting dangerous. It is not like the movies there aren't any John Waynes here. We're all scared Marines who fear booby-traps and an enemy we hardly ever see, but we do awful funny things when we're scared like a frontal assault into a machine gun position or walk right into an ambush run after the gooners with an E-TOOL (shovel) & pistol & just chase their asses. I have seen it & believe me it's not bravery, it's down right stupidity with luck. I never thought I would assault, but when I saw my fire team leader get hit I didn't even think. I was up front yellin' & firing like all the others, after it gets over then I start gettin' scared.
Fuck the war stories, I hate to tell them I went through it once & that's enough. Have you seen Kryda lately?...Tell Greenfield hello for me,...If you see Denise... tell her I love her, do that for me Tim. I'm gonna marry her when I get back, you're invited...

Maybe it was stories of our own parents' relationship that fueled the constant attention Johnny put on his future with Denise. Similar to Denise and Johnny, my parents had lived in the same neighborhood, just a few blocks from each other. Both were raised in comfortable homes and were well cared for.

My dad had had eyes for my mother as soon as he saw her. My mother played coy, but even when she told me about it when I was a young girl, I could tell she was taken by him. From pictures, I could see my dad was handsome with his dark hair and athletic physique. My mom was a beauty herself, with sparkling blue eyes and a big white smile. Mom was a senior in high school and Dad was a college freshman. She was dating another man in the neighborhood when my father asked him if he wouldn't mind if he also asked my mother out. There were no ill feelings between the two men. My father was gallant in the way he handled it, and the other man was gracious. A friend of my father's with artistic ability drew a funny cartoon of this encounter. In this drawing, my mom and her former boyfriend were on a park bench, while my father, chest protruding, was leaning toward the boyfriend asking if he could date his girl.

May 17

We lost it all at once and in the span of months passed from boyhood through manhood to a premature middle age.

—Philip Caputo, *A Rumor of War*

Johnny's squad was expecting a fresh load of recruits and their squad was short leaders, so he was assigned to take on more responsibility. Along with the struggles that came across in Johnny's letters to Dad, the foreboding topic of booby traps appeared multiple times. He shared his latest accomplishment:

...Well the Capt. decided to send me to Land mine and Booby-Trap Warfare school. He said probably some time in

June I would be going. It lasts about a week and you learn demolitions and the setting of booby-traps.

In this letter to my parents, after his usual report of the rain and heat, Johnny thinks of what his age really means with his birthday drawing near -

Well Ho Chi Minh's birthday is the 19th so we are suppose to be in for it. Don't worry my squad is squared away and will be O.K. Pretty soon the responsibility of managing this squad will be on myself and 2 other men...so I suppose I'll be very busy in the coming months watching over the behavior and lives of 22 men. I'm going to close now I miss you all, and I sure don't feel like 20 yrs. Old, maybe 40 would be more like it.

Love,

John

Johnny Gallagher was five years younger than Johnny and the oldest of seven children. He looked up to his older cousin as a role model. Johnny was like the older brother Johnny Gallagher never had. He had always been told he was named after his dad, Jack, until my brother Johnny convinced Johnny Gallagher otherwise.

"You weren't named after your dad because your dad's name is Jack," my brother Johnny had told him. In fact, Johnny Gallagher was named after his dad. John was his dad's real name and Jack just a nickname. After the Gallaghers moved to Michigan, Johnny Gallagher continued to get reports, from his parents, on what his cousin was doing. It was always positive. They told John Gallagher that Johnny was very good in track and cross-country and that he was the captain of the team. Johnny Gallagher joined track his freshman year of high school because of Johnny. Track was a spring sport, and Johnny Gallagher's team was in the middle of its 1970 season when Uncle Jack and Annie Laurie attended one of their son's meets. During the middle of the mile run, Uncle Jack stood in the bleachers, next to his wife who was cheering on her son, and turned to her.

"Annie Laurie, he's last," Uncle Jack said.

"C'mon Johnny!" she shouted from the bleachers as her son tried desperately to keep up. She turned to Uncle Jack.

"He's always last," she said, then turned quickly back to the track.

"C'mon Johnny!" she shouted again.

Johnny Gallagher knew he was last, he knew he was usually last, but the crowds cheered. That was one of the things that kept him going. The other impetus was his prayers. He prayed to be like Johnny. And he was, not only because he finished every race but because he was the oldest boy and very responsible.

May 19

In your letter you sound pretty depressed about things that have to do with mom and & dad. Well, ya can't very well go off & join the Marine Corps like I did, but maybe you can try & do something a little more intelligent & better.

—John A. Guldan, May 19, 1970,

to Mariann

Johnny felt the unrest within his family through my father's letters and heard it from Mariann. Johnny learned through Mariann's few letters that her spring semester at Mount Mary was one of emotional turmoil. She did not feel she was where she was supposed to be and tried to explain that to Mom and Dad.

Mariann had a scholarship to attend an Illinois school, where she would study teaching, yet my parents said she had to go to Mount Mary College. She didn't push it because this would be just another battle with my parents she chose not to fight. Besides, she thought, what if she went her chosen way and failed?

Most did not know exactly what fueled the Vietnam War other than the United States' aversion to communism. Was it not the same thing that was happening within my own family? Not to say at all that the two were at the same level of seriousness. I am only pointing out the control factor. The United States wanted control over the choices Vietnam was making as a government, and my father wanted control over the choices Mariann and Johnny were making for their lives. In both cases, I believe the desire for control was based on good intentions, yet no good came from either.

When Mariann was born in December of '51, my father was still in Okinawa serving in the Army's Dental Corps. With three feet of snow on the ground and Mom in the hospital, Grandma stated, "She wants to be home by Christmas," and ordered her sons to go get my mom and Mariann, overriding Grandpa's suggestion to wait for the snow plows. My young Uncles Jim, Mike, and John went to the hospital to bring Mariann and Mom home. Mariann was three months old when our father returned from Okinawa in 1952, and he held her for the first time. He was a stranger to her, and always remained a stranger.

- - -

At a café in San Jose during the spring of 2006, Mariann recalls trying to explain to our parents what she wanted in life.

"I remember writing a letter to our parents at 17 when I was at Mount Mary and trying to figure out what I was all about and where I was going. I used a lot of 'I' statements in that letter because I had to. It was about me and I was trying to reach out to them, maybe hoping for understanding and guidance. Well, it didn't come. In fact, it backfired on me and reinforced all those negative messages I had been getting ever since I was able to remember. My father said all that was in the letter was I this and I that. How selfish I was. So naturally, I believed him. I didn't step up and defend myself with words to match my feelings. Instead, I shut down and closed up. I protected everything inside and held in the tears. I wasn't going to show him how deeply my hurt went. I knew then I had no champion in my corner. They didn't or couldn't see me no matter how much I wanted them to. I'll never forget that. They were so critical of me. Their emotional whips scarred my heart and soul. Never knowing how to break out of my shell, John helped me. He encouraged me to keep going and that was good."

- - -

While he encouraged his sister to follow her heart, Johnny had his own metamorphosis. He was developing a sense of self away from our parents' control.

You see, little sis I felt the same you do, ma never acted like she trusted me and resented the fact that I was seeing too much of Denise and I might get Denise into trouble...I joined the Marines cause I did what I really wanted to, I did what I felt was right inside me & Marianne there wasn't anybody in this world (maybe Denise but she wanted what I wanted) change my mind. Not Dad, not Ma, not anybody. I tried a year of college for THEM, not me and I didn't want it. I gave their wish a try, I didn't dig it so now it was my turn to follow through with my wish. You tried Mount Mary you did what they wanted once, now it's your turn, do what you want the most. Right now I could be smoking herb and screwing girls for a pack of cigarettes, but I do not. Why? Well, cause whether Ma or dad has trust in me or not I don't do it cause it isn't right inside of me. I developed these morals. I have they did not, it's me that did & I developed that way for Ma & Dad to be proud of me, Dad knows, but Ma lacks trust for some stupid reason. Ma & Dad have given us a lot and I owe them a lot, but now I owe myself & you owe yourself your life to make of it what you want. We are old enough now, it's time for me, you & Pat to be on our own and Ma & Dad should start worrying & trusting the younger kids.

Johnny's empathy for Mariann in her struggle with my parents was one of the things that bound them tightly together. Yet Johnny was growing up, his struggle was losing its intensity, while Mariann's ravaged on.

Marianne I'm gonna go to Eastern, Ill. Univ. when I get out,... I will most likely do that cause I want to do it. So do what you want kid & say what Denise and I say when the folks break heavy "Fuck em' all Sammy Small" do what you want. Ask Dee about that saying. Take it easy Mar, if ya

*get anymore static tell me & I'll write to Dad about it & tell
him like it is.*

Love,

John

P.S. Don't worry kid

everything will work

out O.K. I'll see to it!

Tell Denise I Love her!

Johnny used that saying about Sammy Small a lot. I thought he made it up because it was so goofy. I guess there was actually a fighter pilot song called Sammy Small. It was unpredictable what my brother Johnny would latch on to and make popular among his friends. Of course, he did not use this phrase around my dad.

Dad was not the type of father who tossed a ball with his sons or coached little league. He had his jobs and hobbies that he included my brothers in by demanding them to help. They mended fences, harvested the alfalfa (hay), and cleaned the barn. When the wagon was stacked with the bales of hay, my dad or Johnny pulled it into the barn with the big, shiny green John Deere tractor. Together we all helped unload it. Johnny, hay fever mask adorned, unloaded each bale from the wagon onto the conveyor belt, with the help of Bill and Jim. I clicked the counter as each bale traveled up the conveyor belt while Joe and Mickey lifted them from the moving belt and stacked them neatly, according to Dad's instructions. If we had visitors, they helped too. For me, this was fun. I'm not sure it was as much fun for my brothers.

Putting this in perspective—a twenty-year-old son, the oldest boy, an eighteen year old daughter with set ideas, and a strong disciplinarian as a father is the recipe for rebellion. Another ingredient: it was 1970!

May 20

..., well you poor, sorry co-k sucker. I've only been here 3 months and in that time I've seen enough of war, bullets & mortar shells so that I'll never watch COMBAT or any other war flick again. I'm sick of gooks, of crud, of jungle rot, of heat, of no sleep, food in cans, rats & snakes (they like to sleep with me), the fuckin' flies & mosquitoes (maybe some day I'll get malaria & I can go home) I'm sick of the smell of myself, of sweat (I sweat from the time I get up till all time), of the utilities rotting off of me with parts of my skin and most of all I'm sick of seeing my buddies loosing their legs, arms, balls, and eyes by these fuckin' booby traps. My advice is to skate...3 down 8 months & 20 days to go SHIT!

—John A. Guldan, *May 20, 1970,*
to Neal Beatty

Johnny's close friend, Neal, had written to him that he had been drafted. Neal was quietly against the war. He watched the nightly news reporting the body count. Neal changed his opinion from pro-war to anti-war after reading Johnny's letters yet never let Johnny know he was against the war. That opinion of the war was continually reinforced by what he read and saw in Time and Newsweek. He was especially affected by the reports of the massacre at My Lai. The My Lai Massacre and the Tet Offensive were both notorious and brutal Vietnam events of 1968, the highest casualty year of the war. Tet Offensive was presented as an American loss even though our troops created a greater loss in the North Vietnamese army, number-wise. The culture, the perseverance and resilience of the North Vietnamese was underrated when it came to the 'kill more of them and we will win' strategy of the Vietnam War.

Although the U.S. continued to kill a larger number of the NVA and VC, it did not reduce the intensity with which the North Vietnamese fought. They were like an ant colony; working on and on, together, united, their pace never altering. Even if there were only one of them left standing that one would have continued on as if his whole army was behind him. The American servicemen didn't notice there were any less of the enemy no matter how many of them they killed. Whether there was one or there were one hundred still lurking in the jungles, the fear was still there. The land mines were no fewer. The poisoned bamboo shoots, sharpened and waiting at the bottom of a camouflaged hole, were not any fewer either. The man-eating tigers continued to stalk at the same rate. The bloodsucking leeches in the rivers the troops crossed and the centipedes delivering sickening bites were no fewer in numbers. The constant, torrid downpours, jungle rot, and temperatures well over 100 degrees, still came. Their number dead meant nothing to the North Vietnamese army because they'd be fighting fiercely until the last one of them was dead.

May 23

Tuesday's child is full of grace.

—A.E. Bray, *Monday's Child:*
Traditions of Devonshire

Johnny celebrated his twentieth birthday on May 23—a Gemini like my father and born on a Tuesday, also like my father. From time to time, my mother reminded us what day of the week we were born on and recited the poem "Monday's Child." [1] She believed the day we were born was significant to our destiny.

Monday's child is fair of face
Tuesday's child is full of grace
Wednesday's child is full of woe
Thursday's child has far to go
Friday's child is loving and giving
Saturday's child works hard for his living
And the child that is born on the Sabbath day
Is bonny and blithe, and good and gay

The Vietnamese people believe the year someone was born is significant. Their calendar has a twelve-year cycle, and each of those twelve years is represented by an animal. Each of those animals represents a set of characteristics, both positive and negative. When I traveled to Vietnam in 2007, I learned Johnny was born in the year of the Tiger. The tiger represents strength, power, and leadership.

On May 23, knowing my mom missed her son on his birthday, my uncles reminisced with her about when Johnny was born. They all recalled his baptism.

Johnny's baptism took place in the basement of Christ the King Elementary School. Christ the King church had not been built yet, so the basement of the school was used for mass and all sacramental services. My mother did not attend Johnny's baptism. At that time a Catholic ritual, which is no longer practiced, required that a mother go through a purification process after her baby was born. Another Catholic ritual was to have your baby baptized within days after its birth. Since the mother was not yet considered purified, she was not allowed to attend the baby's baptism. All members of the family, except the mother, attended. Everyone else was considered pure, I guess. In addition; most mothers were happy to stay home because this was the time for them to prepare for the party after the ceremony.

Father O'Meara, the priest who performed the baptism, was a humorless man and a stickler for detail. He had been a Navy chaplain during World War II and saw a lot of action. My aunts and uncles believed that Father O'Meara was on two ships that were torpedoed and sunk and that he was involved in a couple of big battles on the beaches of Tarawa.

- - -

Father O'Meara's background explains the demeanor of this man portrayed in my aunts' and uncles' retelling of the infamous baptism.

"When you were an altar boy under Father O'Meara you knew your stuff. There was no foolin' around." Uncle Mike says.

- - -

My father was educated by Jesuits, and my mother's brothers had been taught by the Christian Brothers. This was the basis of a light-hearted rivalry between my father and the Bansley men. One of the differences between these two orders were the prominent saints, which set the stage for the memorable baptism of my brother Johnny.

The baptismal font was located in a windowless room with a low ceiling and a laminate tile floor. There were four babies to be baptized that day, all with their families in that basement room. The saints Johnny was to be named after must be from the Christian Brothers' order, the Bansley men thought, as they waited anxiously for Father O'Meara to pass down the line of infants to their nephew and grandson to be baptized. They could hear each of the families responding to Father O'Meara as he asked them what saint their baby was to be named after. My father was holding Johnny as Father O'Meara approached.

"Well now, his name is John Anthony. What saint is he named after?" Father O'Meara turned to my dad and asked.

In most circumstances, my father was not to be intimidated. Yet with Father O'Meara demanding an answer, Dad was on his way to being intimidated. Uncle John swore he could see the wheels turning in my father's eyes as he tried to think of a Jesuit St. John. Without a clue for an answer, my father looked, wide-eyed, to the sea of dark-suited in-laws crowded behind him. On cue, all of the Bansley men commanded in unison, "St. John Baptist de la Salle." My father turned back around to face Father O'Meara, giving him a slight nod. With that Father O'Meara continued, "And which Saint Anthony do you name this child after?"

My father, again caught off guard, turned to his brothers and father-in-law with raised brows of expectation at this point. Uncle Jim had the honor of being Johnny's godfather since he was Mom's oldest brother.

- - -

Uncle Mike describes what Annie Laurie also vividly remembers:

"Doc kinda' turned around and before he could really say anything Jimmy (Uncle Jim) says," Uncle Mike couldn't help but laugh, "'It's John Baptist de la Salle, Anthony of Padua, Guldan!' Now that I remember," Uncle Mike interrupted himself again with laughter, "it's just a competitive thing. It's not a nasty thing at all." Uncle Mike finishes.

Just boys being boys, I think to myself.

- - -

So that was it. My brother's full, Christian name was never known as just John Anthony. It was John Baptist de la Salle, Anthony of Padua. At least that's what my uncles called him. I never knew the story behind that long name until Annie Laurie's interview in December 2007. Annie Laurie said she had never heard a baptizing priest ask for the specific saint for which a child was named.

More children were born to my parents, and many more baptisms took place. Annie Laurie had been very close with the three oldest children in our family, while they lived in an adjacent neighborhood. When Johnny was five or six, he visited Aunt Annie Laurie and Uncle Jack on Green Street. It was during this visit Annie Laurie taught Johnny how to tie his shoes. My mother was thrilled. She had tried and tried to no avail. Johnny would not be allowed to enter kindergarten without this skill. Annie Laurie later became a teacher. It was her calling.

May 24

What's this crap about Marianne at an antiwar rally?
She told me she got in a little trouble with school, but
she didn't say why. Ya better tell her I'm disappointed
in her if she's doin' that stuff.

—John A. Guldan, May 24, 1970,

to my father

Johnny had been hearing about Mariann's anti-war sentiments from Denise and a few others. He learned from my parents that Mariann had been out after curfew at an anti-war demonstration at Marquette University. Although Mariann tried to strike out as an independent adult, it was these same actions that tightened the noose around the artery that still connected her to Mom and Dad.

Mariann was vaguely aware of Johnny's concern about her protesting. Although he never said anything to her directly about it, she had always claimed she was never involved in any organized protests. She never demonstrated or marched. I never did determine how she exhibited her anti-war opinion. Back then, when I was a very patriotic ten-year-old, I would have been appalled had I known my sister protested the war.

- - -

"But she was a protestor. She protested her family," Aunt Barbara insists during my interview with her and Uncle Jim.

Uncle Jim and Aunt Barbara have been married fifty-four years when I interview them in December 2007. Aunt Barbara was disheartened by the lack of awareness the public had of the young boys fighting in Vietnam. She refers to it as "The Forgotten War." Society was frivolous and rambunctious. People were carrying on like there was no war, instead of the conservative reverence one would expect while young men were putting their lives on the line for their country.

"You have to support him [the President]. He knows more than the average person. You just got to have faith that he'll make the best decision with that knowledge," Aunt Barbara says to me.

If we are not a united front, then we are not the United States. This is Aunt Barbara's stance.

- - -

After Mariann's first and only year at Mount Mary, she moved back home for the summer, where she lived unhappily. At this time, Johnny had been in Vietnam for several months. Mariann's boyfriend, Bruce, came to our house and met my parents for the first time. It did not score any points with my mother that Bruce addressed my dad as "Mr. Guldan" rather than "Dr. Guldan." When I met Bruce for the first time I saw a tall, skinny dude with a big Afro and the widest, worn out bell-bottom jeans I'd ever seen. He was bent over, peering into the fish tank in our living room, as if it had something interesting swimming around in it. We had neon tetras, the most common fish around. I noticed this guy my sister brought home had a strong accent that told me he wasn't from around Beverly, or probably anywhere in Illinois. He didn't sound like he was from Wisconsin either. Bruce, we all soon discovered, was a New York Italian. At eight years old, my youngest brother Chris sensed disruption around his big sister's new boyfriend and was certain he had a motorcycle outside waiting to whisk Mariann away.

- - -

Chris tries to recall why he felt tension between our parents and Mariann and Bruce. He thinks this was based on Bruce's anti-war attitude.

"I don't blame him because it was a messed up war. Should'a never been over there. Just like what we're dealin' with now," Chris says. He was referring to the wars spun out of the 9/11 attacks on our country.

"I know. At that time, I remember thinking anyone who was against the war was a bad person. Now I see. It definitely was wrong," I say.

- - -

Mariann and my father's battle of wills was never loud. Mariann did not accommodate Dad's rules like the rest of us. My dad said, "No smoking," and Mariann smoked in the house. Dad said the album "Hair" was sacrilegious and we were not allowed to listen to it. Mariann brought the album home and listened to it in the living room when my parents weren't home. My mother made the choice to remain silent when Mariann disagreed with my father's rules. I think she hoped to show support for Dad and at the same time not make Mariann mad at her. That hope was not realized. Dad did give in a little and eventually told Mariann she could go to Eastern. But maybe it was too little, too late because we had our own little war going on at 9029 Oakley.

Mariann confided in Bruce that she was an outcast in our family. Bruce DaCosta offered Mariann every ounce of sympathy and support that existed in his emotional arsenal. Bruce, a young man of twenty-two, was defending an eighteen-year-old damsel in distress. Together they were united against my father. Bruce appealed to Mariann's rebellious side. Although, by the age of eighteen, rebellion was no longer just a side of her, it was becoming her whole being.

What none of us realized was that Bruce did not speak out against the war. He just looked like he did. And he did not dodge the draft. Due to physical issues he was not considered fit for service and, therefore, was relieved of the burden to make that choice. Although he had heard enough stories of the Vietnam War to know it was not where he wanted to be, he would have followed his brothers' leads had he been called to duty. His oldest brother Joe had served in Korea while his brother Bobby was in the National Guard. Another brother, Randy, was drafted in the late sixties, yet narrowly escaped deployment to Vietnam. I'm sure my parents were not aware of all of this. How perceptions get twisted when fear is involved.

Bruce called the house one evening to speak to Mariann. Dad answered, but since Mariann was expecting the call, she was nearby. Dad told Bruce he could not talk to her. Mariann heard this and protested, of course. Bruce, hearing Mariann trying to get to the phone, called my father a son-of-a-bitch. Dad was flabbergasted that a child, and a boyfriend of his own child, called him a swear word. None of us had ever spoken back to my father, at least not within earshot.

Bruce grew up in a middle-class Long Island family as a son of an alcoholic immigrant. Treatment of his own father occasionally included physical brawls, to keep him at bay until he sobered up. So to Bruce, calling a parent a son-of-a-bitch was not so unusual and did not warrant my father's reaction of barring him from our house.

In 1970, us kids thought of Bruce as a hippie. Margie didn't understand how Mariann, her prom queen heroine, could date someone who looked like a radical and a war protestor. From the looks of the two of them together, they were as different as chalk and cheese. With Bruce's Afro and bell-bottoms, an anti-war sentiment oozed from his large Italian pores, while Mariann's whites and pastels, her hair usually in National Velvet style, and her nose often buried in a classic novel, emitted a Norman Rockwell-esque air.

Margie attended Academy of Our Lady (AOL) High School, same as her older sisters, Patti and Mariann. I think it was the twelve-block walks to school each day, even in the snow, in their penny loafers that bonded Margie to her older sisters, like soldiers who endured a lot together. When Eileen and Margie started high school in 1968, Mariann was a junior. By the time Mariann had graduated, she left her younger sisters big shoes to fill as valedictorian, class president, and homecoming queen. Although neither was close to Mariann, Margie and Eileen were in awe of their big sister.

It was difficult for Margie to understand what drew Mariann to Bruce. With his anti-war image, Bruce was clearly making a statement against the very purpose Johnny was fighting for. Given that Johnny and Mariann had such a strong bond, Margie never understood how Mariann could keep up both relationships. She didn't understand a lot about her big sister, who was brooding and quiet and distant from the rest of us, except Johnny. There were a lot of confusing things going on.

We have also one blonde Marine who traded over and is leading a squad of VC. I have encountered him once on patrol & we missed him, but I know we wounded him.

Seventy soldiers in every one thousand deserted between the years 1966 and 1971. In this same letter to my father, Johnny told of a whole black platoon that had traded over, sabotaging the U.S. Marines supply depots in key areas.

...Those people are the ones I would enjoy killing.

And the very next sentence, he writes:

Tell Nan I got a package from Mrs. Carroll and the squad ate well once again.

- - -

"When your life is at stake, you're going to do things you regret," Uncle John says as I interview him. His head and heart are full of somber memories about Johnny's months in Vietnam.

- - -

I got the birthday cards from Bonnie and they were cute.

Mom did not fail at having that card arrive in Vietnam on his birthday.

The gooners have a new booby trap. It's a ZIPPO cigarette lighter just placed on the road. A Marine picks it up, strikes it & it blows up. They fill it with NITRO and now cigarette smoking is really hazardous to one's health. We've already had one medevac cause of it and the guy was only in country 2 weeks. I told the nit wit not to pick anything up at all...

Having said goodbye to his teen years a whole day earlier, Johnny had acquired a callous attitude toward the deadly "booby trap." He disregarded the pact he had made earlier not to tell my folks anything. He was a witness and it seemed he must tell someone what he saw.

I almost got busted by our capt. today because we killed a woman out after curfew, she had an interesting cargoe. 2 mortar rounds and an AK 47 rifle. The Capt. Couldn't get it through his silly head that she was VC so I picked up the rifle & fired it into a tree & said to him that this AK doesn't fire blanks & that they have a habit of killing Marines whether fired by male, female or kid. Dad he is an ignorant fool, he's in the rear all the time unless something happens to the villagers. He doesn't even come out to us when a Marine is wounded. All he wanted to know was when my buddy Peeler got killed was if he had his flak jacket on. Dad he just doesn't know what's goin' on, it's like he is blind ...I shouldn't have said that.

"Puppet soldiers" was the name the North Vietnamese gave to the South Vietnamese soldiers. This term meant that these soldiers were controlled by the imperialistic United States to do their dirty work. It had a mocking connotation. Johnny may have felt like a "Puppet Soldier," controlled with strings held by others. He signed off this long letter, aware of the strings:

if I get busted it's only $8 difference,...Oh well, I have the lives of 3 other men plus my own I have to watch over cause I was made first fire team leader. The capt might have different ideas though. My men have confidence in me & I have confidence in myself so screw the capt.

Thanks for writing Dad, I wish I could write longer letters,...I miss you all, this summer will be hell without you people.

Love,

John

"Cha mon yadda fellas!" we yelled as we ran down the basement stairs. Snowball had grandchildren. Derf, her daughter, had a litter. It was the responsibility of Joe, Mick, and I to give them milk and water. We gave them lots of cuddling too. They were all so cute when they stampeded toward us every time we chanted "cha mon yadda fellas!" We were responsible for the lives of these puppies yet we could not have understood the enormous responsibility Johnny had while protecting the lives of those men.

May 25

> *"I've seen war psychosis, and I've seen guys in combat who lose all fear for some reason,...it makes you wonder about who we are..."*
> —Nelson DeMille, Up Country

In a May 25 letter to Denise, Johnny attempts to put the insanity of war into his own words:

Dear Denise,

Wow, it's hotter than hell around here now. I'll never forget this heat Denise, there isn't even any wind either. Last night was a bad night for us Marines Angel and it was one of those times I felt how precious life is & how terribly much you mean to me. The gooners hit us with a suicide squad (zappers, we call them) and they hurt us, they even stole our M-60 machine gun so now we have to be extra careful where ever we patrol. That M-60 can cut a man in half. After we examined their little bods we found out why they were so brave. They were all doped up and they had wires running through their skin from bone to bone and were wrapped tightly with tape at the joints, so when we shot them & blew them up they kept coming by the strength of their final reflexes. Do ya see that shovel I got in my hand in that flick, well remember the Sand Pebbles & how Steve Mcqueen used that axe? Denise I got sick all over, I emptied my whole magazine of 20 rounds into him & he still kept comin'. I couldn't believe he was still runnin' at me with just a bayonet, he was screaming so loud my ears were ringing, something made me pick up that shovel and start swingin'. God Denise these gooners are out of their minds & don't care about life. One of them had dynamite tied to him & jumped in the fightin hole with the gunner Allen and blew himself and Allen to hell. That's how they got the gun. Jesus Denise I've never been so scared or so sick in my life. On top of that our corpman caught it in the neck and besides killing I had to patch men up too. We called in the medevac and the Doc will be O.K., but Allen wasn't as lucky. Denise after last night I'm convinced that God is with me in this hell hole, especially when rockets hit, I mean Darling what keeps that rocket from landing in the hole with me is a lot more than just luck. Denise if I could be any place else in the world with you now, any place at all is my wish. If this gets any worse I'm gonna go off my rocker. Maybe I ought to cross that thin red line that separates sanity from insanity, maybe they will send me home to you then. Oh Denise I need you so very much, please stay mine forever, I know if you are waiting and will be my wife I can make it. I know I can Denise. I'll love you till I die and I'll Love you into eternity.

I must close Darling take care of yourself I miss you so much my insides hurt.

ALL OF MY Love
And
Heart,
John

I had always hoped that my brother did not kill. This was the first letter I read from Johnny that clearly stated he killed another human being. He took another life. I no longer wanted to write this book when I read this in 2008. Believing he did not kill was the naiveté of an eleven-year-old. I kept writing. Something pulled me back to it. A story still needed to be told. But I no longer knew what story.

May 29

Dear Jim and Bill,

Thanks for the letter and ya better quit sending me those pictures what the hell, do you want me to get a hard-on?

—John A. Guldan, *May 29, 1970,*
to brothers

So much for that idea, Jim thought. Billy and Jim wanted to take Johnny's mind off his current hardships and being teenage boys their minds went one way to solve that problem. They sent pictures of provocatively posed and barely clad beautiful young women they had cut out of magazines.

Johnny was making a conscious choice not to get involved in the unhealthy activities, such as sex and drugs, offered daily to him and his platoon mates. It was a tempting escape to deal with the harshness of life around him. Drugs and dissension had become a big issue among the men Johnny was fighting alongside. He would not turn his back on some men in his platoon. His toiletries, his writing supplies and even his gun went missing at times. My parents replenished his supplies the best they could, sending them in packages he received regularly. My father attempted to send a gun. One of the most valuable things Dad sent was that pair of binoculars, yet they took a long time getting there.

I haven't received the binoculars yet, but I'll watch for them. Dad, those things will be as good as gold, the snipers are doing a lot of damage to our company. Somebody up there really likes me.

While President Johnson was pouring more troops into Vietnam to support the efforts of war, Mayor Daley was doing all that he could to prevent war in the streets of Chicago. The young adults of the seventies were not inhibited about exercising their right of freedom of expression. The Black Panthers and the Chicago 7, notorious entities known around the country in the late sixties and early seventies, spurred on the young activists. The Chicago 7 was a group of radical motorcycle riders who participated in anti-war protests that took place in my home city. Many of these events became violent, and conservative members of society, my parents being two of them, viewed the group as criminals. A famous trial was held in 1970 that centered on this group's responsibility for deaths and property destruction in the Chicago Democratic convention of 1968.

Uncle Jim was thirty-seven years old and working night shifts as a stationary engineer at Children's' Memorial Hospital. There he had plenty of exposure to the anti-war sentiment. Often there were young demonstrators on Michigan Avenue and Lake Shore Drive when he went into work each evening. He noticed how most of them were young kids. He never saw forty- or fifty-year-olds. It was common knowledge that the young protested the Vietnam War. But for my Uncle Jim, who was busy raising a young family and working two jobs, he was just beginning to realize, back then, that there was a whole movement of young people speaking against the war. When he was the age of many of the protestors Uncle Jim was in the Marines Officer Training reserves. It was during a time of peace but he would have been ready to fight if our country was at war.

The protestors in front of the hospital always made Uncle Jim think of his nephew, who was putting his life on the line for these kids' freedom of speech. If he could only explain to them, Uncle Jim thought. Instead, one night after passing through the crowd of them, he sat down on his lunch break and wrote a letter to Johnny. He told Johnny how proud he was for what he was doing and that, although it was wrong that the Kent State students were shot, he didn't agree with the anti-war demonstrators. He wrote that the freedom enjoyed and taken for granted by those protestors exists because of guys like Johnny.

Our young citizens fighting for us 13,000 miles away also consisted of protestors. Two more men from Johnny's platoon had traded over to the NVA:

Dad you wouldn't believe how low the morale is here. . . . It's no fun to have Marines kill Marines, but God these guys are traitors.

The South Vietnamese army lost 120,000 each year to desertion. There were graphic public displays depicting burning villages, mutilations of "the enemy," torture, beating, killing, and shooting civilians. A year later, in a 1971 march on the Capitol, 700 Vietnam vets threw away their medals. That same year, there were 20,000 members in Vietnam Vets Against the War (VVAW). In the United States, the threat of riots and violence over race, the draft, and the war, rumbled like an active volcano any time three or more people gathered in one spot. Ironically, while racial wars surged among the U.S. civilian population, where the real war was going on, in Vietnam, Johnny and his platoon mates were colorblind. Johnny's letters never mentioned color when speaking of the men within his own platoon. There were whites, blacks, Filipinos, Mexicans, all watching each other's backs, entrusting their lives to each other. They had a business card made calling themselves the "Mod Squad" of Mike Company with all of their nicknames listed: Gil, Raleoscar, Smiley, Blue, Prof (Johnny), Oruis, Bear, Chico, Deck, Perry, DTGN, Stretch, Doc, Chief, TGN, and Bear Dog.

Thousands of miles away, news of all the upheaval reached Johnny. To him it must have felt like the alien invasion in H.G. Wells' War of the Worlds.

...I guess the morale will get lower if race riots start up this summer. Dad, it is sickening, if anything happens to you people or Denise, I'll swim home I'm not kidding. There's enough killing and hate over here, why can't they leave it where a war should be fought. They gave us the May 15th

issue of Life Mag and that crap about KENT. Dad 3 people out of the 4 weren't even in on the protest and they got it... it makes me awful mad. That could have been Pat, Marianne or maybe Denise. Dad it even scares me more than going out on a killer team at night. They tell us not to think about it & grab your rifle ya gotta job to do now, but I can't get that fear outta me. Boy, Dad this is bad I got fear for my life and for those 13,000 miles away. I really got into a mess...

The headlines of the Kent State tragedy had reached the NVA as well. A village boy taunted the Marines of Hill 55 with the cover of an American magazine showing the bodies of the students on the campus lawn.

Johnny brings up the topic of his love and fierce protection for Denise, who lived only a few miles away. She didn't not come over to our house much but my parents heard a lot about her in Johnny's letters. Dad most certainly can relate to being a young man in love with the woman of his dreams.

...I know you and Ma probably think I'm too young to be so gone over one girl like I am over Denise, but contrary to your good or bad thoughts on feelings you have of her she means as much to me as you people. She said she would wait, I told her it would be better if she did not, but she would not even listen to me. She said to shut up and that she would wait forever, so when I get back & get a little squared away & settled I'm gonna marry her.

I have to close now take care of yourselves, Happy Memorial Day too.   Love,
                                                                                                                                John

Despite these heavy topics that filled Johnny's mind that day, he had room for advice to his younger brothers Jim and Bill –

...So you quit in the 2 miles, Bill, well no sweat track doesn't mean anything at all, don't get tied up in it as much as I did. I don't believe you two assholes don't have a girl yet. When ya get one make sure she is fine and send me a picture of her.

I hope you guys did O.K. in school and I hope ya have a great summer, and if ya see Denise or Margaret her sister slap them on their fine asses for me.

Ya better not get too drunk at least don't get caught at it...

When growing up Johnny took advantage of his reign as an older brother. Jim, Bill, Joe, Mickey, and Chris did not escape being terrorized by Johnny and his friends. Johnny was true to his astrological sign, Gemini, the twins, with two sides to his personality. He had a sensitive, caring side, which showed in his letters to Denise, and he also had a tough, bullying side that came out when he teased his younger brothers. He and his friends routinely intercepted the younger boys in the alley on their way home from school.

"Ouch!" they hollered at the sting of hard-thrown ice-packed snowballs when they smacked against their legs and backs, causing welts beneath their wool slacks and winter jackets. Joe stood there and took it. Due to the large age gap of eight years—and perhaps the snowball attacks—Joe did not have a close relationship with Johnny, though they definitely looked like brothers. They were both runners. They were both proud, both sensitive. They both had that thick, dark-brown wavy and coarse hair of the dark Irish. Johnny's relationship with Jim, however, was on an equal, almost competitive level. It would be safe to bet that

Jim was not in that lineup of snowball targets. It seemed that deep down Jim admired Johnny without openly admitting it, whereas Bill openly looked up to Johnny.

- - -

"I was always getting beat up by him." This is Bill's first comment when I ask him about his relationship to Johnny, yet he says it with an endearing tone.

"Him [Johnny] and his friends, Neal and Pachol, as we got older they used to line us up against the garage wall in the alley and just beam us with snowballs an' stuff." Bill laughs heartily. "We all would do what he told us," Bill says and laughs again.

I ask Bill why he didn't run away when he was getting snowballs whipped at him. Bill, still laughing, says Johnny, Neal, and Pachol told them if they ran they would get it worse. "These older boys had things figured out," I say. We both laugh.

"They were probably fourteen or sixteen. So I'm five years younger than Johnny...yeah, we were like nine and eight," Bill says. No hard feelings—no one got hurt other than their pride.

- - -

The uncles and cousins gathered at the Kellogg elementary school playground or Grandpa's backyard for what they called the "Annual Snow Bowl." This was a football game initiated after a significant snowfall. My dad did not take part in these games. Although athletically inclined, he was not a fan of contact sports. He enjoyed watching along the sidelines, ribbing and chiding our uncles, his brothers-in-law. During one game, Uncle Mike instructed Mickey to stay put in one position. Mickey obeyed, digging a little hole in the snow and securely planting himself. Johnny came running his way and ran right into Mickey, who grabbed his big brother's leg and held on tight. This brought

Johnny down. Uncle Mike would not stop teasing him that day about his little brother tackling him.

Even with all of the antics Johnny perpetrated against his younger brothers, they stayed connected with him through letters. In 'Nam there was no censorship of mail like there had been in boot camp. One week after Johnny's twentieth birthday, he taught his brothers Jim and Bill more about his stay in Vietnam. Johnny and his platoon mates were not only stalked by the NVA and VC, they were stalked by Asian tigers, living right there in the jungles with them.

...Yeah that is my M-16 and it is suppose to be small cause of the jungle and quick-kill techniques. Me and another Marine in my squad killed a tiger 2 days ago. The thing was trackin' us for about a mile on patrol, we heard him rumbling in the bush and then we saw it, God it was the biggest thing I ever saw. Almost as big as Snuffy, well we emptied 20 rounds into it & that was that. The villagers were happy and they took the skin...

Snuffy was our Shetland pony. Johnny used to hitch Snuffy to the pony cart and ride us around the farm for hours, taking turns in the cart with him. Johnny and Snuffy were pretty tight. However, once Snuffy stepped on Johnny's foot accidentally and Johnny punched Snuffy in the jaw. Poor little Snuffy, who stood only four or five hands high, was not hurt by this as much as Johnny, who broke his hand.

In the same letter that began with Johnny telling Jim and Bill about killing a tiger, he ends telling his younger brothers about his plans for the night:

Well you guys take it easy, take it any way you can get it. I have a killer team to go on so say a prayer if ya know how, I almost forgot how to, there's no room here for them.

Your Bro,

John

Bill thought all this stuff was cool when he read these as a young teenager in 1970. It was the same kind of things he saw in movies. Jimmy wasn't so sure how to take the accounts of war his big brother was sharing with him. My parents? I think they hoped and prayed he would come home. They would worry about his faith later.

May 30

We are the unwilling, fighting for the unskillful, doing the unnecessary, for the ungrateful.

—Konstantin Jirecek,
Slavic scholar (1854-1918)

Johnny had scribbled this quotation on a small scrap of paper that was wrapped up with a letter to Uncle Jim and had also included it in an April letter to my parents. Johnny was in the midst of mankind at its worst. He and the other Marines were willing to give their lives, but for what? It seemed they no longer knew.

Johnny began his May 30 letter to Uncle Jim—

We had to find the supply routes down to Dodge City. That's where my company is at now.

One of the strategies of the American servicemen was to cut off the supplies being sent to the North Vietnamese. Dodge City spanned a five-mile radius south of Da Nang, filled with hamlets and tunnels. It was called Dodge City because of the cowboy-style fighting tactics carried out in that area.

We have been getting heavy resistance from the NVA since we moved into Cambodia. The VC and NVA are running back with as much weapons as they can carry, right into the old stronghold we took away from them two months ago. We gave these areas we secured to the Army and now of course the "doggies" let go and we have to take them back. I am Fire Team Leader now and I have a lot more responsibility. Not only my life but three other men I have to watch and lead. I'm still a PFC, but you know rank doesn't mean a thing in the bush. I am in charge of two Corporals and one Lance Corporal. So you can see it doesn't mean a thing. My squad is due for a rest soon but maybe it's just talk. I hope it isn't just scuttlebutt. We found that supply route. Most of it was tunnels. I rigged charges on a trunk line all the way down. They ought to be slowed up a little bit by it. I set booby traps all along their route. Now they can taste what it's like to hit booby traps. I know you won't tell my ma that we did this. Cuz if I wrote it to her and dad they would worry like heck so don't tell them. It's 110 degrees out now and the monsoons have just about started. I freeze when it rains because the temp drops to 80 and I'm use to high temps.

This letter to Uncle Jim followed the one he had sent Johnny about the Kent State shooting. Although it was the only letter Uncle Jim had written Johnny, it made a big impact. He assured Johnny that he supported him.

Your letter made me feel good. I let the men in my fire team read it and it made them feel pretty good too. I wish I could've been at the annual get together. I'm sure Denise and I would have been the deciding factor in the game. Well next year we will be there. I have to go now. Thanks for the letter Uncle Jim. It was good hearing from you.

Sincerely,

John

At the time Johnny wrote this letter to Uncle Jim, the big Memorial Day bash was taking place at Uncle Jim and Aunt Barbara's house on 93rd and Longwood in Chicago. It had become a tradition for the Bansley gang to get together on this holiday. This event was not only in honor of Memorial Day it was also Uncle Jim's birthday. Memorial Day was extra special that year, because we had something—or someone—to commemorate: Johnny was fighting for our freedom. All the cousins and a few close friends came. We put softball teams together with the aunts and uncles as captains. Each team competed against the others at the Longwood Park baseball diamond. A winning team was determined at the end of the day. It was very competitive. Arguments between the aunt and uncle coaches arose and were forgotten by the end of the day as the adults all sat around a backyard fire drinking beers and laughing about the day's events.

We took a picture of everyone, including Grandma and Grandpa. They were right in the middle, Grandma in her wheelchair. It was a feat trying to fit us all in. Of course, not everyone was looking at the camera. My Uncle John tugged on one of my braids and I turned around just as a neighbor snapped the picture. As soon as the photo was developed, Mom sent a copy to Johnny.

June 8

Dear Dad & Mom,

Thanks, Dad for those binoculars, they are great. They are the best things since the eye-ball.
—John A. Guldan, *June 8, 1970,*
to my parents

These binoculars were what Johnny had asked for as a birthday present, and finally they arrived. I too had just celebrated a birthday. On June second, I turned eleven. My sisters Margie and Eileen had planned a birthday party for me. I was now at Kellogg yet Margie and Eileen invited the girls that were in my Christ the King class because they knew their older sisters. I felt a little awkward, because we didn't go to the same school anymore but was happy they came. My cousins Anne and Jean came, too, and told me about a letter their dad had just received from Johnny. I think they wanted me to be interested, but I wasn't. It was my birthday and I wanted it to be about me. At 11 years old, I couldn't understand where he was, nor what he was going through.

The fire team leader, whose position Johnny had taken a few days earlier, was fired for refusing to obey an order during combat. The U.S. Marines were having difficulty controlling their own men and the South Vietnamese Army. Many of them were unwilling to fight to save their own country. This was exasperating and did not help the low morale. In this letter to my parents, Johnny writes:

> *I took out a killer team on the night of the 4th and it consisted of 4 Marines & 6 South Viet soldiers, I got 100 meters outside our perimeter and the South Viets sat right down and refused to go on,... After I spoke to their leader (I have picked up the language pretty good and it's even easier than Latin) I found that they were too scared to go on. Well, we left them & went on our task, when we got back they weren't there just weapons & helmets were laying there. The next day the South Viets were suppose to go on a sweep with us, they refused, and again we went on by ourselves... it's their war & they won't even fight it,...*

He was a little bold to tell my parents that he went on a killer team after it was clear they did not want to know. But what could my parents do? I guess he couldn't help but tell them the truth.

June 9

I don't know this Bruce dude or what he is like, but if
Marianne likes him then he's alright.

—John A. Guldan, *June 9, 1970,*

to Patti

"He didn't understand what was goin' on with Mariann and why nobody liked Bruce. Ya know, that kinda shit. That's in one of the letters I got," Bill tells me.

- - -

Bruce, born November 28, 1948, was the youngest of six. He grew up in the middle class town of Hicksville, on Long Island, New York. To this day, Bruce has a strong East Coast accent despite having lived on the West Coast for almost ten years. His father was born in Jamaica and came to Ellis Island at the age of twelve. Somewhere between his youth and his adulthood, he became an alcoholic and remained one as he fathered and raised six children. Bruce's mother, the daughter of a potato farmer, was a native of Long Island. She was a housewife and his father a plumber, neither having made it to high school. Bruce was one of the few in his family who went to college and got a degree. He was attending the Milwaukee School of Engineering (MSOE) when he met my sister Mariann at a Marquette party, in the spring of 1970.

The back porch housed all of our boots and coats and probably some lawn tools. With its white siding, this small room was an obvious addition to our brown brick bungalow. It had a couple of large screened windows that could be slid open to provide some fresh air and offered the cheeriness of sunlight during the day. The triplets used to hang out on this porch from time to time with one or two of their friends. When I came through the back porch after a long day of play, I had to pass through this small crowd. Bill, about thirteen at the time, was sitting on this porch when Mariann, a quiet woman of action, came flying through the door, shoes in hand, not on her feet.

"Good bye," Mariann said to Bill.

"Where ya goin?" Bill asked.

Mariann was upset. Her face was red and tear-stained.

"I'm leavin'!" Mariann answered.

She ran down the steps of the porch and Bill watched her continue down the driveway and disappear somewhere down Oakley Avenue. Bill went inside to find out what happened, able to fill my father in on what he had just witnessed. Dad got right in the car and drove around the neighborhood looking for Mariann. She was only a few blocks away when he found her walking alone, down the sidewalk. He pulled her into the car kicking and yelling. He then went so far as to, literally, drag Mariann to a psychiatrist, thinking she had a "screw loose". His words.

Back home, Mariann wrote distressed letters to Bruce, telling him of her inability to endure car rides with my father and her refusal to work at his office. Bruce, as were the most of us, were perplexed as to how this ultra-sensitivity had developed. It was understandable to be angry about some of the things my dad did. But Mariann seemed to be angry with everything he said and did. The summer of 1970, Bruce had planned to live in New York with his family, but Mariann's letters changed his mind. Believing my parents had done something unjust to cause the rift, Bruce moved from New York to the Chicago area in hero-like fashion. He rented an apartment in Forest Park, a suburb fifteen miles northwest of Beverly, and got a job at a nearby GoTane gas station.

Upset about the family commotion caused by Mariann seeing Bruce, Johnny was skeptical of Bruce's motivation for writing when he received his letter. Still, Johnny was compelled to write back. A seed of negativity had been planted by the consistent message he had gotten in letters from Denise yet he wanted to give his younger sister every benefit of the doubt. He decided to reach out to Patti on June 9 to get her opinion:

So Marianne's boyfriend is nesting in Chi-town this summer. Denise met him and said he was a nice guy, but a creep (don't tell Marianne) ...That little sister of mine is smart and she knows what is right & wrong by now.

In his few letters to Bruce, Johnny tried to develop some kind of bond, in the best interest of his sister. But he was torn as to what was really going on and whether the boyfriend she had chosen was good for her.

- - -

In a conversation with my brother Bill in 2000, my father talked about the incident. Dad explained why he dragged Mariann into the car; he described her as stubborn and bull-headed. He added: "It's funny. Back then no one called the cops on you if you touched your child. I was surprised nobody did."

"Dad wanted his kids to do what he wanted them to do instead of allowing us to do what we wanted to do, and support us! That's where Dad was terrible. I'll never forget I wanted to buy and play guitar and stuff and he didn't want me to. Come to find out, when he was a kid, Nan made him take trumpet lessons, piano lessons and somethin' else. And he HATED it."

Bill finishes with, "Well, you don't find too many families like ours anymore. Everybody's divorced and married three times over, kids from different fathers."

Silence follows. He was right. There have been many divorces in our family now; I have been divorced twice myself. We realize that a family like the one we grew up in displayed admirable loyalty and strength.

June 12

When I reached manhood, I married Anna, a woman of our own lineage. By her I had a son whom I named Tobiah.

—Tobit 1:9, *New American Bible*

It was my parents' 22nd anniversary. Mom and Dad had known each other from a young age. Dad and his family were living on 94th and Leavitt when my mother's family moved into the neighborhood in the 1940s, only two blocks away. My father, a striking young man with jet black hair and a six-pack physique, was hard for my mother to resist when he finally got up the courage to ask her out. Although my mother played coy, she was love struck. Once she got to know him, it was his intellect, his devotion, his upbringing and his faith that inspired her love. My father, like my mother, attended private Catholic schools. Over the course of their courtship, Mom went off to Mount Mary College in Milwaukee and Dad to dental school at Northwestern University in Evanston, Illinois. Dad couldn't bear their separation and proposed. He insisted Mom quit college, so she finished her sophomore year, got married, and never looked back.

Years later it was very important to my mother that I followed my dream to go to college. When I was trying to figure out how to pay for school, Mom took me to Northern Trust Bank in Chicago. We met a friend of hers who worked there. He took the forms I had filled out and made sure they were processed. I got the loan and went to Illinois State University.

Mom and Dad were married at Christ the King school on June 12, 1948. There was no church at that time. Their marriage service took place in the basement of the school, with my mother's brothers John and Mike attending as altar boys. The church, where we attended weekly mass and where all of us kids made our sacraments, was built many years later. Despite being married in a basement, my parents had a large, formal wedding with extravagant gowns and silver and crystal gifts from many well-to-do friends of their parents. Grandpa could afford this because he was a successful entrepreneur and accountant. However, despite this fairytale beginning, difficulties were as much a part of their marriage as good times. Soon after the honeymoon, my mother learned how tightly my father was attached to his mother's apron strings. Dad spent a lot of time at the home of his mother rather than with his wife during the early part of their marriage. Nonetheless, the children came quickly. Patti, Johnny, and Mariann were born before my parents celebrated their fourth anniversary.

June 16

Dear Dad & Ma,

Ma, I got your cookies and they were the best I ever had, I thank you & the squad thanks you. I got your letter about telling me not to worry about you people at home and it brought my morale up quite a bit...

—John A. Guldan, *June 16, 1970,*
to my parents

Mom had Margie and Eileen bake cookies for Johnny in our little farm kitchen. I baked a batch of cookies, too, but used salt instead of sugar. Needless to say, I was told to just watch as my older sisters did the baking. Once done, they shared a fresh one with me just like Johnny shared the treats he received from home with his friends on Hill 55.

We had packed up and made the seasonal exodus to our farm in Waupaca, Wisconsin that summer, removing ourselves from the media and the incessant body count. Life at the farm rarely included watching TV for anything more than the local news at 10 p.m. Jim, Joe, Mick, myself, Chris, and Mimi were all excited about spending our summer at the farm. Bill was disappointed, because going to the farm meant he'd miss the summer baseball leagues. Bonnie was happy to be there as long as her mom and sister Mimi were there too. Johnny, on the other hand, was now in the ominous place he had referred to earlier—Dodge City.

Well I am now a fully qualified demolitions expert, I went to school for it & passed with a 96%, it was very interesting, they even gave me a diploma. We are now in a place called Dodge City and the monsoons have started. I feel like one big drip. It is impossible to stay dry and when the rain stops for a few minutes the steam dries me off only to get wet again...

North Vietnam was industrial, as a result of its Chinese influence, where South Vietnam was agricultural.

...Supply has been hard to get cause of the rains so we have been eating a lot of rice and herbs, the water we drink is from rice paddies so the halazone tablets make the water taste wonderful, almost like from a bubbler back home.

On our first weekend at the farm that summer, we celebrated my dad's birthday, which was June 14. Dad went fishing and was happy just to be at the farm for his birthday. Someone made a cake and frosted it with chocolate frosting, his favorite, and we all sang "Happy Birthday."

...I'll say again Dad, your binoculars are great, on a bright night they are even better than a star-lite scope (infrared) we have...

In the early part of summer, there seemed to be more rainy days than sunny ones, up at the farm. When the rain kept us in, the younger kids played combat games in the barn. We made foxholes out of bales of hay stacked in the barn. I loved making these hiding places. We played combat for hours, using croquet mallets for guns. That had been Johnny's idea.

...take care and say hi to all my brothers & sisters, tell me when I should start writing to you at the farm, I forget the address.

Love,
John

When Johnny used to play the barn war games, he gave my sister Margie, who was a three-and-a-half-years younger than him, the role of medic.

- - -

"I thought he was old. At that time I never thought about how young that was. . . . He was the boss," Margie says.

"The boss even over Patti?" I ask.

"Yep. He decided what we all watched on TV. We watched what he wanted," Margie clearly remembers.

Like Margie, Eileen remembers times when Johnny ordered her around, too.

"I remember him putting us in gunny sacks, with Jimmy and Billy [helping]." Eileen says this with an "it didn't bother me" attitude.

- - -

Patti and Eileen worked at my dad's office during the week, while Mariann took the train downtown to work for Grandpa at Bansley & Kiener, his accounting firm. Denise had begun a summer job at the Chicago Transit Authority (CTA). Each morning, she took the train into the city. Denise had waited anxiously for his first letter to arrive from Da Nang. When it finally did, she was relieved to know he was somewhere and safe—safe enough to write, anyway. Since that March day when he landed in Vietnam, she had received several letters a week, yet it never stopped her from being anxious each day. So, each night when she got home, the first thing she did was check the mail. There was usually a letter or a package with a cassette tape from Vietnam. Yes, Johnny also managed to send flowers and tape-recorded messages to his girl.

A few dried stems from these flowers were in the container of letters, cards, cassettes, and mementos Denise entrusted to me when I began this book. As I speak to her today, she doesn't remember the particular occasion for which Johnny sent her these flowers.

"Knowing Johnny, they were just because," she tells me.

This sturdy box contains her remains of Johnny. It hurts too much to keep him in her conscious memory.

The first time Johnny brought Denise to the farm, she accompanied him as he carried out many of his farming responsibilities. One afternoon, Denise was standing in the barn and watching the boys and Dad unload a wagonload of baled hay that had been gathered from one of the fields. The heavy cubes of straw traveled slowly up the conveyor belt evenly spaced, as I stood nearby and clicked the counter with each one Johnny loaded on to it. One of my brothers at the top removed each bale and stacked it neatly next to the others. This machinery and activity, including the barnyard smells, were all a first for Denise.

Chris realized Denise's fish-out-of-water situation.

"Do you want to go for a walk?" He asked Denise.

This six-year-old boy took Denise, a woman eleven years older, to the river and beyond where they explored our farm property. When Chris and Denise returned from their walk, Johnny was upset with Chris. Johnny had wanted to show Denise the land and river he had spoken to her about so often.

- - -

Chris had a good chuckle recalling that he had tired Denise out, when he was only knee-high to her, and she didn't want to go on another walk with Johnny.

"Did you feel bad that Johnny was mad at you?" I ask.

"Yeah, I'm sure I did," Chris answers without hesitation. "But I was bored, and I always liked going down by the river," he adds.

- - -

From the day he was born, Chris was social and loyal. He was a kindhearted child, as trustworthy and honest as the day is long. Today he is very much like our father was; rich in friends and integrity.

June 23

Dear Sis,

I would have written sooner but my squad was on an operation up on Charlie Ridge for a week. I got that form you sent for the exemption of my loan.....Dad & mom are probably buggin you and Pat probably isn't helping matters at all. Well don't let them get ya down I'm on your side and when I get home nobody is gonna give ya any trouble. I don't think I will be meeting Denise in Hawaii for R&R, her mom & Dad said no. I guess they are right...

...tell Ma I got the package with the mashed potatoes & stuff in it. I ate good again for a day.

—John A. Guldan, *June 23, 1970,*

to Mariann

The situation between Mariann and Bruce was heating up at home. Other than Bruce, Johnny was the only one who seemed to be on Mariann's side. Mariann looked out for Johnny too. She researched his options for getting his school loan taken care of while he was fighting for our country.

June 30

Dear Ma & Dad,

I am back at the school we rebuilt and the VC blew up, we are suppose to rebuild it only this time we are Booby-trapping it.

—John A. Guldan, *June 30, 1970,*
to my parents

Through demolition school and practice Johnny became skilled with booby traps, often keeping his buddies out of trouble by spotting the booby trap before it got them.

- - -

Johnny's good friend, Tom Wernig, tells me of the times when Johnny's knowledge of this ominous topic saved his skin.

"'Wernig put on your Gad damn flak jacket, Wernig get over here, Naaw Wernig! Don't touch that!'" ...and sure enough, it would turn out to be a booby trap," Tom says.

- - -

There were half as many letters between Johnny and my parents in June than in April or May and Johnny recognized this. He mentioned this in letters to Denise, his friend Neal, and Patti, saying he was not going to write them. He breaks his silence with this June 30 letter to my parents. It is a long one.

I am sorry I missed Father's Day Dad but it snuck by. I was out in Dodge City when everybody started talkin' about it a day after Father's Day. So Happy Belated Father's Day.

He guessed that the farm was keeping them from writing to him. His thoughts traveled to the farm with them in anticipation of another holiday he would be missing:

...Also have a nice fourth of July, are ya gonna be up at the farm for it like always. I don't know what the 4th will bring me, but I'm sure they won't be just shooting off fire crackers...

We were well into life at the farm that summer. It was finally starting to warm up and we were able to float down the river. We'd hike up the road, rolling our inner tubes over the hot black top road, drop them in the water and let it take us back to our bridge where we'd climb out and do it all over again.

From 13 Sept. to 26 Sept. I am being sent to non-commissioned officer school. I am suppose to get promoted on 1 JULY and if I get high enough marks on the tests they give I could come out a Sargeant [sic]. Also when I get back from that school I am suppose to take the place of our present squad leader. That means instead of being responsible for 4 other men I have 21 under my command. Really all the rank means is more money, but the stripes don't mean a thing if the privates aren't behind you, let me tell you I know. If the privates aren't with ya nothing can be accomplished. So I'll let ya know what happens.

Dad could relate to troops not following their leader's command; after all, one of his troops didn't seem to be following his suggestions—Mariann.

I was going to take an R&R, but the more I think of it the more I think I will pass. If I did go I would probably go to either Tokyo or Hong Kong. Everybody goes to Australia that's all I ever hear about. Heck I'll save $500 by not going and have a better time when I get home.

That's about all the latest news here in hell the temp keeps rising and the enemy never sleeps neither do we for that matter.

Love,

John

P.S. Everytime ya send a package send vitamin pills.

(Letter continues on back)

I just got your letter and I'll answer some of your questions. Yes Dad we do have SNAKES & BUGS! That's like asking if there's snow in the North pole.

I can only imagine how my father would have replied to this. Probably stating a scientific fact about how it doesn't actually snow at the North Pole, it's too cold. Or that the P is capitalized in North Pole.

All but 7 species of snakes are poisonous and the seven other can swallow you whole. There have been stories of Marines being physically beat up by mosquitos. I do take Malaria pills every Sunday; the corpsman gives us all one. The only PX we go to is on a truck sponsored by the Red Cross and it comes maybe once every 2 months depending on enemy activity.

...Also $450 of the money I have in Bell Savings is Northern Trust's Loan I took when I went to Defiance. I only used $450 of that $1000 loan so I gotta pay it back if I don't use it when I get home. I might use it along with the G. I. BILL if it's possible. I'm gonna go into medicine & I think the G.I. BILL helps.

As June turned into July, Johnny was unceremoniously given the rank of lance corporal. The Marine Corps gave him an 8-by-10 paper certifying this, which he mailed home.

July 4

Lover,
Happy 4th of July sweet-heart, I would have never known it if it wasn't for the gooners and their loudspeakers. They keep telling us, "Poor Marines, what were you doing last 4th of July, too bad you will never see another one, this is your last day of life." Of course it scared me so much I puked all over my scummy body and went into a state of shock. We got so sick of

listening to their threats I rounded up my fire team and we went looking for this gooner with the big mouth who likes to harass us homesick Marines. We found him and 3 others having a party, laughing & everything. We surrounded them, but seeing as it was the 4th I told my men not to open up, so we took 3 prisoners and a loudspeaker. As soon as we got back another loudspeaker started again, well this time we all stuffed our fingers in our ears...

—John A. Guldan, *July 4, 1970,*

to Denise

Choppers carried the mail to Hill 55 on a daily basis, usually. Whenever Johnny received a letter with the CTA logo it brought a smile to his face. Those letters were from Denise. There were periods of time when the mail was not delivered because the choppers were being shot down. On the Fourth of July, they were to have girls flown in to Hill 55 for USO entertainment. This did not happen because it was too dangerous that day as choppers were under fire. Most of the men were disappointed about the girls; Johnny was disappointed about his mail.

The effects of war had begun to numb Johnny. During a 4 A.M. watch from a foxhole Johnny thinks back on how he missed our parents when he was in boot camp and now he misses only Denise. He thinks a bit more . . . he misses Mariann too.

Another friend of mine died yesterday, he was a sergeant. I was talking to him 10 minutes before he got hit. It's kind of Ironic I talk to a person, a good friend, he is breathing, talking, joking, laughing, showing me flicks of his fiancée, and tells me of his plans for the future and in the next few minutes life stops and everything is shattered. Damn it Denise, I hate this God damn place, I hate it with a burning passion, I wish I could blow this hell right off the face of this earth. It's nothing but an ignorant, wretched smelly, hateful, death-pit. Life here is cheaper than a lousey stinkin' pig. It costs more for a pig than it does to bury a human being. I must be lousing my feelings or something. I didn't even flinch when I lifted him into the chopper, my emotions must be dying, maybe I will never cry again, I hope you will still Love me. I gotta get out of this morbid mood, I'm suppose to be gay & happy it is the 4th of July, that's right I got the fireworks to look forward to tonight.

Johnny ends this letter with:

I will have to close now Princess the fireworks are starting. Luke the Gook has got another loudspeaker workin' again.

July 5

Dear Dad & Ma,

I got your letter wrote on the 18th of June & I got it on the 4th of July, so 16 days isn't too bad is it? The reason it got goofed up was cause the choppers were getting' shot down before they got here, but they are back to normal now...

—John A. Guldan, *July 5, 1970,*
to my parents

Johnny and my dad had their letter sequencing down to a science. Each time they wrote, they let the other know when their last letter had arrived and put the date they were writing in the upper right hand corner of their own letter.

I trust your 4th of July was fun it was a lot of fun here. Some little girls brought some candy and signs of peace to my squad and after a little bit of suspicious interrogation we found out they were sent by the VC to see how many men we had & how many weapons. Also I checked the candy again & sure enough bamboo shavings & glass were in it along with water buffalo crap.

Although the Vietnamese children threatened his life at times, Johnny never showed resentment toward them.

"I love the kids. They are so cute, Denise. I wish you could see them. I love 'em and I can't trust 'em,"

Johnny told Denise this in his tape-recorded message. He chuckles as if he understands this phenomenon. Three-year-olds smoked cigarettes. The kids walked barefoot on stones with 80- and 100-pound sacks on their shoulders. They had scars. It was sad. Johnny did not know exactly what the scars were from, but he figured it was shrapnel from booby traps or mines.

Johnny was not only impressed with the resilience of these children but also how smart they were:

"Ten year olds know two languages and can tear apart and put back together our weapons."

The kids translated better than paid military personnel. For this reason, the Marines would often use the kids as interpreters.

Fang was very good at this. Johnny spoke of him with reverence and talked to a lieutenant about getting Fang a job in Da Nang. Unfortunately for Fang, the lieutenant had only seven days left in the country, so nothing ever came of it. In his recorded letters, Johnny taught Denise the Vietnamese terms the kids used like "Tee hee" for little, "buku" meant much, "leep leep" for sleep, and "waki'" (wah-kē) was the word for the world. America, where the Marines were from, was "waki," a place beyond the children's imagination, like the "Land of Oz".

While back in the world where Johnny grew up, his baby sister, Bonnie, almost three, had a muscle spasm in her neck. We were visiting a relative's horse farm in the far southwest suburbs of Chicago. While we were petting the horses, standing on the wooden rail fence that separated them from us, Bonnie suddenly started screaming. We all thought a swarm of bees was stinging her or that she touched a live electrical fence. My mom, very worried, brought her to the doctor the next day. We learned Bonnie had suffered a muscle spasm in her neck. That is the level of trauma children in our world had to suffer. In our "waki," children had parents that attended to their needs.

Johnny went on to write that day about Joe Heeney. Before leaving for the farm My mom and Mrs. Heeney had visited each other often, sharing news received from their sons, Johnny and Joe. Because of these visits, Mom knew Joe Heeney would be coming home soon. By July 5, Joe was what Johnny called a "double-digit midget"—he had less than 100 days left in Vietnam.

Joe Heeney is going home in 72 days. Gosh, I don't see how he got so short, heck he only went in 3 months before me. Anyway, he's been kidding me about my rotation date, he says I'll be leaving with the barbed wire.

Joe sensed that John was having a difficult time in the letters they exchanged. Johnny had acquired a leadership position at age 20. This was the result of attrition that didn't come about through the retirement or advancement of experienced officers. Joe knew the attrition "in-country" was due to death, or better known as KIAs (those killed in action). In his letters, Johnny questioned everything. He had little tolerance for decisions made and directions given by his superiors. He was tired of his friends being killed, children starving and maimed while the brass only cared about the enemy body count. In his letters back to Johnny, Joe did what he could to encourage Johnny to hang in there and to let things go.

- - -

Two months before my March 2007 trip to Vietnam, I interviewed Joe Heeney. Our family was having a funeral service for my sister Mariann, who had passed away after a long battle with breast cancer. Joe's brother Mike was the funeral director. As soon as I spotted Mike, who was busy orchestrating and delegating, I went over to ask him to let his brother Joe know I would be going to Vietnam.

"There are some questions I'd like to ask him about Johnny and his location there," I told his brother Mike.

"You can ask him yourself," Mike said encouragingly, and added, "He's here."

Mike directed his hand, in a way I imagined he had done throughout many funeral services, toward a tall, trim, dark-haired, mustached, unassuming man standing a few feet away. I had never met Joe. I walked up and introduced myself. I've never known a man named Joe who was not a nice guy and Joe Heeney was no exception. I told Joe that I would be going to Vietnam with a group of Vietnam vets and family of veterans and that I would be going to Marble Mountain, the base where he had been stationed.

I wanted to know Joe's side of the story, the story of being over there, being part of Johnny's decision to go over there, being a pen pal of Johnny's. All the while I was aware that I was trying to nab an interview from an old friend of my brother's while he was paying his respects to my sister. I imagined them both looking down on us from a puffy white cloud, sitting next to each other with their feet dangling over the side of it and their chins resting contently in their hands. Something deep within me told me they wanted this story told.

Joe Heeney went into some detail about ambushes and firefights, but it was all technical, telling me the naming conventions and number of men involved. Joe, like Johnny, was raised in the Catholic Church and taught in Catholic schools, where the Commandment "Thou Shall Not Kill" was something to be viewed with caveats. At times of war, it was the Old Testament that seemed to take precedence.

I ask Joe if he kept any of these letters.

He says, "No, I didn't bring any of them back with me. You can only take so much home."

I take this to mean there was nothing of value Joe wanted to bring back from Vietnam. He tried to leave it all behind.

- - -

Back on the home front, the relationship between Mariann and Bruce created a tension almost every member of our family could feel. My brother Chris, eight at the time, was playing with his GI Joes on the screened-in porch. He overheard my mother speaking uncharacteristically loud, and he looked up from his world of play.

"Mariann you cannot see him anymore!" Mom insisted.

"How can you tell me that? What kind of a place is this that you don't care about what I want?" Mariann responded.

Chris was staring now, and not at his GI Joes. He had forgotten about them. Mariann's voice had gotten louder than my mother's. My dad's response quieted everyone.

"You're acting crazy and he's part of the reason! You're not allowed to see him," Dad said.

As soon as Mariann was back in Chicago after the holiday weekend, she called Denise, upset that my parents had told her to stop seeing Bruce. Denise in turn wrote to Johnny about our parents' reaction to Mariann and Bruce's relationship. At this point, Johnny had gotten multiple sides of the story. He approached the topic with my parents:

... I guess you are pretty sore at Marianne, I don't know what's goin' on with her & this dude Bruce, but it sounds like a lot of static is in the air.

He could only spend so much attention on the troubles at home. A lot was going on in his world. From mid-June forward, there was an underlying sense in Johnny's letters that he was wearing out, physically and emotionally. He repeatedly wrote, "The morale is low," or "Activity is high." This July 5 letter to my parents continues:

...I know you are still sore at me for joining this green machine but Ma & Dad, I had to do it, not cause I was trying to find myself but cause I hated school and ever since I graduated from grammar school I knew I had to come here. It is an experience I will never forget & it's made me see many things I was blind to before. I will kick myself quietly.

Early July

"You can do anything you want to me Denise. I'll do it. I don't give a crud except for one thing—wearing bell bottom pants."

—John A. Guldan,
July 1970 audio recording to Denise

Denise had received money from Johnny to buy a tape recorder and that's what she did. By July, Denise and Johnny had expanded the format of their communication to sound. The tapes they exchanged were in addition to the daily letters Johnny and Denise wrote each other. Thanks to his generous platoon mate Tom, Johnny had use of his tape recorder any time he wanted.

Denise told Johnny that she wanted to make him a "Joe-Cool" instead of a collegiate type. Johnny was OK with that, except, bell-bottoms. Tom immediately starts mumbling something in the background while Johnny is still speaking into the mic.

"Why wouldn't you wear bell bottoms?" Tom asks.

"Because they're for squids (sailors)."

"No, they're not. No, they're not," Tom argues. Boston, Tom's hometown, was a little ahead of Chicago in fashion.

"Yeah, some guy comes up and cracks my ass..."

"I doubt it. Sh-t!" Tom says.

"Watch the language," Johnny says.

"All right, all right," Tom laughs. *"I'm sorry."*

Tom pops back to a lighter mood, and they both continue to joke about bell bottom fashion, each defending their stance on it as if fighting for the last c-ration on Hill 55. Johnny says he will also not wear anything from the Marines when he gets home. Yet he is willing to make an exception if Denise wants him to wear his dress blues when they get married. Maybe they could just elope, he adds.

Johnny had already sent Denise a few tapes by the time he received his first one from her in early July. In his recording, Johnny had taught Denise terms like "squid" for sailor and "cover" for helmet. When she sent her messages back it sounded funny to his Hill 55 buddies, Tom Wernig and Jim Hornsey, to hear Denise call my brother "John." Tom and Jim had only known Johnny as Prof. Yet Tom Wernig reassures Denise on the next tape that he will call him John if that is what she preferred.

"I think it's because of my glasses," Johnny explains to Denise.

Johnny continually urged Denise to talk about the future she wanted. He wanted to know her plans and perhaps needed assurance that he was included in those plans when he returned. When Denise replied with, "Time will tell," Johnny reacted strongly:

"I Don't like depending on time. Ya know what I mean? Maybe that's you but it isn't me. Time will tell sounds like fate rides in the winds. I wish you would cut it out because it tends to make a guy think over here. Especially when the goin' gets rough and a guy feels like shootin' his foot off... then I want to get home and see what time says ya know. I wanna get goin'."

Denise, hesitant to plan, said she didn't know what was going to happen after next year. Johnny's response:

"I'll tell ya what's gonna happen, you're gonna be with me. We're gonna be together. I'm sure everything's gonna

work cuz we're gonna be together. I'll make sure. Everything works out just fine. Nothing bad could ever happen because I can't stay mad at you."

Denise continued to be fearful to put her hopes into a future with Johnny. She would not even allow herself to articulate why. All she knew was that she loved him more with each passing day and since no one could guarantee he would make it home she could only think about a day at a time. So to appease his pleas to think about the future, Denise asked what profession he thought he would take up. He replied:

"I know I keep changing my mind about what I want to be. I've never been so close to what I wanted ya know what I mean. I like workin' with kids and takin care of 'em. Pretty sure I'd like to be a pediatrician. I know it will take a long time but I want to do it. I wrote for information on aviation but nothing hits me like pediatrics. Bear with me as I keep changin' this fool-hearty mind."

Johnny says this last sentence with an attempted English accent.

"Who are you supposed to wake up?" Tom interrupts.

Tom Wernig, still beside him in the foxhole, reminds Johnny that it is time for them to be relieved of their night watch. Johnny says that he isn't sure who is on next watch and didn't make an effort to find out. His shift turned into the next shift giving some Marine extra sleep. He remained in that dark, damp foxhole and continued recording his message to Denise.

"We can do anything we want, Denise. I know we can. It'll be hard but I know we can do it. I love you more than anything."

He saw a clear vision of their future and he so wanted to know Denise saw that same vision.

"The days go by fast when you look back but when you're going through them it's very slow. Then I see guys like Leo and Sullivan, short-timers, and I've got time left to do. Time left to think. It makes me sick. What can you do, I asked for it. Here I am Fourth of July, New Year's, every blessed holiday over here. But what can you do now, I did it. Heck Denise I don't want to talk about it."

July 11

Well, it is the 11th of July and the big push is just about over, the V.C. are pulling back now. We lost 8 men in 3 days and a total of 38 men in 2 weeks, in short we are getting whipped. More than half of the casualties were due to booby-traps. Remember our lieutenant who was suppose to leave in a week for Okinawa? He lost his damn leg cause of a stupid move, I told the asshole not to step on any cardboard that is on the ground, the dufus jerk says,"WHY" and plants his foot right on it. I wish he was conscious when we put him on the medevac chopper I would have cussed his sorry body into shock.

... a lot of my friends are going home now, not the way they wanted to but they are going. Enough of this morbid talk...

—John A. Guldan, *July 11, 1970,*

to Denise

Denise's mom knew how important these letters were for her daughter and began to become anxious herself when the postman came by. That particular day, not only had Mrs. Racky's concern been relieved, but she was excited when several letters had arrived from Johnny. One was addressed to her and one to her son, as well as Denise. Denise grabbed her letter from her mother's hand, ran to her room, closed the door, sat on her bed and ripped it open like she had done most days that summer.

Dear Denise, she read and immediately burst into tears. This had become her nightly routine that summer of 1970. If she didn't receive a letter, she'd cry; if she did, she'd cry. Although the summer was only a few weeks old, it seemed like she had been doing this every day of her whole life. Then she'd read on as he began to tell her the things that were happening that day. When she was done with the letter, she'd read it all again, and then individual parts. Then she'd be worn out. The contents of this particular letter, like many others, reminded her there was a very real chance that Johnny might never hold her in his arms again.

When her mother called her for dinner, she dragged herself to the table and went through the motions of eating. At the dinner table her mother and brother told her about the letters they had received. The topics weren't as heavy as the ones Johnny had discussed in his letter to Denise. In fact, Mike, her brother, even had to laugh about some of the things Johnny wrote to him.

The older girls were at the farm with Dad for the weekend. They probably had things on their minds similar to Denise, like Johnny and their next school year approaching, which was much different than what was on my mind—exploring, riding horses, playing hide and seek in the barn, and scaring my sisters and brothers.

"Boo!" I yelled as I threw open the vinyl curtain of the little metal shower stall.

There was a screech, and just when I was about to laugh, I heard a crack close to my ear and felt a sting on my left cheek. Patti had smacked me across the face. She stared at me with wide-open eyes and her hand clamped over her mouth as if to hold back further screams. I stared back in disbelief and stepped out of the small shower in our tiny farm bathroom. I had been hiding in there waiting for someone to come in.

"Don't ever do that again," she scolded me.

I won't, I thought, as I stepped out of the shower and walked past her.

In Vietnam that July, being frightened had a whole different meaning for Johnny. Fear was likely a constant companion twenty-four hours a day. He finished his letter to

Denise:

P.S....there is no man on this earth yet who can kill me, I can feel it as long as I have you to come back to My Darling, my hope & Love will give me strength to make it.

P.SS.
We were just informed over our radio that the death toll has just hit 43,000 since the start of Viet Nam. I wonder

now if it is really worthless, or that it is too late to be worthless. In my eyes, too many men have died for it to be completely worthless, to die with no meaning is the most worthless thing in life. What do you think Denise?

Mid-July

> *Some men could not withstand the stress of guerilla-fighting: the hair-trigger alertness constantly demanded of them, the feeling that the enemy was everywhere . . .*
>
> —Philip Caputo, *A Rumor of War*

Johnny sat in a foxhole with his buddy Tom and they chatted to Denise and each other on tape, as if she was right there with them. Denise had been sending tapes she made from the recorder bought with money Johnny had sent her. That night, Johnny had just listened to her voice on one of her tapes and felt homesick. While Tom was getting some shut-eye back on "The Hill" Johnny was recording from the foxhole, alone.

"Ya know I detected something Denise. When you sent me this tape tonight [pause]... I detected a little bit of self-pity there, which is very bad. Because when you start feelin sorry for yourself over here, you start feeling like a baby. Ya don't wanna work or ya don't wanna, ya don't wanna fight against 'em. If he hits ya all ya do is feel like throwin

your arms up and you just wanna go home. I kicked it outta me as quick as I could. Had it out on that ambush and I was scared Denise. Self-pity is very bad to have while you're over here. Very, very, bad to have. I keep tryin' to get rid of it […] I want to get home to you Denise. As long as I keep my guard up I'll be ok."

Johnny noticed, from Denise's recorded messages and letters, how she had grown closer to her father since he had been in 'Nam. He is happy for that, yet admits a twinge of jealousy. His letters and recorded messages were like a rope he was throwing to her as if she was being sucked into a black hole. This communication was his lifeline back to reality, to home to which he was desperate to stay connected. It was during these tapes he told her how he felt after he made that first phone call to her. He could tell in her voice she was happy he called. That same spirit in her voice remained constant, through her letters and her tapes.

Denise's days started early in downtown Chicago but she didn't mind because that meant she got out while there was still a lot of the evening left. Denise had written to Johnny about the parties she went to while away at school, but at home for the summer, it was a much quieter life. Johnny didn't like it when Denise wrote to him about parties with guys.

"The first thing a guy thinks when a girl drinks is that she is gonna give in to him, easy. I'm not kiddin' ya! Remember you got to promise that you got to keep with me. You'd make me feel awful bad if you didn't. I know you probably think I'm actin like a father. But I love you baby. I LOVE YOU BABY! And I just don't want anything to happen to you. I don't like drinkin'. And uh, I want you to stop it but if you don't. It's up to you. Im not gonna love you any

less if you don't I keep loving you more and more anyway."

Johnny finished on a lighter note, telling Denise that they will drink together when he is back. Actually, Johnny didn't like drinking, let alone taking drugs and smoking pot. In fact, he hadn't had a drop of alcohol since he arrived in 'Nam. He had smoked a cigarette once but quickly realized the lit, red end of it made him a target. Yet there were members in Johnny's platoon that were tempted by any substance to escape the constant stress they endured. Some guys were placing others in even more danger by smoking marijuana or taking speed while on watch.

"... they didn't give a crap about anybody on the squad all they did was want to smoke their weed. We got rid of them. Right now they are probably back in the world smoking weed, growing their hair and stuff."

In addition to drugs, venereal disease was another big problem for some of the Marines in Johnny's platoon. So big they had to be "restricted," Johnny called it. The Marines had run out of penicillin and were not able to treat those who came down with it, so they tried to keep them away from the population in Da Nang and Saigon. Johnny and his close buddies thought it was pretty funny. The remaining squad dealt with this disappointing situation the best they could.

"Our squad still has some rough points like a few guys that want to do things easy for their bod..."

"I owe it to my bod" became a phrase that the slackers used as a reason for not going out on an ambush, walking point, or some other dangerous or dirty job. "Walking point" meant being in the front on an ambush team, the most vulnerable position. Chief Red Eagle was changing into one of these "owe it to my bod" guys. Or rather, he was "fading away," as Johnny called it. Chief used to be his best friend.

> *"...All they want to do is take it easy, go to the hill, eat chow and stuff. We're gonna kick them out of the squad too but right now we need as many men as we can keep. I'll tell ya, uh everybody here feels the same way about the war. Feels the same way about losing their friends, about watching them die and stuff. I don't want to talk about it over this tape."*

The prologue of Ronald Winter's memoir, *Masters of the Art: A Fighting Marine's Memoir of Vietnam*, about a 1968 Marine helicopter pilot and gunman, describes the intense impact the people the author fought with side by side had on his life. This was a brotherhood that cannot be known in times of peace. At the time I read this, I thought about how Johnny did not get to experience this positive side of war because of the drugs among the troops. Yet I learned, through his letters and tapes, of the few within his platoon he trusted and experienced the type of relationship Winter speaks of. Tom Wernig was one of those.

Suddenly, while recording a tape for Denise:

> *"Shit, you're steppin' on my freakin' foot. What are you gonna do?"* Johnny says to his foxhole mate, Tom.
> *"Get some whadduh,"* Tom says in his string Boston accent.
> *"Get some water? Get me some steam too. Cuz that's what it is,"* Johnny says.

Pop—which we called it, and known as soda to others—was expensive at $1 and beer even more, Johnny complained.

Aside from the few owe-it-to-my-bod guys and varying personalities, Platoon 55 they worked well together. Whatever food Johnny received, he shared with his platoon mates. He wrote of a new kid who would not wear a flak jacket even when Johnny insisted. Johnny said he was "cocky." He soon left. Johnny did not say what happened to him. The group of five or six Johnny was close to made life bearable throughout his months in Vietnam. He wrote home about these guys, sent photos, and gave some of them even got some airtime on his tapes to Denise. In addition to Tom Wernig; Jim Hornsey, from a small town in Southern Illinois, was one of those voices.

- - -

Forty years later, Jim Hornsey wrote to my family. I had not met Jim at this point and did not think to interview him. Yet when he offered this description about life I knew it was valuable in understanding what life was like for Johnny in the U.S. Marine's Mike Company during the summer of 1970:

> *Sgt. Jack Gilbert was somewhat of a quiet person. I don't think he had much in the way of family. I used to pick up our mail all the time and he very seldom got any. He had been in the Marines a while and was on his third tour in Vietnam. He used to make up little signs saying bad things about the NVA/VC. He would leave them at the entrance to whatever village we happened to be working in at the time. I think Gil thought of the Marines and us as his family. He would do his best to make sure we were OK and had what we needed to do our missions. In turn, we trusted his judgment and probably would have followed him anywhere. John seemed to have a special relationship with him. They would often talk about ways to do our*

missions and where we should go next. I feel he looked at John like a little brother.

"Doc" Brown was our Navy Corpsman. Like many corpsman he should of gone on to be a degreed doctor. He definitely had a OJT (on the job training) degree. He is one of the kindest, gentlest people I have ever met. But if you messed with one of his Marines he would go up against a General. Usually around ten days before your rotation date they would not make you go on any more long range patrols. I was a "Company" radio operator my last four months in VietNam. I had gotten my hand split open and infected on a two-week patrol in early December. The company c/o we had at that time wanted to force me on a four day patrol a week before going home. "Doc" Brown bandaged my hand and wrist until it looked like a football and told him I would not be going anywhere until I went home. In the squad picture I sent, Doc Brown is standing between John and Tom.

John "Professor" Guldan ranks right with "Doc" Brown in the kind and gentle department. It was always pretty obvious by the way children reacted to him. In almost every picture that I have ever seen in a village we were in, the kids would be around John. He would of made an awesome father. You could tell John was focused on family and raised well. I was aware of Denise and that he planned to get married when he got back from Vietnam. John was a very good Marine and also cared very deeply for everyone in our squad.

We actually were not on Hill 55 very often. Someone, a lot of the time it was me, would go there every afternoon to pick up the mail and maybe a few things we needed. If *we were close enough I would go by myself. When I think back on that it was probably pretty dumb. If we were a little further out 2 or 3 would go. You have to remember we only had about 12 guys so you couldn't let too many go. If we did stay on Hill 55 for a few days we were able to sleep on cots in metal roofed hooches (huts) with screened sides. We were usually out in villages. Most of the time it was Bich Bac or Chau Son 1 or 2. We would sleep under the stars or we would make small tents like pup tents out of poncho liners and bamboo. That was if you weren't on watch or an all-night patrol or ambush. I really don't recall where Johnny slept but maybe close to Tom W.*

- - -

Back in my "waki" (world) many of my siblings and I enjoyed the long summer days at the farm while our older sisters kept busy working in Chicago. Patti worked for Dad and Mariann worked at Grandpa's accounting office. My sister Mariann worked briefly for my dad, but could not tolerate working for him, so Uncle Mike hired her. My father was just happy to have her kept out of trouble and under the watchful eye of a trusted relative.

During these years, Margie and Eileen exchanged gigs between babysitting at Uncle Mike and Aunt Diane's in Evanston and working in my father's office. When Dad drove back for his long weekends at the farm, the sister that worked with him came back with him. At sixteen, they were too young to be left on their own in Beverly with only their older sisters as their guardians. I think if my dad could, he would have had my sister Mariann come back to the farm with him each weekend too. That would have taken nothing short of binding and gagging her.

Newspaper photo when triplets where baptized Jan. 1954, at six weeks old, L to R: Mom, Johnny (3 yrs. old), Dad, Mariann (2 yrs. old), and Patti (4 yrs. old) Triplets: Eileen, Jimmy, Margie

The Guldan home in the Beverly neighborhood on the Southwest side of Chicago

Portrait taken at farm of Guldan girls, about 1965. Farmhouse in background. L to R standing back row: Mariann, Patti, Front Row: Eileen, Terri, Margie with Mimi on lap, Missing: Bonnie

Portrait taken at farm of Guldan boys, about 1965. Farmhouse in background. It was later painted it charcoal grey. L to R standing back row: Bill, John, Jim Front Row: Joe, Chris, Mickey

Aunt Nora and Uncle Bill relaxing at the farm.

The farm, in Waupaca, Wisconsin, after it was painted, some time in the mid-seventies.

Bonnie, about four years old, with her favorite puppy, Pretty-Ugly

L to R: Neal Beatty, Johnny, Steve Pachol. Photo courtesy of Denise Racky.

John Guldan showing his winning form.

Johnny crossing finish at a Marist Cross Country meet

Johnny at Denise's house December 1968. Photo courtesy of Denise Racky.

John Guldan graduation from USMC MCRD San Diego, CA 1969.

Chicago's 91st Street Train Depot, in Beverly neighborhood, where Terri's father picked Johnny up Jan 1970.

Freedom Hill - DaNang, Vietnam Marine base 1970. Photo courtesy of Jim Hornsey.

Johnny writing and reading letters in Vietnam. Photo courtesy of Jim Hornsey.

Johnny with binoculars Dad had mailed to him. Photo sent to Denise in late July. "I'm ready to go home, war stinks," he wrote on the back.

Johnny and Tom Wernig in foxhole on Hill 55. Tom was wounded. Photo sent to Denise days before Johnny was killed.

Standing Rear L to R: Bob Face, "Doc" Brown. Standing Front L to R: Chief, John "Prof" Guldan, Tom Wernig. Sitting L to R: Gary Orvis (Machine gunner), Squad leader, Unknown. Sitting Front: Sgt Gilbert. Photo courtesy of Jim Hornsey.

Memorial Day 1970. Not all are listed. Back row L to R: Barbara Bansley (Aunt), Bonnie (Sister) on Johnny Gallagher shoulders, Jean Bansley (Cousin), Terri (Author, in braids), John Bansley (Uncle), Mike Bansley (Uncle, in glasses). Row 2: Jim Bansley (Uncle), Eileen (Triplet, holding Lil' Mike), Mickey (Brother), Standing far R: Annie Laurie Gallagher (Aunt). Row 3: Joe (Brother, Bansley baby on shoulders), Grandparents (Sitting center), Mrs. Guldan (kneeling), Diane Bansley (Aunt), Margie (Triplet). Front row sitting: Patti (Sister, L of Grandma), Mimi (Sister), Mariann (Sister) with Bansley boy to R. Missing: Dr. Guldan, Jim, Bill, Anne Bansley

Johnny with Vietnamese boy, 1970. "Here stands the future of this war torn land, Jack," Johnny wrote on the back of this photo he sent to Denise.

Jim Hornsey, USMC radio operator for Johnny's platoon, 1970. Photo courtesy of Jim Hornsey.

Johnny with DaNang area village kids. Littlest is Bug-Fuck, with his brothers. Biggest one suspected V.C. squad leader. Photo courtesy of Denise Racky.

John Guldan Obituary Notice.

Swing set Johnny helped Uncle Jim put up in Bansley backyard. Standing today.

THE KING'S PAGE

CHURCH OF CHRIST THE KING

14th Sunday after Pentecost — August 23, 1970

JOHN GULDAN III GIVES LIFE FOR FLAG AND COUNTRY

The picture on this page shows some of our school children lined up before the Church holding small flags as they awaited the flag-draped coffin of one of our boys who made his whole grammar school course at our School, Lance Corporal John Guldan of the Marines, killed in Viet Nam, and buried after services here on August 14th. This young hero, John Guldan - just twenty years old and the oldest of a family of thirteen - had volunteered for one of the most dangerous missions possible in the war field, the detection and de-fusing

Cover of Christ the King August 23, 1970 church bulletin, showing kids outside the church, holding US flags at funeral

Standing on the neighbor's driveway about 1971. Our station wagon in background. L to R: Johnny Gallagher, Terri, Margie, Joe, Tommy Gallagher, Billy, Mom, Eileen First Row: Mimi, Bonnie

1976 weekend at farm. Back Row L to R: Joe, Chris, Mariann. Front Row L to R: Dr. Guldan, Mrs. Guldan, John DaCosta on Terri's lap, Mimi, Mrs. Wernig with Bonnie in front, Bruce DaCosta

Terri getting a rubbing of brother's name from Wall in Washington, D.C.

Christmas 1978 in Palos Park home. Mom, Dad, Bonnie lower left, Mimi lower right.

My parents' 50th anniversary celebration, June 1998. L to R: Dad, Mom, Aunt Alice, Dad's sister, and husband, Uncle Paul.

Terri on Hill 55 in 2007, holding remnants of US Marine poncho found on the hill. Photo courtesy of TOP Vietnam Veterans.

Terri in Vietnam in 2007, on Johnny's spot, gathering dirt in pill box. Photo courtesy of TOP Vietnam Veterans.

2007 Bich Nam, Vietnam. Terri with TOP group following and supporting as they near Johnny's site of death. Photo courtesy of TOP Vietnam Veterans.

July 14

I got a tape from Denise and she sounded beautiful. She was worried about her voice sounding too nasally, but she sounded outstanding. I listened to it a hundred times and it made me so lonely for her I almost cracked up.

—John A. Guldan, *July 14, 1970,*
to Patti

The evening Denise arrived home from work and saw the package containing this cassette tape, she quickly opened it and popped it into a recorder. She laughed as Johnny coached her in English and Psychology. She had told him she did poorly in those subjects the previous semester. His platoon buddies spoke to Denise, while Johnny censored them on the spot so nothing disrespectful was said to his girl. He included teachings about the area and the culture. He mentioned the places of Bich Bac, Duc-Ky, and Chau Son. "Chau Son was no good," he said.

Denise was not as comfortable as Johnny recording her message and instead recorded songs of the times to fill much of the tape. Johnny enjoyed these, especially the politically edgy ones from Credence Clearwater Revival and Bob Dylan. However, he wanted most to hear Denise's voice and scolded her when she didn't talk enough on the tapes. Johnny talked of how he was mentally holding himself together. Guys from his company were in Chau Son and he was worried about them there.

While on a trip to Freedom Hill to refresh supplies, a lieutenant questioned Johnny as to why he was in the bush since he had completed a year of college. He was again offered an office job in the rear. This time, after almost five months in combat, Johnny seriously considered leaving Hill 55. He told this officer that he would like an office job in a couple of months.

"Well, we'll see about it," replied the Lieutenant.

It was not an easy choice to make, to leave the bush and take a job in the rear.

> *"I might end up bein up there and I hope I am. I tell ya, after listening to this tape makes me wanna get the Cripe outta the bush Denise. Cuz it scares me. It's no fun bein shot at. No fun hit by mortars. I mean this is my squad. This is my family out here. All the little petty differences and fights and squabbles and the way they fight the enemy, they're ok. They're ok."*

No matter what disagreement Johnny had with his fellow Marines, he protected them whenever he could. He would not allow his fire team leader to walk point because he would be going home soon.

> *"Every time I listen to your tapes I get home sick. Everyone can tell. Your mind is thinking of something else. You're not paying attention. That's not good. Like tonight on ambush I hadda walk point cuz there's only me and short round and it's getting time for short round to go home and I don't want him walkin point. I mean I was scared yeah but I pretended like you were behind me (chuckle) and I was holdin' your hand and everything was ok. I looked funny holding my hand out and the other one holding my 16 (gun) straight out in front of me. Walkin point is a funny thing Denise. It makes you know how important life is and how important a person means to ya. Especially when ya wanna marry her and I do wanna marry you so very badly Denise. I want so much to have*

everything work out when I get home. I want you to sit down and I want you to tell me what you want for your life. I don't want you to be a career girl. You know what I want Denise. I want you to tell me if there is something inside you that tells you you want to be something that would make you happy...I ain't rich but maybe some day I will be. What the heck money isn't everything but it sure helps a lot. I know the good times will outnumber the bad. I'm sure it's gonna be bad if I end up bein' a pediatrician. I know I'll have to go through a lot of school. But Denise you and I, we can do anything. I'm convinced of it. There's nothing in this world that could ever keep us from doing what we really want. NOTHING at ALL. I don't know if ya ever get sick of me telling you this in all the letters. If I could make you realize how I feel when I'm over here. When I look up at the stars at night and I see your eyes, I close my eyes and I think of you and I want to hold you Denise, so tight, and I can't. All I do is just grab air. I can't even touch ya. I keep tellin' myself, someday soon. Yeah, someday soon..."

The struggle of right and wrong was a constant for Johnny. For his survival, he needed to convince himself that he was there, fighting and killing, because it was the right thing to do. In a July 14 letter to Patti, he owns this choice and defends it fiercely.

Did ya see the draft lottery numbers that came out? I did, I will commence to kicking myself quietly. I can just see Dad now, saying what a fool I was. Let him think what he wants I do not regret joining the Corp or being here and when I get home I will feel much better.

Letters from Mariann slowed. Johnny was very worried about his sister from the reports he had received from others and not hearing from her added to his concern. He was frustrated that he could do nothing to help her. July 14 he wrote to Patti:

> *I haven't gotten a letter from Marianne for a long time. I guess she must be really busy with the dude Bruce. You are right about Ma & Dad not being the only ones with bitter feelings toward him. Beattie & Patch & even my girl has given him thumb down. I'm not gonna committ myself yet about my feelings toward him, all as I know is my little sis has not been writin' so something must be heavy. I can't believe she is working for Gramps, is she working in the place I used to? Well, I will be home sooner than ya think and then I will see what the word is on all this hassel. Is Marianne going to Eastern next fall?*
>
> *...and I'm not gonna write to Marianne till she writes to me...*

Patti, Johnny, and Mariann's natures were clearly distinct. This was obvious at a young age as the dynamics began to take shape between them. When they were toddlers, Uncle John arrived at the house to babysit the three of them. They all ran up to him, demanding his attention right away. They grabbed his hand and led him. They would have dragged him if they could but he was almost six feet to their three feet. Uncle John felt like Gulliver in the land of Lilliput. They brought him into the living room to where a phonograph was. Johnny began setting up a record to play when all of the sudden Mariann covered her ears and went running out of the room. Johnny threw the shiny, vinyl record down. With a burst, he stormed after Mariann to convince her to come back. Patti explained to Uncle John this was because it had been really loud last time Johnny turned on the record player. She calmly closed the phonograph's top, picked up the record, and put it neatly back in its case.

July 16

> *Dear Mariann,*
> *... Make sure and tell Ma I got the package. I lost my apetite for about 3 weeks and then I started taking those little green vitamins Ma sent and now I am always hungry.*
> > —John A. Guldan, *July 16, 1970,*
> > *to Mariann*

Johnny had not stopped writing to Mariann. And for the first time he spells her name correctly, with no e at the end. I wonder if she had finally corrected him or he just figured it out. Attempting to manage the war on his home front, he tried to get some information about Bruce, yet he continued to be supportive.

> *...I have been getting a lot of biased opinions and views on this guy of yours, Bruce. What can I say? I can say this if you like him and you really believe in the dude and ya absolutely know he's not just leading you on then follow this, the one I follow with Denise: FUCK THEM ALL SAMMY*

SMALL, I learned that in boot camp & it seems to help when everybody is against ya...

In this same letter to Mariann, Johnny gently pointed out that the Bruce situation does not seem to be leaning in Mariann's favor:

...I never heard of the old man ever forbidding one of our friends to come into the house...

Johnny never swore in front of my parents but the Marines brought out an expressive side that had been there since he was a young boy—Fuck Them All Sammy Small.

- - -

A chuckle pops out of Eileen as if it were a hiccup, as she claims in a confessional tone that it was she who got Johnny kicked off the altar boys. The nuns were covering the lesson on not to take the Lord's name in vain, when Eileen proclaimed, "I don't listen to my older brother swear." She thought the nuns would see this as a good deed on her part. From what Eileen knew, it was acceptable for older brothers to swear.

- - -

While at the farm—It was this weekend we went to the annual Portage County Fair of Amherst. All summer I looked forward to this fair. Not only did I love the fast rides that made me dizzy, but I loved seeing the pigs, sheep, cows, and bunnies. I especially loved the horses and watched, with reverence, as their 4-H owners not much older than me, showed them. I petted the huge pigs as I walked by their stalls, paying special attention to the ones with the blue ribbons proudly displayed. My sisters Margie and Eileen took me on the rides. However, this month it was just Eileen because Margie was staying with my cousins in

Evanston, babysitting. The previous summer, before they had their jobs and they were able to stay at the farm all week, they took swim lessons with us. They passed the basic classes and advanced to lifesaving class. I stood on the beach and watched Margie and Eileen perform their final lifesaving test. They were able to remove their jeans and blow them up while treading water and use them as a raft, like female James Bonds. They were so brave, I thought. I still think that.

July 18

> *I have heard it said lately that a well-seasoned rifle soldier is your basic, functioning psychotic. . . . I was not simply a witness but an integral, even dedicated, party to a very wrong thing.*
>
> —Larry Heinemann,
> *Black Virgin Mountain: A Return to Vietnam*

At home, normal was Mom putting her already chewed Wrigley's Spearmint gum in a tiny, blue porcelain ring dish that sat on the kitchen window sill. We never knew how long a piece of gum might have been sitting in that little blue dish. This was my mother's sacred ground. That and the drawer that held her candy corns.

Johnny and the others in his platoon had to forget the normal they used to know or their daily life would have driven them crazy. However, Johnny allowed himself to hold on to some future dreams of the normal he once knew:

> *Darling,*
>
> *You asked me in your last letter what kind of name I could think of for a boy, and after coming to the conclusion that anything would be better than SEAN, this is what I chose: DAVID ANTHONY. How do you like that for our first son's name? I think it has a type of strength when I say it. Let me know if you like it or not O.K.? I wish I would have never left you, Denise, I wish they would let me get back to you right now... when I get back I will show you how much you mean.*

Denise had gotten home from work and found this letter on the front desk, where her mother or brother would leave every letter that arrived from Johnny so that she would see it as soon as she walked in the door. Denise grabbed the letter and rushed into her bedroom after saying a quick hello to her mom. She sat on her bed and read. She stared at the words. What is this vast space that lies between us, she wondered for only a flicker of a moment. She would not allow herself to linger on such thoughts. She too had to stay with a normal she could live with. She kept reading his words. She could hear his voice as if he was right there with her.

> *...I cannot explain why I turn down 3 typing jobs & one mail room job, it's me Denise, do it the hard way, that's me, I must be a fool or something. I'm afraid of dieing for only one reason and that reason is you, Denise. Life would be death without you, dieing doesn't hurt it's just that feeling of emptiness not to be able to live my dreams out. I am afraid and life is so precious because of you Denise, just*

you. I still keep staring at death & tempting fate. Why Baby? Everytime we get hit or make contact my mind goes blank, my dreams hide somewhere & you Denise you hide somewhere too and I must be a fool I sneak up on gooks so close I Can hear their hearts beat, myself & 2 other South Viet soldiers while the other Marines stayed behind. I go on every patrol, killer team & ambush and I don't know why Denise. I gotta stop it cause everytime I go I loose all interest, hope, faith & trust in my dreams of you & me together...

Robert Jay Lifton, a psychiatrist who studied the psychological effects of war, explained this process in his book, *Home From the War*. The military's basic training takes an enlistee and breaks down his learned beliefs around killing. What they have learned from their family and society is undermined and replaced with a "warrior identity," the main purpose of which is to remove the enemy. Mr. Lifton says that with this training, the "warrior" is able to kill without feeling nor concern of dying as he commits to the role.

It seemed Johnny was trying to achieve the psychological state of the warrior in order to defend his buddies, his family, his country, yet he told himself that it was temporary.

...I wish there was no such thing as war Denise, it's like a nightmare, so many times I wanted to squeeze that trigger and blow my toe off to get back to you, so many damn times. So many times I wanted to throw my rifle down when I had a gooner in my sights and run all the way back to you. Denise, I don't know how the hell you can Love me. I'm such a big, ignorant, jerk. Here I am spilling tears about it and I'm short of breath & I can hardly keep my hand

steady (I'm glad I didn't make a tape on this I'd be sounding like a little baby) Denise, My Love, I am so close to you and yet so far. I close my stupid eyes and I am squeezing you tight, so damn tight. I don't know, maybe God is watching and caring for me, I don't know why. I'm mean, I hate, I kill and all I feel is recoil from my rifle. I swear, I curse, I don't give a damn about my family, I'm selfish. And I'm a big, stupid, silly jerk who doesn't know when the hell to quit...

Johnny was physically sick on this day. He had a fever, stomach aches, and his bones ached. The platoon doctor said he was delirious and had been calling Denise's name in his sleep. Maybe this illness contributed to the tearing down of an emotional wall that kept his psyche in check, yet this truth seemed determined to escape him. Johnny thinks again about how long it is until he can go home—six months to go.

P.S. This letter probably sounded bad, Denise. I am in a very lonely mood, I want to be with you, and I miss you so very much.

July 22

I am now on Hill55, the company pulled my squad out of the bush we have been making heavy enemy contact for the past month and I guess our Capt. Is afraid of another Mai Lai. We already had one just like it in a place called CHAU SAN but I guess it never hit the papers.

> —John A. Guldan, *July 22, 1970,*
> *to Dr. Gallagher*

Johnny wrote several letters on July 22. One of those letters was to Dr. Gallagher, a close friend of my parents. Dr. Gallagher had sent Johnny a package of treats that he had shared with his platoon mates. Johnny sent this letter in response to thank him and, as usual, had other interesting things to share that had happened recently.

And here is something you will not believe... We uncovered an underground NVA & VC hospital in a hill on an operation. We got 4 nurses one was from Canada, yeah Canada and the supplies, plasma, utensils, bandages and all the goodies were in crates & boxes marked with: "Compliments from us at Berkeley California who are with the oppressed." Isn't that the sweetest thing you ever heard of?

This was not a brick and mortar hospital. It was a mud cavern discovered after Johnny's squad had blown out the side of the hill, uncovering part of the 155 miles of the elaborate Cu Chi tunnel system (See Appendix). His sarcasm is showing here. He really did not mean, "the sweetest thing..."

Believe me there is a very big credibility gap over here, the papers don't tell anything but the good news. For instance, I read in the STARS-N-STRIPES we get over here about one of the squads in my platoon when they got hit by the Viet Cong, it said we beat them off but failed to mention 2

Marines and 5 South Viets got it and also that the gooners
stole our M60 machine gun. Did you know that we are
actually supplying the enemy over here? They use
everything we drop or leave behind when we move.

There was a discrepancy between what the news was reporting and what was actually happening. Johnny's platoon had traveled into Cambodia yet the American public was being told that there were not troops positioned outside of South Vietnam. Adding salt to the wound were the U.S. celebrities who spoke out against the war. At the time, Jane Fonda was married to Tom Hayden, one of the Chicago 7, and had been putting together some anti-war play and speaking out against the war on college campuses. Johnny and his platoon mates were aware of her stateside activities and sympathizing with the North Vietnamese. To put it mildly, they were not impressed. And this was two years before her trip to Vietnam when she was dubbed "Hanoi Jane."

"We are not fonda' Fonda," was a common saying among the troops.

- - -

Eileen has read every letter we have from Johnny and remembers the details within them.

"Jane Fonda was over there," Eileen recalls, bringing up Johnny's dismay and disappointment in one of his letters about the Berkeley supplies found in an enemy hospital. I see a sad look on Eileen's face as she recalls getting that letter of Johnny's. And then she ponders for a second and I catch another quick look— 'Does it even matter?' I see this question on her face for a fleeting moment.

- - -

Johnny continued to keep sight of what was good. He never stopped planning a future for himself, one that would ensure a sense of reward, and he communicated this in his letters. Once he wrote about being a policeman, another time it was a dentist, and in late May he mentioned optometry. Yet the profession he mentioned most often was pediatrician. To Dr. Gallagher he wrote:

...I would like to ask you a favor Dr. Gallagher. I am interested in pediatrics, I wonder if you could recommend any school or schools I should try & get into when I get back so I could start getting ready to dive into this and make up for the time I have lost in the Service.

Denise's and Johnny took advantage of the current technology as much as they could. Johnny wrote:

...I love your voice the way it is, I melt into puddy everytime I hear it. I wish we had a telephone our own private phone that we could talk to one another on every day.

It was twenty to thirty years before cell phones and cell towers would become ubiquitous around the world. Today, service men and women can not only call home and hear their loved ones' voices within minutes, but they can stream a live video and see them as well. What a jolt of encouragement it must be to hear your loved one's voice on the other side of the world, to see his or her face, smile, and know for sure he or she is okay. Yet nothing could fill the void:

...all the time I wake up I feel empty, so damn empty.

Was Johnny becoming a student of war's toll? Did he see that wearing out was deadly? Like falling under the spell of the poppy seeds in The Wizard of Oz as the wicked witch, a.k.a. NVA, watched in anticipation from her crystal ball. He saw his friends getting killed and maimed. He seemed to be looking for the common element that was a part of those who were hit and not a part of those who remained on the battlefield. There had to be something, something that would make some sense of the senselessness.

Ya wanna hear something funny, Dee, I mean something pretty hard to swallow? The Marine Corp is going to give me a medal, yeah a stupid ass medal for acting the way I was trained to act under enemy fire one night. Listen to this crap "For acting bravely & gallantly while under intense enemy fire, L/cpl Guldan courageously stayed behind & covered his fellow Marines as they pulled back. And with the radio on his back called in a fire mission on top of the enemy and adjusted effectively on top of them by himself while still under heavy volume of enemy fire." It's called the Navy Commendation Medal & I am now up for meritorious Corporal. But guess what sweet-heart I blew it out of my rear cause when they were givin' me the damn medal I told the Colonel to stick it up his ass and to give it to Steve Cummings, my buddy, who died along side of me that night. I told them he deserves the Medal of Honor and if he paid the supreme price, he's the damn hero. He had a wife and a baby girl he never saw, it makes me sick to my gut...When I get home and look for a job nobody is even gonna care whether I was in Nam let alone get a medal so the hell with it. My Sargeant said he is gonna give it to me whether I like it or not cause he says I earned it whether I know it or not...he said if he had his way he'd give me the Silver Star. Fuck em' all Sammy Small!

I just want Denise Star of Love, that's the kind I want, that will get me through this.

Johnny apologized for what he wrote in his letters and asked Denise to save them all. He promised in a tape to Denise that he would write his book and then he wouldn't talk about it ever again.

"If you tell me it is too much I won't write it anymore. Just let me know. I will remember every detail."

- - -

As I sit with my Aunt Barbara and Uncle Jim in their home, interviewing them in 2007, it is difficult for Aunt Barbara to hear that Johnny hated the war, hated being in Vietnam, and that he just wanted to get out.

"Was this true?" she asks me.

"Yes. Very true," I say.

I ask Aunt Barbara why this realization bothers her, even forty years later.

"Well, because I thought...Ya know, ya just think—they join to protect our country, and it's just disheartening when you hear that they had a turn-around and I'm sure one day in a, um, what do they call it? Fox tread, trench or whatever..."

"Foxhole," Uncle Jim says quietly.

"...would turn you. You'd be scared to death," Aunt Barbara replies, ending this explanation in a high pitch. Is she now thinking about the reality of fighting in a war for the first time? Uncle Jim looks at me with a grim smile and points out statements in Johnny's letter that indicated his deteriorating patriotism. Aunt

246 | T.M. Guldan

Barbara seems to be hearing this for the first time. I don't go into the umpteen movies and Vietnam vet memoirs that tell of the same phenomenon, yet I want her to know. Johnny wanted us to know. In 1970, morale was low, it was a terrible situation to be in, and Johnny's letters painted a clear picture of it.

Uncle Jim tries to explain how this situation developed.

"They cut the budget. Ya know, Democrats got in and they wouldn't fund the war. I mean it's really sick when you get down to it. They cut off your money so ya gotta get out..."

At this point, Uncle Jim and Aunt Barbara do not know my stance on the war, or war in general. Do they assume I believe what my parent's believed? I am careful not to display my opinion. It is a strong one and I don't want to strain our communication. What I feel or believe does not matter at that moment. I carefully interject a little of what I've learned about this particular war.

"But ya know what, having been in that country, I don't know. They could've poured in any amount of money. Those people [Vietnamese], they're like ants. They're resilient—they find resources out of nowhere!"

I say this with awe and respect. I know my aunt and uncle are kind people. They would help a stranger struggling. If I could pry into their patriotism and fierce protection of their loved ones to expose a glimpse of the people struggling on the other side of that particular war, I think it would be a step toward peace. A step toward not letting this happen again.

- - -

While Johnny's spirits were wearing out half a world away, we were at the farm, oblivious to his plight—at least us younger kids were. We enjoyed our comic books and playing in the river and in the barn with the cats on rainy days. The cats weren't allowed in the house. Grandma, a superstitious woman, put the fear of cats into my mother. They were bad luck and would scratch your eyes out, she told Mom. We had several roaming our farm, including a black one. So when the bird flew into our picture window and laid dead on the porch that day in late July, Mom freaked. It was a bad omen she told us, and had my brothers Joe and Mickey immediately take it off the porch. I think they buried it.

For Johnny, a bad omen came in the form of sentences about Mariann and her boyfriend. These sentences were in letters from Denise, Neal, and my parents. What was happening between Mariann and Bruce was still unclear to Johnny, but his loyalty to his favorite sister remained clear. To Denise:

> ...O.K. the guy is a creep, maybe Marianne likes creeps, I'm not the coolest Rock Hudson either and would you like it if Tom or your folks tried making you go with somebody else,...Besides that if ya try and cause static between them what does it do? It brings them closer together and then the naughtiness of secrecy sets in, you know what I'm saying Denise. Marianne's your friend right? Well then that's it...

Denise had written to Johnny how she had faith in him for choosing to do things the hard way. She knew it was his choice. Just as she knew it was her brother's choice not to request to go to Vietnam. Tom Racky, who was also in the service, had orders that placed him in the states. She told Johnny she trusted he knew that being in combat was the way he needed to do it. Johnny replied:

...Ya know you've got faith & trust in me & Denise I have so very much faith & trust in you, are you sure we aren't twins?

Although he had gotten four letters from Denise on July 22 alone, it had been a few weeks since he heard from my parents.

...as a matter of fact, Lover, I haven't gotten a letter from the old man in a month or more, I don't care. He must be having a ball at the farm, FUCK EM' ALL SAMMY SMALL! I have Denise & I don't need anybody else.

July 23

Sweet-heart, you said in your letter that I sounded proud of being wanted by the V.C., well I am not proud to kill Denise, I hate it and, if anything, I am ashamed to do it but, Denise, I have to do it to get back to you. Please don't be mad Dee, it is my job for a year and it is a sickening job.

—John A. Guldan, *July 23, 1970,*
to Denise

The My Lai massacre and the execution of the North Vietnamese soldier bound and on his knees were imprinted in Uncle John's mind. He imagined what Johnny would be suffering, not only from what might have been done to him, but for what he might have done to others.

> *...I'm not even gonna watch war flicks when I get back. The reason I sound funny or maybe sarcastic about it in my letters is cause it helps a little Denise to keep me from going nuts. It's not so bad to kill the enemy & see him dead, but to see a Marine even hurt a little not only makes me sick, it makes me blind, raging mad and I want to tear things apart. Christ, Denise I never thought I would ever find it in myself to hate enough to want to destroy, but I guess it was hiding inside and it took a war to bring it out. I know it will be burned out of me by the time I get back to you, so don't worry I will be my old nice self again with a little help from you.*

There are a few theories on our involvement in Vietnam. One of them begins with the American support of France in Vietnam. In the early fifties, France was on the verge of being ruled by the Communists. The United States' fear of Communism propelled efforts to prevent Communist officials to be elected in France. The United States provided military support to de Gaulle and France to keep the Communist Party from ruling. Ho Chi Minh and his Communist guerrilla forces attacked the French at Dien Bien Phu after moving artillery up and over the mountains surrounding the airstrip. The French were caught off guard, never expecting it was possible to get heavy equipment up the steep-walled, jungle-covered mountains surrounding Dien Bien Phu. As a result of this defeat, Russia, a Communist political state, came into South Vietnam.

France, then Russia, and then the United States, all wanted control over South Vietnam at some point in history. There is a story about Ho Chi Minh going into the American embassy in Paris. There, he laid out a constitution that declared his plans. "Vietnam is not Communist. We just want to be our own country and this is our program."

Ho Chi Minh presented documents detailing his program. The American ambassador appeared to be listening to him. When Ho Chi Minh departed, the ambassador threw all of the documents in the wastebasket.

- - -

Uncle John sympathized with Ho Chi Minh while Uncle Mike heatedly questioned the political maneuvers spanning 1950 to 1970.

"When you negotiate with a dictator or a Communist who don't have any morals, ya know they just change things around whenever it suits their benefit. But I think there was a certain amount of data about that war that never surfaced. The Kent State: who prompted all that? Who prompted all the riots in Chicago in '68? . . . But, ya know, I think we were victimized by a lot of different propaganda that came up. I think years from now, your grandchildren will analyze the war with a heck of a lot more objectivity." Uncle Mike states.

Both Uncle Mike and Uncle John were well informed on the details of the politics during the fifties and sixties. They were young adults at a time when our country lived with fear of the volatility around the world and they naturally wanted to understand it. The generation after them stirred up conflict by challenging and criticizing policy rooted in the fifties and sixties. By the seventies, our country was weakened and vulnerable from this conflict within it. Now a bit older, my aunts and uncles' focus was on their own lives.

"We were at a point—not that we didn't know what was going on—but we were all busy raising kids then so it wasn't a focus for us. Our children weren't going to war cuz they weren't old enough. And so, ya know, it just kinda was part of what we were doing and we were caught up with raising children and going to school," Aunt Diane says.

I dig deeper toward my aunt and uncle's memories of what happened during that time. I see these memories as hidden treasures, jewels that had been stored away, forgotten until now, their value finally realized. Their memories provide explanations that allow me to understand the truth of that time like the clarity of a priceless gem. Their memories provide explanations for why Johnny would have voluntarily joined the war and what my parents were going through at the time. Some of those memories seem to be locked behind defensiveness, like a serpent guarding a treasure. A serpent that could be tamed by a flute playing music. That music to tame the serpent is us talking about it together, listening to each other.

- - -

It was a confusing time for young and old. No one was able to get a clear picture on what was going on over in Vietnam, not even the young men fighting in it. The news was negative toward our country and soldiers while at the same time portrayed them as heroic and glorious with each increase of the VC body count.

...Well I haven't gotten a letter from my old man for a pretty long time, I guess they are REALLY having a good time this summer, oh well no news from them is GOOD news, and besides all they would talk about is how nasty Marianne is and why I haven't written in so long.

I guess my parents were caught up in their lives or their letters were getting lost on the way to Johnny. My dad was busy going back and forth between the farm and Chicago. When in Chicago, he tended to his patients. When he was at the farm, he tended to his farm duties and hosted visits from friends and family. My siblings and I played and explored many of the farms' acres every day and tubed down the river when it was warm enough. On weekends, we'd pack lunches and spend the day at Lake Emily or Sunset Lake.

July 26

"Stripes don't mean a thing in the bush."
—John A. Guldan, *recorded July 26, 1970*

Johnny was now a lance corporal but hadn't seen anything yet to prove it. He was told he would get an additional thirty dollars pay in each monthly paycheck. He was also to attend NCO (non-commissioned officer) school. All of this would give him another stripe. The thirty dollars was more important to him than the stripe or the title. He had thought he might not get promoted because the captain thought he was disrespectful when Johnny replied over the radio, "Negative, I don't have a Mickey Mouse," when asked him what time it was. "Mickey Mouse" was Johnny's tongue-in-cheek term for a watch, originating from Disney's Mickey Mouse watch. Another time Johnny questioned his

Captain as to why he seemed more upset that they shot a VC mama san than the fact his friend Peeler was killed.

Their squad had been reduced from twenty-three to fourteen. This was not all deaths and injuries. Three were discharged because they were on drugs, some for psychological reasons, and a few had served their time. Others were just mishaps like his lieutenant Johnny wrote about, in his July 11 letter, who had picked up a piece of cardboard and caught a booby-trap.

Mariann continued to be quiet about Bruce in her writings to Johnny. She provided no help for Johnny to understand why my parents were reacting so strongly against him.

...I am not getting the true story and it's making me very mad. I am telling you cause I Love you and I want you to find out, find out from Marianne what the hell she is doing, how come my old man hates this dude so much to tell him that he will break him in half if he caught him hanging around. If this was happening to Pat or anybody else I would not really care, but it's happening to Marianne and I am getting mad & worried about what the hell is going on. I want ya to talk to her by yourself & find out for me why, why the whole god damn family, cousins included hate this guy and why they think my sister is nuts. Will ya do that for me Denise, I keep getting one sided letters even to the point where they become actually hateful. Either tell Marianne to write & give it to me straight or you tell me. I have written to her and she beats around the bush, she doesn't say anything. If the letters I get from my family get any worse I'm just gonna burn the lousey things and not even open them and I WILL NOT write back to them, then if they want to know what is happening to me over here they

will have to keep in touch with you. I want to know what in the hell is going on in that stupid family, it sounds like it is breaking up from the few letters I do get.

Johnny sees that the end is in sight and began to get excited about coming home. Did Denise feel that the end was in sight?

We got a whole mess of new guys in the company today and again I feel good cause it makes me feel like I'm getting closer to you & I AM. I figured it out Dee in a little while I will be down to a DOUBLE DIGIT MIDGET how do ya like that...

Was Denise able to celebrate yet? There was still too much time to go. She was still afraid to hope.

& I also figured out I only have 6 more pay days left here in Nam (which means 6 months, but it sounds better & feels better to count the pay days) I'm goofey, aren't I? All I do every day is think of you & ways to make the days go faster. Here's a tip Denise, never count the days, just the months, when I get down to DOUBLE DIGITS then I will count the days. WOW! DEE I LOVE YOU, I can almost feel you now soon we will be together and then WOW, Denise, yeah sure here I am all sure of myself and telling myself what a lover I am gonna be when I see ya for the first time, and when I first see ya I will probably wet my pants and shake all over the place. God Denise I could squeeze you till ya pop, I need you so much & when I get home, well actions speak much, much louder than words, except I might be a little weaker than usual. I won't be the big

*healthy Marine like I was on leave, but I am sure under
your Tender Loving Care and delicious MEAT LOAF I will get
back to my HOT DOG self.*

The foreboding reality of where he was remained in both
Johnny's mind and Denise's as she read his P.S. in this same letter:

*Have you heard of a place called THAN MY' on the news
about Viet Nam? If ya have, let me know, Denise, that was
a hell, it was definitely a hell on earth after that it makes
me wonder how God would allow something like that to
happen.*

By July 26, Johnny broke down and wrote to my parents.
He corresponded on the usual topics and did not ask why he had
not heard from them. At the same time, Mom was mailing off
another package to Johnny with all the things he had asked for,
like socks and cookies and more. In this letter alone, twice he
admits to being homesick. He is weary from the enemy and the
rain's constant aggression and yearns for a place to rest.

Dear Dad & Ma,
    *I know it's been a long time since my last letter but I
am on hill55 now for a couple of days before they send my
squad to a different area of operation, it is pretty secure so
I can put my eyes down on this paper and not have to look
up. I got 2 packages from you Ma & one with the picture of
all the cousins and it made me kind of homesick, next year
Denise and I will be in it....*

Johnny had finally received the picture we had taken on
Memorial Day.

A lot has happened since the last letter, the enemy had an offensive for about two and a half weeks, I was put up for a medal for acting the way I was trained to act under fire...

He doesn't go into the detail surrounding this medal that he went into with Denise in his July 22 letter.

...the rains are here...I can stand being wet, but I hate wet feet, all day and night my feet are sopping wet.

Uncle John thought of his nephew constantly. The young boys he taught at St. Mel's high school each day reminded him even more of Johnny because many of them would soon be going off to Vietnam. St. Mel was in a poor neighborhood, where kids couldn't afford college. These were typically the first victims of the Vietnam draft. Five of his students who had entered the service after graduating were killed in action. Statistics showed that if you could survive your first ninety days in Vietnam, your chance of survival dramatically increased. Uncle John marked off the days on his calendar that hung on the otherwise bare wall of his high school office hoping for those ninety days for Johnny. The counting of days was a constant topic in Johnny's letters.

Joe Heeney is going home in about 50 days, I didn't think he was that far ahead of me...I might take an R&R, I probably won't take one but heck I only have 6 more pay-days here ... I was going to arrange it to meet Denise in Hawaii, but I decided against it, that wouldn't be too smart. Then I was checking on coming home for 5 days but I don't think that would be too smart either. That's when I was really homesick, now I have cooled down.

That's about it on the news here, I sure wish I was
home, well I am in my 6th month and it won't be long now-

Love,
John

By the end of July, I started counting the days too. But I dreaded for the days I counted to get smaller, because that meant how many days before we went back to school. Yet as July was wrapping up we were still doing what we had done all summer long: Dad and my brothers harvested the hay, Mom grocery shopped, did laundry, and cared for Bonnie and Mimi. We continued doing the fun things we did at the farm including Saturdays at Lake Emily. I had been at the beach and came home complaining about my eye hurting. It stung like a bee bite. My dad laid me out on the porch couch, where there was lots of light. He looked and looked and wiped it with a wet cloth but it still hurt. He worked on my eye again and again, until he finally saw it was a grain of sand. I lay perfectly still, not blinking, while he carefully picked it out of my eye. It felt so much better. I knew he could fix everything.

July 28–The Letter

> *No matter what you say, children won't' listen*
> *No matter what you know, children refuse...*
>
> —Into the Woods, song lyrics,
Disney

My father sat down on July 28 and wrote a letter full of homeland topics, keeping Johnny informed on what was happening. Johnny's July 26 letter was in transit home and the drought of letter writing between them ended. It had to. They had clung to each other over the months with the threads of ink laced across their letters. It was a tenuous, day-by-day existence for all of them.

7/28/70

Dear John,

Your letter written 5 July arrived several days before the one dated 30 June. I guess like everything else—SNAFU.

SNAFU is a military acronym meaning "Situation Normal All Fu-ked Up." The simple act of receiving letters from his son was fouled up due to the government's SNAFU, and his son's life was in their hands. This war our government had the Americans believing in, this use of our innocent young men, was a SNAFU.

It sounds good to hear you talk about only six months to go. I'd say you have it figured right. I calculated you'll go home before January 1st and maybe for Christmas. It seems as though they're rotating at ten months from there, unless the situation changes. Let's say a few beads it doesn't—or changes to 8 months.

My father had no control over when Johnny would return home from Vietnam. He prayed, resting his hope in a few beads of the rosary. Dad was brought up with the rituals of the Catholic Church and the heavy-handed hypocrisy that came with it. My father believed in God but didn't work at that relationship via the religion he had known. As a result he stayed away from the practice of any religion with the exception of the rosary. He and my mother said the rosary whenever they were traveling. My father and mother clung to their faith and respect of a higher power. These were fundamental beliefs they shared.

I don't know if I congratulated you on your promotion, but if not, consider it done. You're now a Lance Corporal. You mean if you score high enough in that school in September you will be a Sergeant?

As I read this letter decades after it was written, I can sense my father's arms reaching up from the paper to lasso Johnny with the ink on the pages and pull him right back into our living room at 9029 Oakley. This is fantastical thinking. This is desperation. This is hope.

If I were you I'd take the R&R as long as you have the chance you should see as much as you can. You can bet I'd head for Australia. In fact I wish you would. I've been thinking of immigrating there. You could look it over and let me know what you think of the place. I've got all the dope on dental practice. If Jimmy and Bill have to go over to that manure pile you're in I'll not be able to stand that much more letter writing . . .

"Letter writing" was my father's substitute for crying out, screaming, or any number of heart-wrenching activities he was fighting at home while his child was fighting half a world away. My father lightens the mood with this term, "letter writing." I love that.

. . . so it'll be easier to cut out of this place. I was in Tokyo and I can tell you it is for the birds. You can have Hong Kong too.

My father loved our country but was so determined not to have his other sons go to war that he began to make plans to move us all to Australia. He spoke to someone at the embassy a few times. They were encouraging him to move there because Australia needed Dentists. It was several weeks after this letter that my father actually went to the Australian embassy in Chicago to collect application forms for an official departure from the United States, like Baron von Trapp from The Sound Of Music, who led his family out of the country they loved to escape the war.

- - -

"Would you support your child going to war if they wanted to join the service or would you move to a country like Australia to avoid a draft?" I ask Aunt Diane and Uncle Mike, who have since raised two boys and two girls of their own.

"No, I mean I would support 'em. I would certainly let them know my views and feelings; that I didn't want 'em to do this for various reasons. But I would support his decision. I wouldn't like it but I would support it," Aunt Diane tells me.

"I had no idea," Uncle Mike responds after I ask if he knew of my father's plans to move us to Australia.

"You can speculate all you want but he never would've left here . . . cause he was always controversial about that [the war, I assume Uncle Mike meant]. Just his stand on the Catholic Church, ya know? He'll go from one extreme to the other. But that's your dad. I would never take him that serious at all," Uncle Mike says.

- - -

Today a cryptic message arrived from the Plaza bank. It was a duplicate deposit ticket marked July 25th, 100 dollars, balance $946.57. Then written in long-hand pen and ink across it, Error in Customer Deposit. Maybe this has something to do with Denise? You'll have to straighten that all out when you get home. You've lost me on the high finance bit.

Was my father trying to think of domestic activities to which he could relate? Words on stationary were his transportation device used to send his son a part of home. This piece of home possibly gave Johnny something to hang on to, something to focus on. My parents deposited Johnny's paychecks as they came home and tried to keep track of the amount for him yet managing money was something neither of them did comfortably. Mom enlisted my help to balance the bank statement before Dad ever saw it. My father dabbled in the stock market, watching those marks on the television each day, but it never amounted to much. I don't think we had a lot of money but he never seemed worried about it.

John, in one letter you say you are going to study medicine, and in the next you say you hated school. That's a combination that won't mix. I'm sure the GI bill will help. You should be laying your plans and considering priorities. Remember it's more important what you study than where you study. Since learning is subjective it is up to the student to learn. Better equipped laboratories and libraries are nice but not important when compared to individual effort. Rating school was always lost on me. That would be like rating a book by the people who read it.

Such a profound statement lost in this little letter.
Such a little letter lost in a profound situation.
Such a little situation lost in a profound time.

You're right about the Marine Corps being an experience. Now when you're 40, I expect you to advise your son to enter the Marines and get himself two golden years of experience. The other day a yellow jacket landed in a tub of water and mom told Bonnie not to touch it, but she also had an experience. She got stung. I hope some of your learning, as hers and Mariann's, can come vicariously instead of all of it the hard way.

I am now a parent and as I read, I understand much more because of my father's letter. The military has umpteen benefits for a young man. It offers a career with benefits, pays for school, and provides structure, discipline and honor. This is attractive for a young man. A child heads off, unsuspecting.

Although my father was not able to keep Johnny from "being stung," his letters allowed him to be there with his son as he went through this pain. It is my parents' pain too.

Mom mailed you a package from the farm so you should be getting it about the same time you get this

letter. So long for now and take care. We're counting the
days too, even Bonnie.

Love,
Dad

Sometimes I talk a lot about things that I am not sure of, thinking the talk will make it happen, like going to Italy. I have made plans three times to travel to Rome and each time things out of my control have gotten in the way yet I continue to think and talk about going. I feel if I tell enough people enough details then it will happen. That may have been what my father and Johnny were doing in their letters. If they talked enough about future plans, they would happen. Wouldn't they?

July 30

Meanwhile, day by day, Tobit was keeping track of the
time Tobiah would need to go and to return. . . . She
[Anna] began to weep aloud and wail over her son:
"Alas, my child, light of my eyes, that I let you make
this journey!" But Tobit kept telling her: "Hush, do not
think about it, my love; He is safe! . . . The man who is
traveling with him is trustworthy, and is one of our own
kinsmen. So do not worry over him, my love. He will be
here soon." But she retorted, "Stop it, and do not lie to
me!"

—Tobit 10, *Anxiety of the Parents,*
New American Bible

My father did not let go of the hope or belief his son would return home safely. Yet my mother felt differently. Johnny too was anxious. He had written to my parents on July 26, and four days later, he wrote to Mariann's boyfriend, Bruce.

> *I have not gotten a letter from my Daddio or Mommio for about a month so they must be having fun this summer. I don't write to them, I write to my brothers & sisters and I write most to my girl, I don't have too much time, mr. gook does not let me let my guard down too many times. Enemy activity is very high contrary to the credibility gap that I know is present in the news media.*

Johnny may have been trying to win Bruce's allegiance by showing a detachment from my parents. He wrote home again on July 30, to my brother Jim:

> *...How long are you gonna be up at the farm?...The summer is almost over now...I can't wait till it's over that means I will be getting closer to home then.*

Johnny continued to try and understand what was going through Mariann's head. He replied to Jim's earlier letter:

> *...Jim, I do not know what hell is going on with this Bruce dude and Marianne. I have not heard anything about it, you are the first one who has said anything about it. I wish to hell I could meet this guy so I could see what he is really like and find out why everybody hates him so much...*

Jim was the third triplet to leave Mom's womb. It seems to make sense that Jim was the last triplet to arrive into the world as you get to know him. I could imagine him laying back in my mother's belly, all sprawled out, and enjoying all of the room he had after his sisters left. I wouldn't be surprised if they had to pull him out with forceps. He looked nothing like his triplet sisters Margie and Eileen. He inherited our mother's coloring and features without a lick of my father in him. As the triplets went through school, they were held back in first grade. Jim was held back again in second grade as his sisters moved on, ending up in the same grade as his brother Bill. Bill and Jim completed Christ the King elementary school together and went on to St. Rita High School.

Johnny attempted to explain to Jim, from a big-brother perspective, the issues between Mariann and our father:

Dad has his ways and Marianne has hers.

As Jimmy read this July 30 letter Johnny had sent him, it became difficult to finish. It made him sick to his stomach. He was sensitive to the details of Johnny's situation. For Johnny, he needed to be numb to it. It was a matter of survival for both of them.

...Tonight I gotta go on a killer team into Dodge City, it's pretty tense, but I have been on so many I'm not even scared anymore. I've been here 6 months and it feels like a year already, fuck it I'll be outta here soon...

With the thought of someday going home and his re-entrance into society, he wrote to his friend Neal on this same July day:

...Did you know that us grunts are considered temporarily insane from 2 yrs to 12 yrs back in civilian life. We got this word from Gen Chapman the Commandant who got it from Nixon. I'll bet ya they didn't mention that on the

10:00 news. I guess they think once we get the taste of blood we can't live without it. Heck it's just like killin' chickens. We gotta squad called Kincaid's Killer Squad. Remember Mai Lai, well watch for another one, but this time it's legal.

Johnny wrote troubling thoughts to his younger brother Jim and friend Neal on this same day. To Denise he shared more of what he has seen of mankind in the Vietnam War –

I got a HOLY letter from Nanny grandma and did ya know that Novenas & Masses & Sacrifices are being made for me? . . . It's such a paradox Dee, it's so funny & ironic. Say prayers and then take life, I gotta laugh, say prayers and then the worst comes. Ya know Baby, I cannot count the times a man has died begging God for life in his last breathe, and it's just no use at all, and as I watch him close his eyes for the last time he grabs on to my arm and begs Denise, he begs. It is maddening and everytime it happens I feel like running, running all the way back to you, and grabbing you and run some more & never look back. It isn't pretty, I wish it would all stop and there would never be a war again. Life is so very precious to all men and man takes it away. Someday I'll wake up from this nightmare, and maybe someday the whole world will wake up, I just hope the world wakes up before our kids are old enough to have to take part in man's fiasco of war. I don't want my kids to see it, ever. Denise, if all men could just spend five minutes here I know they would open their blind eyes. Like that song says "War, what is it good for? Absolutely NOTHING!" I believe that with all my heart now Denise, I just wish I would have realized it before I had to take part in it and dip my lousey hands in this blood. I believe in the cause Denise, the V.C. are animals even worse than us Marines, ya know why? Cause they kill, torture, and starve their own people. Sounds funny doesn't it Dee, I mean we do the same thing in the U.S., maybe we are no better than the gooks after all, maybe that's why these simple people cannot realize why we are here. A little kid came up to me on a patrol in a village and showed me a picture out of Life magazine of a riot, I think it was at KENT (I don't know how the kid got it, but he got it) he said, "Hey Marine, why don't you go home and kill the V.C. in your own land?" Right after he said that a South Viet soldier killed him. He just killed him, I asked why. He turned the kid over and he was gonna blow me & himself up with a grenade. I guess maybe the kid was right about what he said, I guess I was awful lucky too. Denise that card I sent in this letter. . . I just want ya to save it with all the other crap so I can look back on it and thank God it is all over, and it's a reminder of what man can regress to in war.

Johnny continued to focus on his home connections and his love via his letters, the letters he wrote and the ones he received. He tried, even in the dire moments, to make light of life. On the birthday of his platoon mate Tom, they laid near each other in the midst of a firefight. Bullets whizzed by, grenades detonated, and the ground shook from explosions, yet Johnny sang,

"Happy birthday to you..."

Johnny's drive to help the children was interrupted by and possibly fueled by such incidents as the one he barely mentioned in a July 30 letter to his friend Beatty. As he is signing off of this two-page letter Johnny writes:

> ...*Some kid came up to me while I was on patrol & waved a flick [photo] of a riot at me and said to go home & fight the VC back there and then he screamed something in Vietnamese and pulled a grenade out from his shirt. I had to kill him, it's a good thing I did he would have killed me and 2 others. Don't tell anyone, especially Dee, I don't want her to know that stuff about killing.*

Johnny had become what they trained him to become. He was a warrior and a protector of his fellow Marines. He wanted to survive in a world full of war. There was violence going on in our country too, and much of it was in Chicago. On this same day he writes to Nan and Pop:

> *How is the summer back there, I have been hearing about shootings and riots... Denise works in the Loop & so does Marianne, I worry a lot about them. It's funny I'm in a war over here and from what I hear & read it's like there's a war back there.*

After reading through my brother's letters and listening to his tapes, I have been able to put to rest the uneasiness I have had that he had killed another person. Feelings of shame that my brother killed have metamorphosed into admiration of him, who at nineteen was trying to figure out how to survive in a dangerous and hellish world without losing his soul. His very honest words throughout his letters helped me understand.

July 31

> *Dear Dad,*
>
> *I got your letter you wrote on the 21st. I'm glad you got the hay in alright and that the cattle business is booming. . .*
>
> —John A. Guldan, *July 31, 1970,*
> *to my father*

Letters to my parents left out detailed descriptions that may have exposed my parents to exactly what was going on there. Yet due to what was not said must have left a lot to my parent's imagination, which must have been tormenting. Johnny was their little boy trying to show them he was a man. It was what a good American boy did.

At the time of the Vietnam War, the U.S. adult population consisted of those that had gone through World War II. Most of these adults were also around during the Korean War. When the Vietnam War came, these adults—my parents, my aunts, and my uncles included—were seeing bloody combat fights right in their living rooms. These images were on the television and in every newspaper and magazine. With the reality of war in front of their faces, their romantic version of war was threatened.

- - -

Aunt Barbara says she would not be able to read the letters Johnny wrote to Denise because they were graphic.

"Are you going to write about any of the gory stuff in your book?" Aunt Barbara asks me.

I tell Aunt Barbara that I am not focusing on the blood and guts but that a certain element of it must be told because that is the reality of war. People die, children die, many suffer. I believe that is what Johnny wanted us all to know, what he screamed out in his letters. Aunt Barbara's silence tells me she finally accepts that.

- - -

The topics and moods in Johnny's letters switched between sentences, injecting humor just when the reader thought it was dire, like the Vietnam terrain injected sunlit rice paddies adjacent to a dense, dark jungle. To my father:

> ...I got bit by one of those horrendous centipedes and they are poisonous, it felt like I got stabbed with a knife. It made me vomit & my chest felt like it was on fire. I thought maybe I was gonna get Medevaced, but no, it only lasted an hour. Heck, I thought all the local insects were my buddies, but I guess this one must have been a vc sympathizer.

Between firefights and patrol, Johnny thought about how to make the world a better place once he got back home. He wrote to Denise of his plans to help her brother's kids who parents were going through a rough divorce:

> Listen Baby when I get back we will take Bill's kids on a few picnics and to the zoo & stuff with us. I know they must be unhappy kids, so we can help out a little if we do some things like that. It's hell to be lonely let me tell ya, it's hell and no little kid should ever have to experience it. So you & I will show em' a little happiness when I get back O.K?

Denise was pulled into the middle of her brother and sister-in-law's breakup. It was emotionally hard on her.

I can be certain that the following content in letters to my parents was emotionally hard for them. Again, just enough to leave the rest to their imagination. To Dad:

> ... *Activity in our area has been high and we just got another intelligence report that the 89th NVA zapper battalion is working in our A.O [area of operation], well I hope they leave, the last time they hit us they wiped out that village of PHU THANH, maybe you heard of it in the news. My squad was the one that was pinned down by them while the rest of the gooners slaughtered the villagers, right after that we were pulled out, as a matter of fact we were choppered out while it was still dark. I think they pulled us out so quick cause the Brass feared another "Mai Ly" even though we did not do it. But you know how things can be twisted by the news. . .*

In this July 31 letter, my parents learned the NVA group killed villagers in order to make it look like the U.S. did so. Johnny is fearful yet able to think about Christmas in a land that felt like God had forgotten about it.

> *Gosh Dad, you say I will be home around xmas. I sure hope you are right, damn I hope you are right...I just hope you are right, it would be outstanding to be home for xmas...*

Johnny's focus, once again, quickly turned to the mundane. He has little patience left with my father on these topics.

> *...O.K. now about my checks being sent home. I have sent ONE check to Denise so she could buy a TAPE RECORDER not a record player, she bought one and tried to give the*

balance to you, all my other checks have been sent to you. I am keeping all the rest of my pay starting with the month of July on the books. The reason I am keeping it on the books is cause I might be able to take an R&R if I ever get around to it. I doubt it very much if I will take one. I might buy a car here before I come home, I have looked into it & I can save $1500 if I get it here, now I said I might buy a car so don't start sweating anything.

Aunt Nora held a celebration for us kids at the culmination of summer tutoring at the farm. The highlight of this celebration was the hokey pokey. Aunt Nora waved her arms and shook her legs like she was a kid herself. I was well into my college years before I realized Aunt Nora was not the inventor of the hokey pokey.

Well, the summer is almost gone and I am glad, that means I'm closer to getting outta this place. Again I sure hope you're right about me being home for xmas.

Love,
John

P.S. Have you been hearing about all the weapons being stolen from Camp Pendleton? I think there's gonna be a Civil War & if so I better be back there if it happens or I'm swimming home.

With the thousands of miles between them; Johnny could not protect his family and my father could not protect his son. Their only opportunity was through their letter writing. They could not see each other. They could not touch each other yet they could hear each other's voices in their letters. There was honesty. There was frustration. There was courage. There was love. There was a commitment to stick by each other no matter what. All of this was carried back and forth across the oceans, on the pages of these letters between a father and a son.

August 1

> *I am not going to take an R&R at all. I will NOT be able to make it home for R&R, the Capt's. final words, so there's no sense in me taking one at all.*
>
> *Be mine Denise, I wish this was over and done, and I had you in my arms. Someday it will happen.*
> *I Love you.*
>
> *All My Heart,*
John
—John A. Guldan, *August 1, 1970,*
to Denise

The letter writing between Johnny and Denise never wavered in frequency, nor did the fierceness of this twenty-year-old boy's love. His August 1 letter to Denise told her he was to go on a mission. He would be away from Hill 55 and did not know when he could write again. He begins this letter to Denise with "Dear Baby" and ends it as he ended the hundred-some letters before—wishing he was back home.

Denise lived the war every day with Johnny. My parents did not have the gruesome detail that Denise heard about in her letters, yet they still suffered in their hearts, imagining the emotional and physical pain Johnny was in, knowing at any moment they might lose him. They all suffered together, or I should say simultaneously, silently and alone. We were all suffering in our own ways, yet all suffering silently and alone. Johnny was the only one among us not silent. He was shouting at us through his letters, shouting at us to know what was happening there.

August 2

> *"My child has perished!" She would go out and keep watch all day at the road her son had taken, and she ate nothing. At sunset she would go back home to wail and cry the whole night through, getting no sleep at all.*
> —Tobit 10, *Anxiety of the Parents,*
> *New American Bible*

Johnny did not write any letters on August 2. He was busy dealing with booby-traps the North Vietnamese had laid nearby Hill 55. A month later, on September 5, a platoon mate wrote to Denise as to what Johnny did on August 2.

> *The Sarge and John were blowing a barbed wire barrier. It's called the Da Nang Barrier. Maybe you've heard about it. Well, they blew it. But not everything blew. . . the detonating round was not one of the blown traps.*

While at the farm, preparations for the new school year were beginning. Mom had plans the following week to take us on our annual trip to Stevens Point to buy all of our new school clothes, shoes, and supplies. We usually packed up at the farm and returned to our home in Chicago right before the start of school in September.

August 3

Sometimes people leave you
Halfway in the woods...
　　　　　　—Into the Woods song lyrics, Disney

As Johnny and Dad had been hoping, Nixon finally began to pull troops out of Vietnam in late July. It just wasn't soon enough. Those of us at the farm took advantage of the last few weeks of the 1970 summer. We played hide and seek in the cornfields, spied on the Bible campers, floated down the river, and rode the horses.

It was another beautiful summer day at the farm. Dad had another day to enjoy his weekend before he packed up for his weekly trip to Chicago. Eileen was already prepared to head back to work with Dad and looked forward to some social activity in Beverly that week. The long weekends at the farm were lonely without her sister Margie. The week of August 3 was Margie's turn to babysit at Uncle Mike and Aunt Diane's and Eileen's turn at Dad's office.

The sun would soon be going down that Sunday evening. Several hours behind Vietnam, it was still August 2nd in the states. My mother was taking laundry off the clothesline outside while she reviewed some weekly plans with my father. He had a farm to run and needed Mom to greet the vet that week and make plans for his next weekend visit with a local farmer. While they were in deep discussion, a cat brushed up against her leg. She screamed.

"Oh, Eileen it's just a little kitty cat. C'mere kitty," Dad said.

"John! You know how I feel about the cats," Mom said.

At the same time, it was the morning of August 3rd nearby a South Vietnamese village called Bich Bac, a small town north of Da Nang. Johnny and his sarge went out early that morning after blowing the Da Nang barrier the day before. The sarge wanted to check on their work.

And then the war took Johnny away...

August 3rd 1970 started out like almost any other day in VietNam. As soon as the sun was up everybody who happened to be asleep would be awakened by the blazing sun or pounding rain. Whichever Mother Nature wanted you to have at any given moment.

I really can't say for certain if anyone knew Gil and John were going to look over that area or not. I did not know they were going. I have never known why they never asked me to go. I almost always went on those little "recon" missions.

I remember standing out by the gravel road that ran north from Hill 55 toward Da Nang. All the sudden to the northeast of our little camp (military talk would be POS which means map position) there was a very loud explosion and a big black cloud of smoke going up into the air. I remember looking around and then thinking where is John and Gil. I think most of us had the same bad feeling. Some of the guys took off running with Doc and I ran to get my radio and tried to catch up. Those radios were pretty heavy back then so I was a little slower than the rest. If we could have gone cross-country it probably would of only been around 500-700 yards. It was a lot quicker for us to go North about 300 or so yards then East about 500-600 yards. On the way to the sight I was on the radio with our company rear to tell them about the explosion and that we were on our way to check it out. When I got close one of the guys came screaming back toward me to get an emergency Medevac mission called in. I did not want to take the time to put the map position into code so I told them something like 800 meters NE of our last POS. That was close enough.

I was about 100 yards from John, Gil, and Doc Brown. When we all got there I was working to get the birds there and Doc was doing what he could for John and Gil. Someone was constantly running back and forth giving me updates. About that time one of the guys came back to me and said, "Professor's gone and Gil is real bad."

At about the same time I looked toward Da Nang airbase and you could see the birds coming toward us. There were two Cobra gun ships and two CH-46 choppers. The Cobra pilot contacted me about five miles out so I could visually guide him in. When they get to you the CH-46's always stay high until the gun ships make a couple of high speed runs over you to check you out. The CH-46 pilots can hear everything you say but they worry about safely getting on and off the ground so they very seldom say anything.

I think everyone was in shock! They always said never to shoot when the birds were coming in because they would feel they were under fire. We had a guy who had only been with us a few days. He was off to my right. For some reason, I think he was just scared, he let go with a full-auto burst from his M-16 toward the small village to our South. The gun-ship pilot saw it and wanted to know what was going on. After I threatened him with great bodily harm I was able to assure the gun-ship that everything was OK.

I tossed a smoke grenade on the gravel road where I wanted the bird to land. As the CH-46 came in he could see Doc and the others working on John and Gil. He landed with the tail ramp toward them and the nose toward me. When they got them on the bird and started to take off I lost it. I sat down in the middle of that road and sobbed much as I am doing now as I try to write this. I made eye contact with the pilot and begged him through my tears to please hurry. He raised his hand slowly like a salute I guess to say I'll do my best.

When the birds left none of us really knew what to do. I remember that the gravel road made a ninety-degree turn to the North. There was a small village of four or five huts a little off that road. No villagers came out there. They would usually try to stay out of the way. They did not want to be seen as the enemy even if they were. To the East where they [John and Gil] were was a small rise off the road, which was overgrown with grass and bamboo. Beyond that a ways was the river. We walked into that village and sort of collapsed next to a couple of the huts. The villagers were terrified, I guess they were probably afraid we would do them harm. About that time I got a call on the radio that Gil was dead on arrival at the hospital ship. They also said for the whole squad to get all our gear and come to Hill55. I walked with Doc to Hill55. He told me John was killed instantly and surely never felt a thing. He also told me that the only words Gil would say was that of worry about John.

The next day, Capt. Kincade, who was the C/O of Mike Co at the time, called in Doc. Brown, myself, and a few others to get our story on what happened. He had monitored the Medevac mission like he did everything we were involved in. We were also told at that time there had not been any U.S./ ARVN activity in that area for a long time. They said that the "mine" was probably a "bouncing betty." I've often wondered how long it had been there, just waiting.

—Jim Hornsey, *2010 letter to Guldan family*

For forty years, I had imagined the scene in my own head: a daisy chain of small, metal fragments, shooting out at the two men and them lying and suffering for hours. Jim Hornsey's letter finally told us about the moments surrounding his death. I learned that our brother did not die alone and suffering. He was surrounded by those who cared deeply for him. This has been a comforting thought.

On June 13, 2015, Denise handed me a letter she had received from Dave Martinez, another of Johnny's platoon mates who was there that day. It was dated September 5, 1970. Johnny and Gil went out the morning of August 3 to check on their previous day's work. Not all had blown. One of them tripped the detonating daisy-chain, spraying mortar rounds upon both of them. A piece of metal was embedded in Johnny's chest, which was considered his mortal wound. Johnny was not wearing his flak jacket. We never learned why that was.

The choppers landed on the hospital ship anchored in the China Sea outside of Da Nang. Johnny's body, along with Gil's, was laid next to many other young, American men who had been killed that morning and throughout the night, their pupils all grey, no life left in them. They all stank. The stink of death. Johnny's wounds were documented and his body counted. One less for our side, one more for the NVA.

The explosion went off about seven a.m. Monday, Saigon time. That was Sunday at seven p.m. in Wisconsin. Eileen and Dad were still at the farm. They had not left yet for their week in Chicago. Eileen had enjoyed her weekend at the farm. The weather had been perfect—Wisconsin summer days of light breezes and blue skies with just enough puffy white clouds for the shade to cool you when needed. Eileen enjoyed one last ride on our horse TC, which stood for Trotting Cindy, our beautiful dark chestnut thoroughbred. While sitting atop TC, she felt a chilly wind blow by, although the air had been absent of any breeze. It sent a chill down her spine and spooked the horse.

Mickey did not sleep well in Wisconsin the night of August 2. There was no startling, waking moment that night for Mickey, it was just a restless sleep. His worries about what he was going to do with the rest of his life kept him awake that night, or so he thought. What else could it be?

After he watched that bird take Johnny and Gilbert's bodies away, Jim Hornsey had to keep enduring each day, keep surviving his service in Vietnam. He did just that, and he has kept on surviving thanks to guys like Doc Brown. Jim hurt his hand a few weeks before his tour was up. He had been given orders to go out on a four-day patrol days before he was to go home. Doc wrapped bandages around Jim's hand and he wrapped and kept wrapping until it looked like the state of Rhode Island sat at the end of Jim's wrist. Doc told the general that Jim wouldn't be going anywhere.

The 1st Marine Division August 1970 Command Chronology entry for that day read:

On 3 August, two Marines from a squad patrol from M/3/1, while moving ahead of their patrol to check out an area for a day position (AT995635), detonated a daisy chain consisting of two M16A1 mines, resulting in two USMC KIA.

III. The News

"American soldiers cried out for their parents when they were dying or injured. We knew the American parents must also be grieving for their children."

—Christian Appy, *Patriots,*
Tran Van Ban interview, NVA 1967-1972

Reflecting on the day we received the news of my brother's death created a collage of memories that shaped into the longest day of our tale.

*

At four a.m. Central time on August 4, Eileen and Dad left the peaceful, green hills and fresh air of rural Wisconsin, after a long, enjoyable weekend. It was a cool, clear morning. The car crept slowly along the gravel drive that wound around the back of the farmhouse, passing the sturdy clothesline that was employed constantly throughout our summer stays. The sheets and white t-shirts hung still in the quiet morning. The heavy denim jeans my father and brothers always wore were damp after soaking in the night's dew without the opportunity of the sun's rays yet. Joe shared the first-floor bedroom with Mickey, who was a year older, and Chris, four years younger. Joe heard the car passing over the grassy drive outside their bedroom window, as he lay in bed. Dad breathed in the country air one more time that morning as he headed back to the city.

We kids did not particularly like that country air. We groaned and yelped at the manure stench, holding our nose as we passed by barnyards and freshly fertilized fields. Dad would laugh and tell us that he loved that country air and then would take an exaggerated inhale. We didn't know if he was teasing us or if the Wisconsin natives had brainwashed him.

Denise and Mariann had already risen for another early day at their busy downtown jobs. Patti too would rise soon. She was to work with Eileen and Dad in his office after they arrived home that morning. August 4 was a typical summer Tuesday in Chicago. The sun was bold even at eight that morning as Denise headed into work with her father, who also worked at the CTA. Each weekday that summer they took public transportation together to the Merchandise Mart in the heart of Chicago's bustling Loop. Johnny was never far from Denise's thoughts. And this morning, his voice from his last recorded message played over and over in her mind, while riding the elevator to her fourth floor office:

"My days for looking for myself are over. I want you to take care of yourself. Stay well until I get back Denise. Remember there is a man over here in Nam that loves you more than anything in the whole world. I need you too. Good bye darling."

He was becoming the man she had hoped he would grow into. He no longer was so determined to prove his father wrong in every matter. He still wanted her and she still wanted him, more than ever. She was amazed at how her love for him could grow over the last seven months when all she had were letters between them. It was now August. Soon it would be fall and then John would be home around Christmas. She was almost ready to allow herself to be excited. She could almost begin to see a future. Knowing he had gone off to do what he needed to do would all be worth it, she thought.

My father and Eileen were due to arrive back in Beverly within the hour. Patti and Mariann were waiting for them. Mom was rising at the farm, as were the rest of us. Bruce DaCosta was tending the pumps at the Oak Park GoTane station, 215 miles southeast of the farm. A military vehicle pulled in with three Marines, dressed in their formal blues. Bruce stepped up to the car to gas them up. While washing their windshield, Bruce asked what kind of business they were doing around Chicago. They said they were there to notify families of fallen Marines. Bruce told them his girlfriend's brother was a Marine in Vietnam. He asked, aware it was a long shot, if they knew him.

"His name is John Guldan," Bruce told them.

Bruce was in disbelief when the one of them replied, "Oh, I think the sergeant is handling that case."

Bruce called our house as soon as he was able, in an attempt to reach Mariann. There was no answer.

Eileen slept most of the way home that Tuesday morning. She had a whole workday with Dad ahead of her and was looking forward to the end of the day when she would have time to reconnect with a few of her girlfriends. Maybe they would go up to Rainbow Cone on Western Avenue and hang out. They'd almost always run into a few more schoolmates up there. However, it was early August, when many of the Beverly families would squeeze in one last trip to Wisconsin or Michigan before the school year began. At the very least they'd chat with the Sapp boys, friends of Johnny and Jimmy. Mr. and Mrs. Sapp were friends of my parents. The Rainbow Cone ice cream store in Beverly was owned by their family. The Sapp boys had visited our farm the summer before. They brought five-gallon containers of their ice cream and scooped it into cones in that famous pointy, pyramid shape Rainbow was known for. Chocolate, strawberry, Palmer House, Pistachio, and orange ice cream scooped in five slabs, pressed against each other, pointing up like a mountain range atop the elegant, long pointed yellow cone.

Margie was babysitting for Uncle Mike and Aunt Diane at their home in Evanston. Uncle Mike and Aunt Diane had two children and one on the way. Michael, their oldest, was born in 1966 with cystic fibrosis. The doctors repeatedly gave my aunt and uncle life expectancy dates, which he proved incorrect until he reached the eighth grade. It was not an easy life for my cousin Michael. My sisters can attest to that. Yet he never complained about the constant effort it took for him to breathe.

- - -

I ask Uncle Mike and Aunt Diane if they were concerned their own children might either be drafted or choose to enlist when our country was at war. Aunt Diane and Uncle Mike admit they did not even think about it because their children were so young back in 1970.

"If we had teenagers at that point or college kids, we certainly would have [been concerned with them going to war]. And we didn't even know anybody who really did except Michael's [Uncle Mike] nephew. I don't even know anybody else that went to Vietnam. It was just where we were at that time," Aunt Diane says.

- - -

About one hour before Eileen and my father arrived home on Tuesday morning, two Marines walked up the front steps of

9029 South Oakley. Patti and Mariann were at home getting ready for work that morning. They were expecting my dad and Eileen to arrive when they heard the clank of our brass door knocker. Mariann opened the front door and saw the two Marines in their full dress, standing at attention.

"What do you want?" Mariann asked.

From their stiff, unsmiling positions they asked for my parents.

"Is it about my brother? Just tell me if it's about my brother!" Mariann pleaded. Her voice was shrill and her eyes were wide. A sudden queasiness hit the pit of her stomach. She left the Marines standing at the door and ran up the long, enclosed stairway leading to the second floor.

"Marines are at the door—Johnny! Johnny! It's about Johnny!" Mariann screamed at Patti.

Patti had been putting her makeup on with orange juice can curlers on top of her head. Patti took charge of the situation, just as you would imagine the oldest of thirteen would do. After shaking Mariann and telling her to calm down and wait in their bedroom, Patti quickly unpinned her long blond hair from the curlers and went to the door. When she saw the Marines, she would not allow her mind to take her to the one place it was insisting on going. It could be anything, she told herself—one voice in her head trying to override the others. She informed the two Marines that my parents were not at home. Patti quickly sensed she was not going to get any information from them. She told them that my dad would be at his office at nine a.m. and gave them the address. They said they would meet him there. After the Marines left, Patti and Mariann, only twenty and eighteen years old, having felt like they aged decades in these moments, sat and waited for my father.

It was eight a.m. Dad had been up for at least four hours and had driven 250 miles. Having slept most of the trip, Eileen felt rested. They were both ready to begin a workday scheduled with patients. Dad and Eileen arrived home in a good mood. As soon as they walked through the door, Patti and Mariann ran to meet them, Mariann in tears, taking in huge gulps of air. All Dad could make out was that Mariann was saying something about Johnny. Patti told Dad that Marines had come to the door looking for him and Mom. My father dropped the suitcases in each of his hands. His face drained of all color and his jovial mood quickly disappeared.

"What am I going to tell your mother?" Dad responded.

Patti knew he didn't mean that as a question directed to anyone there.

"Don't jump to conclusions. They could be here for any number of reasons," Patti insisted.

Patti and Mariann provided Dad every detail about the brief encounter with the Marines. Patti did most of the talking since she was the calmer of the two. She said the Marines would not answer any of their questions. Patti told Dad she had informed the Marines he would be at his office at about nine a.m. and that she had given them the address. She said the Marines would meet him there. Dad and Patti headed to the office while Eileen stayed at home with Mariann. Dad gave them instructions not to call anyone or answer the phone.

The news reached Denise via a 9:00 a.m. phone call from my sister Mariann. It wasn't an easy task for Mariann to locate Denise. She looked up the CTA phone number in the huge Yellow Pages phone book. Once she dialed the central number, she was transferred and put on hold a few times. Denise had been filing employee disciplinary reports in her CTA office that morning.

Although only a clerk, she applied her own judgment in determining whether the reports were worthwhile. When Denise came across one she felt was not appropriate, such as writing someone up for chewing gum, she ripped it up. She even took care to place it in the middle of the garbage can so it was not easily seen. Her co-workers had to track her down when Mariann's call came in. When Denise got to the phone and heard Mariann's voice, she was filled with excitement.

"Hi Mariann! How did you find me here?" Denise asked.

In less than a second, Denise knew this was not fun and games. Once she realized the time of day, that Mariann had never called her at work, and the tone of the voice on the other end, it all hit her at once. Denise went numb. Her whole being, her mind, her limbs melting into her, became nothing.

Denise does not recall exactly what Mariann said to her, nor what she said to Mariann or who was around to call her father as she screamed and fell to pieces on the cold linoleum floor of the CTA office. Her father, working only a few floors away, came to collect his daughter and someone was kind enough to drive them both home. That day and the days to follow became a blur to Denise. She slept a lot.

The Marines arrived at my father's office on 111th and Fairfield earlier than Dad expected. He was in the bathroom, which was situated at the end of a long, narrow laboratory. In that dark, cluttered, windowless laboratory, my father created dentures, developed X-rays, and autoclaved equipment. Patti was in the front office and called back to Dad after letting the Marines into the waiting room area. Dad walked through his laboratory, for what must have seemed like a mile long that morning, and greeted the Marines with a brief hello accompanied by a handshake.

"We have some bad news," was all Patti heard.

The two Marines delivered the news succinctly, using words that would not confuse the message. Marines are trained for this duty. Who would want that job? How old were they? Had they ever been in combat? These two Marines I never met became a mystery to me. Today I think of them as the character Death in *The Book Thief*. After they had delivered the news, my father was inconsolable for several minutes, maybe ten, maybe more. The Marines remained beside him. They didn't flinch or react in any way to my father's outburst of emotions. They stayed with my dad for a half-hour or so after he had calmed down. Then they left.

Patti sat quietly with my dad for several minutes and finally said to him, "Dad, we have to do something."

- - -

Patti was strong and continued to be so thirty-five years later as she hands me the letters Johnny had written to her. When she does so I look for a leaking tear, an eked-out sigh, even a twitch, manifesting her feelings of Johnny's death of long time prior. None of these symptoms are visible to the naked eye. As always, she is strong.

- - -

The phone rang at Uncle Mike and Aunt Diane's home at about 9:15 a.m. Aunt Diane picked it up. It was my sister Patti calling from Dad's office. Patti said nothing more in her phone call to Aunt Diane other than Dad was coming to get Margie. Our father insisted that Patti say nothing if anyone called. He wanted to be certain the news would not spread to Wisconsin before he got there. Uncle Mike was at his office in Chicago. Aunt Diane had called him to let him know something was up. It was too obvious to Aunt Diane that something terrible had happened.

Dad drove himself and Patti back to our house in Beverly. There they informed Mariann and Eileen that what they had feared most was real. When Dad learned that Mariann had already called Denise at her place of work, he went into a tirade, yelling and screaming at her. He didn't want to believe it. He didn't want Denise to hear this news over the phone, let alone at work, and especially did not want any chance of this news getting to my mother, three hundred miles away, before he got to her. This anger, like a quickly formed twister, found Mariann in its epicenter, its winds powered by Dad's anguish and fear. My father later felt bad about yelling and apologized. The apology didn't make a difference to her. He was gone, and I have no one, Mariann thought to herself and knew Johnny would have wanted her to call Denise.

Dad walked past the phone two or three times, finally picking up the phone book. He seemed not to know who to call. Eileen watched him. She was afraid he was going to pull his hair out. He kept running his hand through it, pulling at it, ranting,

"What's your mother going to do? Oh Jesus. What will your mother do?"

Eileen was the one person who was with our dad from the beginning of that day. That seemed to be all he was concerned about, she thought. She had been aware of the argument between our parents about Johnny enlisting, so she knew where this woe was coming from.

Before heading up to Evanston, Dad had contacted his good friend, Dr. Gallagher. There was no relation between Dr. Joe Gallagher and my Uncle Jack Gallagher. My father and Joe Gallagher had known each other for several years, having met through a neighborhood friend who was an obstetrician in the same practice with Dr. Gallagher. There was a ten-year age difference between the two, my dad the elder, but Dr. Gallagher was also the patriarch of a large, Irish Catholic family, and the two of them clicked. Joe was the first person my dad called after he received the news. After telling him of Johnny's death Dad asked him to write a prescription for my mother and anyone else in our family who might need it, including himself. When Dr. Gallagher heard the news and Dad's plan to drive back to Wisconsin, he insisted on going with him. He was at our house in less than half an hour. Their first stop was Evanston, where they picked up Margie.

- - -

An hour or so into my interview with Aunt Diane and Uncle Mike, I bring the conversation's focus to the day our station wagon arrived at their home to get Margie.

"How did that day start for you?" I ask.

"Margie was with us. And, um…" Aunt Diane says.

"Yeah, Margie was with us," Uncle Mike says.

"Margie and Eileen, were they there together or they took turns babysitting that summer? Anyway, so it was probably Margie. I know it was one of the triplets but not both," Aunt Diane says.

- - -

Margie had been sleeping soundly the morning of August 4, the deep kind of sleep that is absent of dreams. The days in Evanston that summer were filled with activities for her and her two small cousins. Going to the beach, changing diapers, making PB&Js, and helping Lil' Mike through his coughing fits usually left her contentedly exhausted when she lay her head down on the pillow each night. When Aunt Diane walked into the bedroom where Margie was sleeping that August morning, Margie shot up in bed, out of her REMless sleep.

"Something happened to my brother," Margie said to Aunt Diane.

Although this was not a question at all, Aunt Diane answered it as if it were.

"No. Patti called and they want you to come home."

Margie kept repeating, insisting something happened as she waited for my dad to come and get her. After an hour that seemed like it could have been eternity or could have been just seconds frozen in time, Margie saw a car pull up to the house. She didn't recognize the station wagon and almost didn't recognize her own father as he stepped out of it. He was pale and looked ill. She could only imagine the worst as to why he was there and why Dr. Gallagher would be with him.

- - -

"When I saw Dad come up the walkway, he looked so horrible, I thought Mom had died," Margie says to me during our interview.

- - -

Aunt Diane stood in the doorway, five months pregnant with her third child. Although she knew something was wrong, she would not allow herself to jump to all kinds of crazy conclusions and upset that baby in her belly.

"Johnny was killed." Aunt Diane's brain registered this as if she had been shot herself. She had been standing on the first step to the stairwell leading to the second floor when she heard my dad tell Uncle Mike the news. She slowly let herself, and the baby she carried, down as her legs gave way under her.

- - -

"I just remember—I believe it was your dad coming to the front door, and we were on Lawndale then, and coming in the hallway, and tellin' us . . . Thank God for the railing," Aunt Diane says as she tells her story, and then continues. "...and we got Margie. She just went upstairs into the bedroom and closed her door. And I was pregnant with Beth. I remember that. I remember . . . It was just very quiet. Ya know, what could ya say. I mean it was just disbelief. We talked about—did Eileen [my mother] know? And they said 'no, we're gonna go up to the farm and tell her.' It was very quiet when he [my father] came and he asked where a pharmacy was and Dr. Gallagher went and got a prescription, I think he said, for Eileen."

There is momentary silence among Uncle Mike, Aunt Diane, and myself.

"It was just very, very quiet," Aunt Diane says again.

"Yeah," Uncle Mike agrees.

At about this point in the interview, Uncle Mike digresses, calling my attention to two dogs in their backyard. He tells me their names, Duke and Duchess. I ask myself: Am I pushing him too far in digging up these memories?

- - -

A deep sense of sadness overcame Uncle Mike. He could not say he was surprised by the news when it finally reached him. Since the day Johnny left for Vietnam, Uncle Mike had had a strong feeling he would not be coming back.

After collecting Margie in Evanston, Dad and Dr. Gallagher drove forty-five minutes south back to Beverly, where they picked up Patti, Mariann, and Eileen. Before they left my dad made another phone call. Pauline, our babysitter, did not know why she was asked to come to our house, especially with no kids there to babysit. My father wouldn't tell her. He needed to get to my mother first. Aunt Barbara was impressed with my father's determination to be the one to tell my mother of her son's death. At that time, Aunt Barbara had not been impressed with much about my father. She didn't like his bullish, intimidating ways with us kids. However, an admiration for him sprouted that day. Arriving at our house to help, she met Pauline, already there. Aunt Barbara realized my father had the forethought, even during the duress of his son's death, to have arranged help for my mother when she returned home.

Once Dad and my sisters were packed back in the car, Dr. Gallagher drove them north, to the farm, to bring the news of my brother's death to Mom and the rest of us. I am told that nobody talked during that long five-hour drive up to the farm. Margie stared out the window, or maybe just at the seat right in front of her, realizing at the young age of sixteen, how in a second's time, things could change your life forever.

- - -

I interview my sister Mariann in a hotel restaurant in San Jose, where Mariann was living at the time. It was spring 2006, and her cancer was getting worse. Patti and I had gone out to visit her. She was still able to teach her third-grade class and be active for a good part of the day. Eight months later, after Mariann had passed, we found a poem she had written about her ongoing unhappiness due to the loss of Johnny. But I didn't need to see that poem to know this was not a topic she wanted to talk about. If it wasn't for my sister Patti bringing up the writing of this book while the three of us were having breakfast, I never would have interviewed Mariann.

I am surprised when she opens up and begins to share what she remembers. Mariann recalls a brief moment of the drive up to the farm to tell Mom.

"I was sitting in the middle seat of the station wagon, looking out the front window. I was trying to conceive what had happened. I couldn't grasp that he was dead and what that meant," Mariann says.

Mariann passed away before I completed transcribing the notes from my interview with her. The cancer she battled for four years finally won out. She died November 26, 2006. Two other sisters and I were at her bedside trying desperately to keep her as comfortable as possible. When she began calling out to loved ones who had preceded her in death, it was Johnny she called to first. She called his name three times as she strained to look off to her right. Her arms, heavy from fluid buildup, could not be lifted easily by those of us caring for her. Yet she reached out to him, as if she could see him, lifting her arms all on her own.

- - -

Although she didn't see him take it, Margie had no doubt Dad had taken valium. Dr. Gallagher explained to my sisters that if they felt Dad was acting funny, his behavior might be due to the drug and not due to Johnny's death. He wanted them to understand this.

"She'll never forgive me."

He repeated this phrase throughout the ride, each time with a quivering voice, on the verge of tears. Tears that, once they came, Eileen feared might never stop. Tears that would engulf him, sweep over him like an ocean wave, a tsunami, and then pull him out into the vast waters. If any one of them in the car started crying, they might all be swept away.

"What will she do?" Dad said over and over. Was this the drugs, Eileen wondered.

They were all dreading the moment they'd have to tell Mom. It was Eileen's second of three trips between Waupaca and Chicago that day. Now the ride to the farm did not seem long, Eileen thought. In fact, it wasn't long enough.

- - -

"I only got one letter from Johnny and I can't find it. . . . It was right before he died," Eileen tells me.

When I ask my sister Eileen about that drive back up to the farm to inform the rest of us of the bad news, she rolls her eyes. "It was horrible" is all she can say. Her focal memory was our father's repeated worry about speaking to our mom. "How am I going to tell your mother . . ."

As we speak about Eileen's memories of 1970, she is waiting for her own son to be shipped over to Iraq. Eileen married Pat Cherry, her teenage crush. Their oldest child, John, a Marine named after our brother, is about to begin his second tour. After he graduated from Marine boot camp and before his first tour in Iraq, he was home for a brief visit. Eileen tells me then that she feels the way Mom said she felt after his visit home before being shipped to Vietnam. Eileen says she keeps touching her son, because she fears she will not be able to touch him again for a very long time.

"He's training with real artillery," Eileen says about his current training and then adds, "He's being sent to an area where many Marines have been killed."

She states this for the second time in our conversation. I try to help by providing any logic I can grab onto that might lessen this worry.

"Just like storms pass, the heavier fighting will shift to another area, maybe by the time John arrives there," I say.

Outwardly, she complies. Maybe I can believe that too. Supporting a positive outcome with unfounded pieces of logic is the best we have knowing Eileen's John is headed into the midst of real danger.

Eileen and her family went over to Hawaii to spend two weeks with her son before he was shipped off to Iraq. It must have been a difficult and long flight home for my sister. That trip home for her may have been very similar to the ride back to our farm in August 1970. All of those hours to think about what was going to happen to her son. The moments prior were a world apart, when her family was all together.

- - -

Throughout the ride, Patti tried to imagine what had really happened. She tried in vain to make some logic of it, put things in order. Those in the car had many hours to grasp what this meant before they broke the news to my mother and the rest of us. It was the longest car ride for some, yet I'm sure it wasn't long enough for my dad—he dreaded delivering the news to my mother for fear he might lose her too. Dr. Gallagher accompanied my father as a close friend, a driver, and a physician.

My father and my sisters arrived at our farm in the late afternoon. For us kids at the farm, it was a happy-go-lucky summer day filled with catching frogs and plans to ride the horses. Maggie, our quarter horse, was latched to the garage. I was tightening the cinch of her heavy leather saddle when a station wagon pulled into our sandy drive, passing me as I stood brushing Maggie, preparing to ride. The car came to a stop a few yards beyond, facing the house. I was very surprised to see my dad get out of the passenger side.

"What's up?" I asked.

Dad looked sad or distracted or something. I had never seen him look like that before.

"Where is Mom?" He asked me.

"She's in town with the older boys, running errands." I told him.

"You shouldn't be riding the horses with no one else around," Dad said.

He was saying this to me but he wasn't looking at me. It felt like he didn't know what else to say. It struck me as odd that my dad should be concerned about me riding the horse. He taught me how to ride, even bareback, putting me on by myself when my legs could not even reach around Maggie's belly. Each summer I lived among the horses. I caught them on my own sometimes, and other times with the help of my brothers. I brought them back to the garage, brushed them, bridled and saddled them for my siblings, my friends, and me to ride. When we were done riding, I took the saddle off, brushed them some more, and let them out to pasture after rewarding them with a bucket of oats. I rode almost every day regardless of the weather. Even in the midst of winter, I loved to catch and ride them in the newly fallen snow-covered fields, the horses with their gorgeous thick winter coats. Maggie, our quarter horse, was the kindest, smartest horse, with a mothering instinct. She tolerated me as I ducked under her belly to quickly get to her other side, as I kicked her to go faster, and even when I pulled her bridle taut to keep her from running back to the house. She even opened the gates with her snout so I didn't have to dismount and do it myself.

As Dad was walking away, the back doors of this strange car opened. I watched as four of my older sisters filed out and headed right into the house, not saying a word. I didn't see Dr. Gallagher. He must've stayed in the driver's seat. My dad and Eileen had just gone back to Chicago that morning. What was going on? It was especially surprising to see Mariann because of the friction between her and my father. Someone must have died, I thought. Who could it be? I thought. It must be Grandpa. Mom would be very sad and that's why Dad was sad, I figured. My mind rapidly ran through all the people in our family who could possibly die and Grandpa was the only one I came up with. Although Grandma had been bedridden since I could remember, she did not come to mind. Grandpa had smoked pipes and cigars and had developed throat cancer. It was horrible. He had surgery that year in February. The doctors had removed the outside of his throat and then tried to make it look better with grafted skin from his thigh. I knew this because when I was visiting him the covers slipped off his leg as he reclined upright in the hospital bed that was in his living room. I saw the big square patch of bloody skin. My mother had to explain to me what it was. Back then I began to prepare myself for Grandpa dying.

From that moment my dad stepped out of the car at the farm, my life changed. It would never be the same again.

- - -

Margie remembers Mom being at the grocery store when they arrived at the farm.

"As soon as we all got out of the car, Dr. Gallagher left us alone," Margie says.

No one remembers seeing him again that day.

- - -

Joe and Mickey were fishing off the bridge when the station wagon arrived. They saw a car pull in the driveway from where they stood on the bridge, the strings from their poles drifting in the river current. Like Pavlov's dogs, we would run up to the house every time a familiar car pulled into our driveway at the farm. Joe and Mick did not recognize the car and so they did not head for the house right away.

We had all started out together earlier that day, but Chris and I stayed with the horse while Mickey and Joe went down to the river.

- - -

While interviewing my brother Chris, I ask what he remembers of that day at the farm when Dad arrived, with our sisters and Dr. Gallagher, to tell us of Johnny's death. Chris, like Joe and I and most of the others, does not remember Mom during this time. He doesn't remember her talking to him or seeing her. He did remember that she had been at the store with Billy and Jimmy, while we were told the news.

"You and me were trying to catch Maggie," Chris says.

"Were you with me?"

I am excited to find someone who remembers catching our horse, Maggie, earlier that day.

"It was just me and you, and Mick and Joe were down by the river, laughin' and jokin' about a green chipmunk or something like that," Chris says.

This makes me smile. Mickey had told me they were catching frogs and tricked Chris by telling him they were green chipmunks.

"We finally caught her [Maggie]. It took forever to catch her that day. I just remember hearin' Mick and Joe laughing and thinking, man, they should come and help us or somethin'," Chris tells me.

His memory becomes sketchy at this point. He recalls that Dad wanted everyone back at the farmhouse.

"I just remember you were always good at putting the bridle and the saddle on. It took an especially long time because for some reason they were so jumpy," Chris says.

Chris remembers that it was a beautiful day.

Mickey describes an eerie feeling coming over him while playing down at the river, once the station wagon was spotted.

"We were just being goofy. And then I remember all the sudden someone screaming from the farmhouse," Mickey tells me.

- - -

The river was within earshot of the house if one yelled loudly. We had a dinner bell outside the kitchen door that was used to call us all in for dinner. This time the bell was silent. It was just me calling.

"Dad's back and Mariann's back!" I yelled.

Mickey and Joe heard me and thought; no, they aren't supposed to be here. Joe had heard the car pull quietly out of the drive early that morning, expecting a long week before Dad's arrival back. Yet here he was, back again that same day. They ran up to the farmhouse. It was odd to see Mariann, and she was crying. Mickey thought she got yelled at because she was still seeing Bruce, the boyfriend from hell. Dad told Mickey, Joe, Chris, and I to go into the house. We followed him into the first-floor bedroom. He sat down on the bed right inside the door. This was the same bed I had lain in a few years before with a concussion. My mother kept watch over me to keep me from falling asleep. In the room was a double bed and a cot. There were two small closets, one at the foot of each bed. One of these closets had housed a boot my brother Jim had peed in during one of his midnight sleepwalking episodes. There were two long, narrow windows encased in wide wood trim that had been lathered with many coats of paint throughout the life of our old farmhouse. These windows lived contently across the room from the door. These were the same windows, open to the fresh country air, which had offered Joe a glimpse of the car leaving in the infant hours of that same day. We stood around Dad, who sat on the bed at eye level with us.

"Johnny is dead."

That was it.

He began to cry and his large body shook. All four of us reached up and threw our little arms around him. He wrapped his arms around us and held us close.

- - -

Mickey begins to cry as he recounts the scene in that bedroom.

"I thought, at my age [13 at the time], when I saw Dad crying, he really does love us."

Mickey cries a bit, pauses, and continues. Unfortunately, he does not remember ever saying "I love you" to our father, although he tells me he felt it, especially at this moment.

"All I know is, when he started crying, [Mickey choking a bit] . . . that broke my heart," Mickey mumbles as he remembers being in that room with Dad.

While discussing this same moment with Chris.

"Do you remember him crying?" I ask.

"Oh yeah," Chris says.

Chris' voice is croaky. He did not attempt to stop or wipe the tears spilling over his eyelids. I rub his shoulder and tell myself that this pain I'm dredging up is helpful. Chris is willing to bear this for me, for this book. He trusts me. I don't know what I did to earn that trust and generosity, but I push on.

"Were you able to hear what he [Dad] said or were you just more upset about seeing him cry?"

"Uh, I remember being there. I think it was surreal, or it wasn't true, it was somebody else," Chris says.

- - -

The words "Johnny is dead" meant little to me at that moment. Seeing my father cry for the first time in my life, and in such distress, was my only concern. This man had been our rock and now our rock was crumbling. With his big arms wrapped around the four of us, he held us close. I was compressed among a tangle of arms and flesh, but I was okay. I did not cry.

At that moment, I created a story in my head. Johnny was still out there, probably in a prison camp beating up all of his Vietnamese captors, like one of the Rock-em Sock-em Robots. I didn't know how to envision the alternative—death, that he was no longer on the earth. I could think of him as a prisoner in a far-off land not knowing when we would see him again, but no doubt that we would. I was certain all the prisoners around him loved him and the enemy feared him. I saw everyone crying and thought I must be the only one that knew Johnny was not dead. Young people did not die. I only knew old people died. Aside from that, Johnny was invincible. The boxer. The track star. The Marine. My big brother. The concept that there were people dying in Vietnam had not entered my world.

Unlike me, Joe got the message Dad had conveyed to us with no room for misinterpretation. Johnny is gone. He understood. Seeing Dad cry for the first time ever brought that message straight to his heart like a roaring freight train.

No one knew exactly when Mom would return from running errands. Jim, Bill, Mimi, and Bonnie were with her. My father didn't want us around when he broke the news to my mother so he told us to go out and stay away from the house until after she returned. Joe and Mick went to the barn, a few of us went for a long walk, Patti and Mariann stayed with Dad in the farmhouse. He wanted them there to take the two youngest when they returned with Mom.

We never did get to ride that day. My brother, Chris, and I put Maggie back in her field. After I unbridled her, letting her go free, I turned to see the disappointed look on my brother's face as he stood by the gate he had been holding open for me. He was upset because we had worked so hard to catch her that day. To me, catching the horses was half the fun. After that, Chris and I followed Margie and Eileen into the back fields. We had one hundred and thirty seven acres of our own land to roam. We walked straight out, to the furthest fields, and talked a little amongst ourselves. Once we got to the furthest field of our property, we turned around. We were mostly quiet. We were all trying to process what had really happened, trying to find a place for it so that our day could continue on the way it started— normal. Suddenly, Christopher burst out, "I don't have a godfather now," and he started to cry. A few of us giggled at this and poor Chris did not understand why we were laughing. "It's not funny!" he said. I welcomed the opportunity to laugh. It was a little bit of brightness added to a serious situation. I envied the innocence of his concern. Chris was only eight years old. I was glad that this was the deepest pain he was feeling. Although, relative to the pain Chris had known in his short life, this was a very deep pain—no more Godfather. To him it was like losing a parent.

- - -

"When Dad said he was dead I mean that hit me, ya know. But it didn't hit me till I was walkin' to the dump," Chris says.

"The dump" was the valley of a small hill in the back fields of our farm where we would throw our garbage that we could not burn.

"I just remember everyone running into the fields and going their own way. Nobody talked. Chris crying. We were all crying. We were all together. We were together but we weren't together. That was the first time I realized how we never really talked. John [her son] even made that observation about our family," Eileen says.

"The girls do," I say.

This was the first time I had been presented with that observation, and there was a subtle defensiveness in my response.

- - -

As we walked back toward our farmhouse I tried to convince my sisters that Johnny was not dead. "How can you be sure he's dead? I don't believe it. How can you give up on Johnny? He's probably a prisoner of war. They just can't find him," I said to them. During this time, Mom must have arrived back from errands, but I didn't see her as we were still out walking.

Jim and Bill had gone into town with Mom to get a haircut, do laundry, and grocery shop. Jim was sixteen years old and about to enter his sophomore year of high school. He had his "blue slip" and was driving my mom all around the country roads of Waupaca, Wisconsin, to log practice hours in order to get his license. Driving for hours with each child when they obtained their blue slip was my mother's job. My father did not have the patience for it. Bill also had a treat in town that day. He was able to get his first professional haircut by a barber. Up to that point, he had had only crew cuts from Dad.

Bill was a little more into his looks than Jimmy. Jim just thought he was naturally beautiful and didn't have to do anything to work at it . . . except for the time he tried to curl his eyelashes. When I caught him doing this with my sister's eyelash curler clamped on his eyelashes and his face an inch from their closet mirror, I asked what he was doing. He looked at the funny little metal contraption in his hand with disgust and said he thought it would cut his lashes, like toenail clippers cut nails. I laughed at him.

Jim turned the station wagon into the farm drive that Tuesday. Mom sat alongside Jim on the passenger seat. Mimi rode in the back seat with Bill and Bonnie. Mimi was six years old, approaching her seventh birthday. She knew Mom was in a crabby mood as they pulled up the drive toward the farmhouse. Mimi didn't know why her patience was worn, yet thought it might have to do with the older boys in the car, one of them a new driver. Or maybe it was dragging the kids with her to the grocery shop. Mimi's bladder was full and she urgently had to get to the bathroom. Maybe that's why Mom was mad, she thought.

Jim was glad to be done with all of those tedious errands, he thought as he brought the station wagon, full of groceries and clean laundry, to a stop and put it in park. Bill was happy he got his hair trimmed and was looking good. Then they saw there was another station wagon in the driveway. Jim and Bill noticed that nobody was around—no kids playing, nothing going on. It was quiet and eerie.

"Where the heck is everybody?" Bill asked Mom.

Then Dad walked out of the porch door. Bill noticed how pale he was and instantly realized that something was not right. He knew Dad had left at about three or four that morning to drive back to Chicago.

- - -

"That look" on Dad's face, a full bladder, and Mom mad is what Mimi still associates with that day. She doesn't remember much of Johnny and has only a few, though vivid, memories of the events that occurred around his death.

"I was lucky . . . being younger," Mimi says. "The sorrow isn't as deep."

Yet, on the other hand, she didn't get to know Johnny. She realizes this and doesn't come to any conclusion as to which is worse or which is better.

"I imagine him like Jimmy but older," she says after a moment of thought.

I interview my sister Mimi at her home in Grand Haven, a quaint town that borders the east side of Lake Michigan. We sit on the Victorian-style chairs placed around the heavy, oval table in her rarely used dining room, and reminisce. This room is furnished with the dining set of our mother's parents. Each piece of the set is still beautiful with its highly shined dark cherry stain.

- - -

Jim thought it very odd to see my father. Dad was supposed to be at his office, the place he had left for early that morning.

"Mom, what's Dad doing here?" Jimmy asked.

Bill and Jimmy jumped out of the car and ran in the house looking for everybody.

"Where is everybody?" they asked Mariann and Patti.

It was startling to see them. They looked blankly back to their brothers, not answering. While Jim and Bill ran through the house looking for the rest of us, Dad walked up to the car and opened the passenger side door, where my mother sat.

"John, why are you here?" Mom asked.

This was said in a demanding rather than a surprised manner. Mimi heard our mother's voice from the back seat but could not see her. Something was wrong, six-year-old Mimi sensed. My mother was never demanding. The words Mom used and the subtext they concealed were two different messages colliding. Between the seconds my mother had thrown those words from her lips and when my father returned the answer, in his eyes alone, time stood still. Her words dropped into the depths of her soul, shouting an unbearable truth. With the car door open and Mom in her seat, Dad knelt down and put his head on to her lap.

"I am so sorry, Eileen."

Margie walked out in time to witness Dad kneeling before my mother. "Eileen, Eileen," she heard him say and watched as he briefly laid his head in our mother's lap. Then Mom got out of the car. It all seemed in slow motion to Margie.

- - -

"She knew it without him even telling. She just hugged him. She didn't say anything. She was good. She just hugged him," Margie tells me as we sip on our coffee at Starbucks.

My brothers' and sisters' accounts of this scene are precious to me because I do not remember seeing my mother from the time she had left for those errands through the next week or so.

- - -

Jim and Bill weren't able to find anyone else in the house, so they came back outside just as they heard Dad say, "The worst has happened. Johnny was killed in action."

It all felt so unreal. Jim saw coldness in the limp body of our mother. She had no reaction other than to be still. She said nothing.

"I'm so sorry," Dad said.

Her arms hung lifeless at her sides as Dad pulled her close to him, smothering her in his barrel-like chest. She didn't hug back. She didn't cry. She didn't say anything. Mimi watched and heard from the back seat. Jimmy and Bill also watched and heard from outside the car and then ran out into the fields yelling for the rest of us. How isolated they felt. It was a silent, cold scene all around.

Although Bill did not fully understand what Dad said, he understood the seriousness of this news. I have to give it to my dad that he did not beat around the bush to explain this to his family. He was clear and succinct in telling us that Johnny was dead and yet many of us still had a difficult time grasping what it meant.

Mickey and Joe had retreated to the upstairs floor of the barn. They watched through the large open window of the barn loft, getting a clear view of Mom's car when it pulled into the drive and the scene that followed. They watched as Dad came out of the house, as Jimmy and Bill ran out of the car, as Dad knelt down next to Mom as she sat in the passenger seat with the door open. Then again, they saw Jimmy and Bill. They came out of the house, stood still for a moment, looking at Dad and Mom. They watched as Jimmy and Bill ran to the small apple orchard that bordered the driveway. They heard Bill yell, "Where is everybody?" Yet Joe had his eye on Jimmy.

"He's like, destroyin' things," Joe said to Mickey.

Mickey and Joe each took a big breath in. They locked eyes, large, frightened eyes. They took off. Joe leading the way, they flew down the loft ladder and ran out of the barn straight to the apple orchard. They called to Jimmy but he didn't respond. He was grabbing at branches and kicked down the small metal post holding up the electric fence wire that kept the cows out of the orchard. Joey ran to Patti to tell her someone better go get Jimmy. Jim looked up to the sky and saw how beautiful the clouds were.

He asked, "How could this happen? How could we hate and have so much death on the other side of the world?"

There was no one with Jim at that moment, only he and God. Patti came out to the field to meet Jimmy. He was still angry.

"Get away from me!" Jim shouted.

He pushed Patti away and ran further into the wide open field, not really escaping. Margie had come out with Patti, concerned for her triplet brother. Margie was afraid he would have to be taken to the hospital because he was so out of control.

- - -

"Jimmy scared me, how angry he was when he found out. He was ripping bushes out of the ground. And we didn't really talk about it," Margie tells me as she recalls this scene.

Joe remembers Bill got a haircut even though Jim insists today that they were grocery shopping and that Dad always cut their hair.

"I remember their hair was cut different. It was weird. . . . They must have talked Mom into it." Joe is adamant.

"I don't remember when I saw Mom again that day," Joe adds.

I ask Bill what he remembers of Mom and Dad's interaction when Dad delivered this news. Dredging up these memories stir emotions out of his control, yet he does not seem to have any intention of pulling back so I continue, cautiously.

"Who was in the car with ya, Bill?"

"Me and Jimmy and Mom were the last ones to find out," Bill says.

He continues to say something about Jim. I think he is saying how Jim ran out, but he is so broken up I can only understand a few words. There is little I can do or think of saying as I sit on the other end of the phone. He is in Colorado without any other family member that can share in these memories with him.

"That's okay Bill. Take your time," I say.

Bill collects himself somewhat and I question further. I want to know exactly how he learned his older brother was killed.

"When did you hear? When did Dad tell you?" I ask Bill.

"When we came back outta the house lookin' around for everybody else," Bill answers.

I persist. I want to know the exact words our father used to communicate to Jim and Bill that Johnny was dead. I want to know if there was any chance that they might have not understood clearly that Johnny was dead. I am relentless.

"Did Dad have to say, to you, Johnny was killed or just saying 'The worst has happened,' was that enough for you?" I ask.

"No, and then he said Johnny was killed, after that. When he first said that I wasn't sure what he meant. I knew he [Dad] was serious because of the look on his face," Bill says.

I tell Bill that the meaning of those words had not sunk in with me either, at first. Bill was on the verge of tears as he spoke to me, yet he did not slow down. He did not hold back. I was in that group Bill was looking for. I can tell him now where we were and why we were there and how we wondered what he and Jim and Mom were doing. I can tell him now that I did not see or hear from Mom either and that this unsettled me, too. I can now tell Bill what happened from our perspective and I am very grateful for what Bill can tell me.

Bill was only fourteen years old when Johnny was killed. He received exactly four letters from Johnny between March and the end of July 1970, and he still has them today.

- - -

Leaving Mom's side momentarily, Dad went out to look for Jimmy. He walked through the orchard, ducking his head below the branches of the small trees, and saw Patti and Margie further out in the open field trying to calm Jimmy down. His cowboy boots carefully stepped over the downed electric fence as he walked over to Jim.

"I hate you! I hate everyone!" Jimmy shouted at Dad.

My father said a few words, trying to comfort him. Dad stood back, remaining quiet, yet remaining, allowing Jim to be angry. This was not typical of my father, but there was something in him at that moment that knew what was best. God's grace maybe. He did love his children, all of his children.

Dad returned to the house to be with Mom, who was there with Mimi, Bonnie, Patti, and Mariann. Patti put Bonnie down for a nap. The rest of us were still scattered about the farm. Dad went into the living room and sat on the couch with Mom, Mimi was in between them. The view from the large picture window at their backs looked out past the front porch on to the solitary country road on which Johnny had often run.

Mimi was not able to conceive the depth of what was going on. Up until that point, her encounters with our father consisted of Dad threatening to trade our mom in for a blonde (jokingly, just to tease us); letting us comb his straight black hair with his small pocket comb; and his famous woe-de-does, where he tossed us up into the air and we squealed with joy, shouting to do it again. Her concept of our mother was singing in the kitchen; placing her chewed gum on the windowsill to be chewed some more later; taking her to dance lessons; and caring for her patiently when she was sick.

"I'm sorry," Dad kept repeating as he and my mother sat on that couch together. Mom sat there, comatose-like, saying nothing, while our father, with his arm around her, cried and begged for her forgiveness. When the time came for my mother to uphold her threat of relentless blame, she laid down her weapons. She had power, yet she did not use it. Another hurt, another piece of hatred in addition to the hatred that took her son from her, would not be found in her broken heart.

- - -

"They were hugging," Mimi says, at first.

She thought some more about that moment back in the recesses of her mind and heart.

"Mom was crying quietly. Tears were rolling down her cheeks. I think, I remember her saying, 'I'll never forgive you. I'll never forgive you," Mimi told me.

Mimi had felt our mother's exhausted spirit.

"I was a sheep in the herd. I just went along with whatever everyone else was doing. I was in my selfish little world," Mimi says of that period and laughs.

"Well you were only seven years old, in a huge family. You were fending for yourself. Man, you couldn't even get to the bathroom," I supply.

We both laugh now. It is settling to hear her care-free laugh when thinking about that time. It is snippets that she pieces together to try to make sense of what happened. The little her memory seems to allow her is frustrating. There is blackness, a void, a chasm where she hoped a self-defining moment might be. Mimi may be disappointed she can't offer me more for this book, yet her few words add colorful pieces to this puzzle I am trying to put together. The letter this book is based on does not say much either. Yet once one knows the characters intimately and the details of the situation, one can read volumes into a few words.

I ask Eileen if she remembers her first sight of Mom after she had been told about Johnny. Eileen is very definite when she says no. But then she remembers after all.

"She came looking for everybody to see if everyone was okay."

I would have thought that the Valium my mother supposedly took that day would have undermined any intention Mom had outside of sleeping, but a mother is a mother and never stops worrying

When Dad had come back to the house in Beverly with Patti, after he was told of Johnny's death, Eileen recalls his concern for Mom.

"He started crying and said, 'she told me she would never forgive me.' But she did."

"Are you sure?" I ask Eileen.

"I don't know, they drugged her pretty good so maybe she didn't think about it."

"Did you see Dr. Gallagher give her drugs?" I ask.

"No I didn't. But I remember her being asleep a lot after that. He gave her a valium shot. He brought the stuff with," Eileen says.

Eileen tells me that she knew, on that day, that Mom was given drugs. I wonder about the moment my mother succumbed to allowing those drugs to be given to her. What was her state before she went under? Did she want to escape? Did she want to go to a deep dark place where she might be able to see her son? I want to know if my mother fainted, if she was stumbling, if she was crying uncontrollably or just quiet. I want so desperately to know how my mom felt when she heard her son was killed. Maybe it is the drugs that had contributed to my mother's absence in my memory during this period as well as the memories of many of my siblings. Even so, I am grateful to whoever gave them to her to help her through extreme emotional pain.

- - -

Mom used to tell us kids, "Don't do drugs. Be strong." My father was always very much against drugs and most medications. He believed the magnificence of the body would allow it to take care of itself. My mother also supported that philosophy. We had to be pretty sick before we got a prescription med from the drug store. Despite this stand on drugs, my parents put their trust in Dr. Gallagher to help them through this day. The adults thought Jimmy should partake in this medication. After he was coaxed in from the field someone had explained how he might feel better if he took a pill, yet he refused. He felt the adults, our parents in particular, let this happen. He had questioned, . . .and he questioned this war that went on half a world away. And yet, no one had ever talked to him about the reality of it. He also questioned the war that went on within his own family. Oh, how he hated both of those wars. They created a current of torment right below his own skin, as if he had his own war going on.

After several moments of sitting with Dad, Mom got up and moved into action. She first went to the barn to get Joe and Mickey.

"Everything will be okay. Just c'mon, we gotta go home. We've got to pack," Mom said.

We all packed up quickly. We stuffed the clothes we needed into our pillow cases and left a lot of things behind. The older girls helped the younger ones pack, then got back into the cars and endured another five-hour drive back to Beverly. There was a two-car caravan going back. Dr. Gallagher drove his station wagon and Dad drove ours. From the beginning of that trip until the end, Margie was concerned about Dad's ability to drive. Not even aware of how tired he must have been, she feared only for his emotional frailness. It had been the first time any of us had seen him cry.

As it grew dark during our drive home, it became dreary and started to rain, much different than the beautiful weather the day had started with. A few of us quietly focused on the racing raindrops on the car windows, picking our winners and watching them gobbled up by another raindrop. Mariann did not notice the raindrops. She stared out, past them, convinced Johnny was on a secret mission that we weren't allowed to know about. Mickey was lying down in the back section of the station wagon. He watched Dr. Gallagher driving. Even as a thirteen-year-old, Mickey was able to appreciate this man's friendship to our family. Mickey thought for a moment about his sisters Patti, Mariann, Margie, Eileen, and was concerned for the multiple trips they had to make that day. And then he, Joe, Chris, and I started to sing the song we usually sang on this long ride, "100 bottles of beer on the wall, 100 bottles of beer, take one down, pass it around 99 bottles of beer . . ."

"Shut up," Jimmy told us.

Other than that, the trip was mostly quiet. Dr. Gallagher offered to Jim, for the second time, some drugs to calm him. Jim didn't want to be numbed. He wanted to remember every sense this hatred had brought upon him. He stared into the darkness the car was speeding through, at what use to be comforting landscape. It was during this long drive that Jim decided he was not ever going to put himself in a position to be hurt again. He was so very angry. He thought about how he hated everyone. He consciously decided to lay blame on society for his brother's death. Jimmy was now very well aware that he was the oldest boy, that he had inherited more responsibility with this loss. He wasn't frightened by this. He'd figure it out as it came, he thought.

Eileen could see the tension in Jim's face as they sat silently in the car. She knew Jimmy had taken the weight of the world on his shoulders when Johnny left for Vietnam. "I have to be the oldest son now," Jimmy told Eileen after Johnny's brief visit home in January. She knew that was troubling him too because that weight would not be lifted.

Eileen had started the day with Dad before the sun rose and had gone through that thousand-hour day with him until after it set. A lifetime of events had occurred during the daylight hours of August 4 before we pulled into our Beverly driveway that evening.

- - -

Eileen does not remember who drove the second car home. Eileen doesn't even remember which car she drove in. The only thing she remembers about the ride back home is that nobody talked.

"I think everyone was numb," Eileen says.

"Do you remember that ride back to Chicago?" I ask Bill.

"Yeah, just a long ride. It was quiet. And uhm—" Bill says.

"Do you remember Dr. Gallagher being there?" I ask when Bill pauses.

". . . Uhh, well I know he drove Dad back—Yeah! I do. I do. We ended up havin' to take two cars back, ya know," Bill says.

"I'm tryin' to figure out who was driving the second car. If Dr. Gallagher drove one, did Dad drive?" I ask Bill.

"Yeah. I think Dad did. I can't remember Terr. I don't . . .I think Dr. Gallagher drove the station wagon with all us kids. And then, I think Mom and Dad might've gone in the other car. I'm not positive. . . I'm not really sure on that one," Bill says.

- - -

No one knew where Dr. Gallagher stationed himself throughout the day. After he arrived with the car load at our farm he disappeared to give us privacy. Dr. Gallagher certainly was a resourceful friend, driving five hours at a moment's notice, turning around and driving back another five hours. He did all of this without us even noticing he was there. As a doctor with a family of his own, he had many pressing responsibilities that he dropped that day. There were many who helped us quietly that day and the days that followed. There were many that may not have been recognized for the support they provided to help us through that day and the days following.

Uncle Jim was finally getting around to replying to Johnny's June 17 letter. He had finished all his maintenance work for the day and had one hour before he went home, got a few hours rest and then on to his night job at Children's Hospital. He got out a piece of paper and sat down at the desk of his Chicago public school office. He had just begun his salutation, "Dear John," when he received the phone call. His wife, Aunt Barbara, told him that Johnny had been killed. His supervisor walked in just as he was hanging up the phone, before the news could fully sink in. Uncle Jim informed his supervisor what had happened.

"Get outta here. Go on home," his supervisor said.

Uncle Jim took on the responsibility to inform the immediate family of Johnny's death. However, news traveled faster than Uncle Jim. Grandpa had been taking a short walk the afternoon of August 4. As Grandpa arrived back at his house, the neighbor expressed his condolences. Uncle Jim arrived at Grandpa's house moments later. Before anything was said, Grandpa pointed to a snapshot of Johnny. Unable to speak, he turned the photo face down. With that gesture and Grandpa's eyes, Uncle Jim understood that the news had already reached his father. Uncle Jim turned to tell Grandma (his mother). He was not able to finish his message without breaking down. Grandpa stepped in to finish. He showed the same picture of Johnny to Grandma and placed it face down, abruptly. She understood. Her eyes filled with tears and something deflated in her, causing her to slump in her wheelchair.

When the news of Johnny's death arrived at Aunt Annie Laurie's home in Fenton, Michigan, she was at morning mass. Her son, Jimmy, who was twelve at the time, received the call from Uncle Jim. Why Uncle Jim left the message with a child as opposed to waiting for Annie Laurie to call him back to tell her directly is an indication of how upset Uncle Jim must have been. Annie Laurie arrived home from church to quite a commotion. Jimmy Gallagher was very upset. Johnny had babysat for the Gallagher boys. With lots of treats and pillow fights ending in nose-bleeds, it was a boy's dream when Johnny was in charge. Jimmy Gallagher especially enjoyed the bedtime stories Johnny told. Young Jimmy Gallagher was composed enough to carry out Uncle Jim's demand to tell his mother (Aunt Annie Laurie) and not to call my mother yet because she didn't know.

Johnny Gallagher was a camp counselor the summer of 1970. When he returned home for the August 8 weekend, his mother broke the news to him. He went outside and sat under a tree. He did not know what else to do. He had been so proud of his cousin when he heard he joined the service. He had visions of Johnny as a war hero, no one getting hurt and no one dying. That Sunday evening he had to make the call to his camp supervisor to let him know he would not be returning to camp. It wasn't until he began explaining why to his supervisor that Johnny Gallagher began to cry.

Uncle John was at Saint Mel High School when he received the news. He had been counting off the days that Johnny had been in Vietnam, on his office calendar, and did so the morning of August 3 and again on August 4. Uncle John knew surviving ninety days in Vietnam was the point where a serviceman's chance of returning home begins to increase dramatically. Johnny had actually been in Nam about 150 days. But Uncle John had mistaken his starting date so the calendar markings had not yet reached the magic number of ninety. Eighty-eight days he had counted when the phone call came.

A fellow brother at St. Mel's, who had been working diligently at a desk in the modest office, looked up. Noticing Uncle John was upset after placing the phone in its cradle on the desk across the room, he asked what was wrong.

"My nephew was killed in Vietnam," Uncle John said.

"Are you okay?"

"Yeah."

The fellow brother placed a hand briefly on Uncle John's slumped shoulder and stepped outside the room to allow some privacy. He stood alone in the office with the calendar of tallied days hanging silently on the wall, staring at the August 3. He'd done what he could. He'd protested the war. He'd explicitly discouraged Johnny from joining. Uncle John left the Christian Brothers order a few weeks after Johnny's death. There was no correlation between the two events. He was thirty-three. He had already announced and planned his departure well before the news about Johnny arrived on his doorstep.

Uncle Jim carried on with the task of delivering the news. Next, he went to Nan and Pop's, my father's parents. They were both home when Uncle Jim arrived. He did not spend much time there.

"Johnny got killed over there in Vietnam," he simply said.

"Johnny, you mean our Johnny!" Pop exclaimed.

Pop then hollered up the stairs to Nan and repeated this message. Their responses were brief. Maybe it was disbelief. Or, maybe they had been prepared to hear it. Nan, unlike my father, was serious about her Roman Catholic religion. Yet, we questioned her Christianity when she referred to African Americans with impatience and the N word. Uncle Jim did not wait for Nan to come down the stairs. He left.

All the while Uncle Jim was spreading the news to everyone, via telephone or a visit to their homes, my father had traveled to the middle of Wisconsin, told my mother and us kids, packed us up and headed home. By the time we arrived back in Beverly that evening the news had spread. It was dark when we all got out of the car, so none of us noticed at first that there was food—lots and lots of food. Glass dishes, plates, and tins filled with food were placed on the steps of our front porch. Margie's eyes followed the food up the porch steps, not able to see where it ended. The plates and pans covered the steps and concrete ledges of our front porch. There were pots of mostaccioli, pans of lasagna and tuna tetrazzini casseroles, plates of brownies and bar cookies covering our porch. We all walked carefully up the steps, around the food. Where did it all come from? Neighbors and friends had poured out their hearts in their kitchens, packaged them up, and brought them to us.

Pauline greeted us at the front door as we all filed quietly into the house, dragging our bags of clothes and pillows from the car. Aunt Barbara and Pauline had been waiting there for us. They were organizing the massive quantities of food in the kitchen. Mickey was keenly aware there was not much talking nor any appetites among us. The plentiful variety of food was good food, the kind Mickey normally would have eaten just because it was there, regardless of whether he was hungry. Like the rest of us, he just didn't feel like eating. Knowing others cared and were thinking of us added some comfort.

We didn't unpack that night. Some went into the kitchen later and ate a little of the food but for the most part we just got washed up and went to bed. That evening, as we were lying in bed, there was a thunderstorm raging. Chris, Mickey, and Joe slept together in an upstairs bedroom. This was the largest bedroom in the house, with hardwood floors and a spacious walk-in closet. It was furnished with two sets of bunk beds and a crib and still had plenty of room for a desk and dresser. At one time, I shared this bedroom with my brothers. When I had shared the room with the boys, Chris slept in a crib pushed up against the wall. Once Chris was old enough, he slept in one of the bunks and I moved to a downstairs bedroom.

That night Chris lay in his bed, the lightning flashed occasionally into the room as he tried to picture Johnny. He was afraid he would forget what he looked like. He eventually fell asleep and dreamt of Johnny. Chris woke from the dream rubbing his chest. He felt bumps. He went down stairs to find an adult. Dr. Gallagher was still at the house, thankfully. He was a child-friendly man, with a clean-shaven face and a head of neatly trimmed, brown hair. Dr. Gallagher diagnosed Chris with the case of the shingles, treated him, and prescribed the needed medications. He was our angel that day. A few days later, Joe also came down with shingles.

- - -

"Ahh, that next morning though, uhm... The reason I knew Joe Heeney had less than thirty days they tried to get him to come home early. And then, uh, Mom told me to go down and tell Mrs.

Heeney. So I walked over there, . . . and, uh, rang her doorbell and she came out. And I said, 'Well my mom wanted me to tell ya—'" Bill tells me.

Then there is silence on the phone, and Bill's voice is choppy. It's breaking up, yet not due to the connection. I want to hear every word Bill says so I repeat what I think I heard him say. I am surprised my mother sent Billy to tell the mother of a boy in Vietnam that Johnny was killed.

"She wanted you to tell her?" I ask.

"Yeah, she [our mother] told me to tell her [Mrs. Heeney] about Johnny so I did, and she freaked out. She came runnin' back to the house with me," Bill is crying as he says this.

- - -

After Bill told Mrs. Heeney the news, in the true spirit of motherhood, she did not leave her home without first writing a note for her son Mike. Mike Heeney arrived home a few hours later to his mom's note on his kitchen table telling him Johnny Guldan had died in Vietnam and she had gone down to the Guldan house. Mike was going into his senior year at St. Rita, the same school Jim and Bill attended. His mother returned upset from our house. Not only concern for our family was swimming through Mike and his mother's minds, but an increased anxiety about Joe, their own, still in Vietnam, was now present.

The next day, my mother and Mrs. Heeney sprang into action. Like their sons, they had developed a bond of friendship that was strengthened as a result of Joe and Johnny together in Vietnam. Together they contrived a plan to get Joe Heeney to escort Johnny's body back. My mother and Mrs. Heeney used the contact information provided by the Marines who had delivered the news to get to a high-ranking officer. Joe Heeney had only thirty days left, so it seemed a reasonable request. However, the men in the military did not feel the same.

Joe had gotten an eerie feeling from the north the day he learned of Johnny's death. After all, Joe had sensed, through Johnny's letters, that Johnny might not make it. Joe's battalion commander asked Joe if he knew a guy named John Guldan. Joe, surprised by the question, nodded.

"He was killed," the officer said and offered no more.

Hearing of Johnny's death was a terrible blow to Joe. Joe and Johnny exchanged several letters over the course of a few months. It had been comforting for Joe to have a boyhood friend so close by in that unwelcoming place, even if they never actually saw each other. Joe learned why his commanding officer knew Johnny was a friend of his when he received a letter from his mother a few weeks later. She wrote him that my mother and her had contacted executive military personnel in Washington. They requested to have Joe escort Johnny's body home. This request was refused and Joe's superior did not discuss any the details surrounding it.

- - -

In my interview with Joe, he attempts to explain to me why he was not allowed to escort Johnny's body home. He does not get a full sentence out when he stops and simply says, "Well, I won't go into that." I don't prod. This was enough, for now. I hope to get a fuller explanation from him some day, if he knows. I think our family deserves it.

In 1973, two years after returning from Nam, Joe Heeney married and is still married to the same woman in 2015. They had a son and a daughter in the late seventies. Joe does not talk to his wife and kids about Vietnam. As a matter of fact, I was the first person he talked to about it since 1971. He says the movie

Platoon reminds him most of how Vietnam was and suggests I watch it. His eyes begin to swell with tears and redden. He sniffs. Joe confides that he felt very guilty about Johnny's death, such that he could not face my parents. It was not until my mom's wake in 1998 that Joe says he was able to finally look my dad in the face. Joe is astonished at how warm and sweaty he is getting as he speaks to me. He felt partly responsible for Johnny's death because he had encouraged him to join the Marines. For thirty-seven years, Joe had been afraid my parents blamed him for Johnny's death. Joe admits now how absurd that fear was. A strong feeling of sadness comes over me as I think how Joe carried such a heavy burden as a young man. I could only hope, by telling him Johnny stated in his letters he wanted to be a Marine since the eighth grade, that this helped ease his sense of guilt. I was relieved to hear him shake his head and proclaim, "It's crazy, some of the thoughts that go through our heads!"

The Body

We know that while we dwell in the body we are away from the Lord. We walk by faith, not by sight. We would much rather be away from the body and at home with the Lord.

—2 Corinthians 5:6-9,
New American Bible

Johnny died in the early morning hours of Monday, August 3, in the Quan Tri Province of Vietnam, twelve hours ahead of Chicago time. Yet it was many, many days before Johnny's body came home to us. Ten days to be exact. We waited and waited.

Friends and neighbors continued to bring dinners and desserts to our house throughout this time. There were chicken noodle casseroles, lasagna, and chocolate chip cookies. Our parents' good friend, Mrs. Grogan, was an excellent cook. It got to the point where we would ask, "Which food did Mrs. Grogan make?" We ate that first. It might not only have been her culinary expertise but her cheery demeanor that made everything taste so good. She always had a big smile lighting up her face when she visited. Her eyes squinted to small slits and her large white teeth competed for attention with her prominent cheekbones. Her famous apple pie and her big, bright, warm smile provided some comfort to my brother Chris while he suffered through his case of the shingles. Mrs. Grogan was another angel in our midst.

Aside from a few gregarious visitors, our house was very quiet during this time. We all moved around without disturbing much. My cousins Jean and Anne came over a few times. They were hanging out with me in one of the first-floor bedrooms one afternoon, sitting on the bottom bunk bed. Jean, a year older than me, brought up Johnny's name. I immediately went quiet. I pretended I was interested in a thread I had pulled from the bed's quilt, acting as if my cousins were no longer there. But they did not go away. I could not say his name. Whenever his name was mentioned it hurt. I was angry and I didn't know who to be angry with. My mother was aware enough of what I was going through to ask my cousins to help.

"Your Mom wanted us to talk to you about Johnny," Jean pleaded.

"What can I talk about? He's not here so I don't want to talk about him," I said.

Talking about it wouldn't change the facts. He'd still be gone. I felt betrayed. Who let this happen? People are in your life, part of your life, you are supposed to love them and care about them and suddenly they are gone! We are supposed to accept that? In addition to this confusion, I felt my mother should come to me, not my cousins. Yet, it was reassuring to know my mother was at least noticing me. As I look back on it now, as a woman of 46, I try to understand my reaction, and all I can come up with is that I wanted my mother, needed her. I wanted her to come to me and hold me for a moment, I think. No matter how close I was with my cousins, they couldn't give me this, although they tried, God bless them. Their companionship provided me comfort during this waiting period.

Aunt Annie Laurie had driven from Fenton, Michigan, to console her sister. While her brood, our Gallagher cousins, were in town, Johnny Gallagher spent a few days at our house. He came downstairs for breakfast, entered the kitchen where my brother Joe and I sat, each with a freshly poured bowl of Lucky Charms cereal.

"Do you think you stay here cuz your name is John or somethin'?" Joe asked him.

Johnny Gallagher was taken aback by this but did not say anything. He must have realized his name alone was making it harder for Joe who was normally a quiet, easygoing kid who got along with almost everyone. I was even surprised by Joe's mean comment. But that morning he didn't want anyone around called John. He didn't want to have to say that name and be reminded of his brother. It hurt too much. The only one who attempted to explain to Joe what happened to Johnny was Nan, Dad's mother. She wasn't one who provided compassion regularly, yet she gave something to Joe in which he was able to find comfort.

"He's in a better place. He wouldn't come back for all the tea in China," Nan said.

This may just have been what carried Joe through those weeks. Although Aunt Barbara had no such words of wisdom to offer, she did come up with an idea to keep Joe and I busy during this waiting period. She put us to work in their backyard to prepare for the after-funeral party, or whatever you called it. We worked in the Bansleys' yard right alongside my cousins Anne and Jean. Anne tugged at dead branches as she thought, how could Joe and I be there helping after what just happened to our brother? While we were busy raking up dead leaves and picking up abandoned paper cups, my cousin Anne yelled out. I looked about ten feet to my right and saw Anne standing in front of a tree stump turned over on its side with its short, dead roots exposed. Anne ran towards the house. She screamed and swatted at her head. I caught sight of a mass of dots hanging in the air, close behind Anne, as she ran into the house. Someone yelled, "It's bees!" I watched in disbelief as the swarm of bees chased her into her home. Annie's scream filled the large house as she ran inside. It was so guttural, that when Aunt Barbara heard it she thought Anne was on fire. The remainder of us in the yard hopped the backyard fence to get out of the yard, afraid to go near the back porch of the house where the angry bees might be lingering. The neighbor's dog was a police-trained German shepherd. I was deathly afraid of this dog, yet I was more afraid of encountering that swarm of bees. So I hopped the fence, running through the neighbor's yard, following right behind my brother Joe. Jean stayed put, afraid to go in the neighbor's yard because of their dog. She watched my brother Joe and I flip over the fence. Joe and I made it all the way home without any bee stings. As for Anne, she had many welts for several days but was okay. Jean later told me that she was amazed we could maneuver over the fence so easily, thinking our loss would have crippled us in some visible way.

- - -

"How could we have been so normal at such an abnormal time?" Anne said to me as we talk about her bee stings years later.

- - -

Aunt Barbara knew it was important to keep routine and that's why she kept us busy in the yard. When my father died in 2003, I went to the health club only a few hours after I received word he had passed, as I would every Thursday. I was afraid not to. I told an acquaintance there that my father had died during the night.

"And you're here?" she asked.

What did she expect me to do? You have to keep going at times like that. If you stop, you might drown in your own pity, be swallowed by the sadness. One must continue to do mindless things like ironing, jogging, manicure appointments . . . until the pain is dull enough to face.

When Dick Barry's mother learned that our family had been waiting for Johnny's body, she asked her son if he could do anything to help find out where Johnny was. There were two stateside military mortuaries during the Vietnam War. The primary one was Dover air force base in Delaware, where Dick Barry had been stationed in 1969. The other one was located in California. Dick called the Delaware base and spoke with chaplain, Lt. Col. Hank Miller, a man he had worked with earlier that year. Col. Miller went to the mortuary and inspected each body, looking for John Guldan. The bodies were identified only by the numbers on their dog tags. There were no names. Dick Barry and Col. Miller had to determine what Johnny's number was before their search began. Dick did the research to obtain Johnny's dog tag ID and discovered Johnny's body was not at Dover. He and the Colonel were perplexed, but Dick did not stop his search. The chaplain gave Dick a contact for the California Air Force base's mortuary.

- - -

Dick begins to retrace the steps he went through many years ago to help locate Johnny, then he stops and I am not sure if he can go on. His wife, Cathy, and I are respectfully silent.

- - -

It was at the Travis Air force base in California where they located the body. This should not have been the protocol, Dick thought, but so many bodies were returning. The chaplain at Travis kept in touch with Dick and paid attention to the care of Johnny's body until it was sent to its next destination, which still was not home.

As the days passed while we waited for Johnny's body, Eileen thought of Kelly Powers, a classmate. That same summer,

Kelly's little brother's drowned body had not yet been found. Although we had to wait, at least we would have a body, Eileen thought. She wondered how many grieving loved ones take for granted the grace of having a body to say good bye to.

- - -

"It took a long time—two weeks or sumthin'—for the body to get home. That was really hard, waiting the two weeks," Margie says.

- - -

Saturday, August 8. Johnny's friend, Pachol, saw the Department of Defense car parked in front of our house. I think they were there to inform my parents of the protocol on receiving Johnny's body and his things. Pachol went in to see what was going on and was told the news. He went straight to Neal Beatty's house. It was not yet noon. The rest of that day and many days thereafter were a blur to Neal. He thought of Denise but he could not bring himself to visit her. We did not see much of Denise either. She stopped by the house once with her sister Margaret and sat in the living room with Jim and Bill. We saw Denise one other time during this waiting period. My parents and a few of us went to the Racky house and listened to the tapes Johnny had sent Denise. She was gracious to allow this so that we could hear his voice again. Also, there were the parents of the boy that was killed alongside Johnny. He was from Oak Lawn, a neighborhood adjacent to Beverly. Johnny was in a very upbeat, jovial mood when he spoke to Denise on the tapes. I didn't listen very closely though. It was too hard. He sounded so alive and at the same time, it was so difficult to grasp the fact that we would never see him again. I did watch my parents and the other boy's parents. I had heard talk at home that one of them had triggered the land mine, causing their mortal wounds.

"Mom, did the other guy trip the wire on the booby-trap?" I asked.

"It doesn't matter. The important thing is that both were killed instantly and did not suffer," she told me.

Today I listen to Johnny's tapes. It is wonderful to be able to hear his voice, to know he was so real for so brief a time.

We had always stayed in Wisconsin until a few days before school started, prepared with all our school clothes and school supplies. Now we were back in Chicago before summer vacation was over. It was strange and very, very hot. Bill went over to Kellogg school and hung out with his friends enrolled in the summer day-camp during this waiting period. When he was home he noticed the radio seemed to always be playing, "War, what is it good for...," all the time, over and over.

Uncle Mike and Aunt Diane rented a cottage in Lake Geneva, Wisconsin, while we waited for the body. They took Margie and Eileen with them to help with their two small children. They stopped by to visit Denise and her family who were also staying at a cottage in Lake Geneva. Before this, Aunt Diane and Uncle Mike had only met Denise briefly at a couple of family functions but remembered how vibrant and friendly she was. They almost didn't recognize her when she greeted them at the door of her family's cottage. How very sad, Aunt Diane thought as she walked away from that visit. Denise was only eighteen when she was engulfed in love and war. She was just nineteen years old when she was given the devastating news that the man she hoped to marry was killed. Her future dreams vanished in an instant.

Dick Barry reported back to my sister Patti as he tracked down the location of Johnny's body. Dick was told by the chaplain at the Travis base in California that Johnny was to be shipped to Rantoul. He recalls speaking to the chaplain's assistant at Rantoul, who understood the distress the family was in and assured Dick he would contact him when Johnny's body arrived. Dick was surprised to hear the body ended up at Chicago's O'Hare airport.

My mother's last memory of Johnny had been saying good-bye to him at O'Hare airport. She had waited as he boarded the plane heading to California. From there, he would be shipped out to Vietnam. Johnny, this boy of only 19, must have seen the worry on her face as she stood there at the gate. He waved and smiled.

"Don't worry Mom, you remember how fast I am? I'll run."

The next time Johnny was at O'Hare Airport, my mother was not there to greet him. It was a quiet welcome home, seven months later, when my uncles met Johnny's remains. It was August 12, nine days after he died. Grandpa encouraged many members of the family to meet the body at the airport. He thought that proper. A few of the Gallagher and Bansley boys went to the airport with my uncles. I was angry that I did not get the opportunity to be there too, to greet my own brother's body. No one from my immediate family was present. Johnny Gallagher watched the plane from the airport glass. He locked his eyes on the flag-covered casket as it was carefully removed from the plane and wheeled over to the hearse, escorted by a lone Marine. The coffin was placed in a hearse. This movement was carefully directed by Mike Heeney. The hearse escorted my family members, present at the airport, back to the Heeney funeral home. It was night by the time their cars all fell in line behind the big black car, making an unofficial procession to the 95th street funeral parlor, where Johnny would remain for the next few days. The slow, steady stream of headlights headed south on the Dan Ryan expressway indicated to any witness that something quietly significant was happening.

Upon arrival at the funeral home, Johnny's body had to be identified by a family member. It was not done by my parents. My parents did not see Johnny's body. No one from our immediate family did. This was considered a sparing gesture. The coffin was opened for Uncle Jim and Uncle Mike to view first. They swallowed hard as they looked at Johnny. His body was not up near the casket rim, as they were used to seeing when paying respects at a wake. He was laying low in the casket with a sheet of glass above him like the ones protecting the mummies at the Museum of Science and Industry. The military had cleaned his wounds and dressed him in a fresh uniform. With a clenched jaw, Uncle Jim made himself look closely. He saw that his nephew's skin was very brown and he was unshaven. His hair was long, longer than the crew cut Johnny had sported, as both a Marine and as a son of John Guldan. This description coincides with the hygiene Johnny described in his letters yet did not coincide with the meticulous detail the Marines are known for when it comes to appearance. Were there too many bodies coming in to take care of them all, or was there such a rush to get this particular lost body back to its home?

My mother urged her sister, Annie Laurie, to go to the funeral home to identify the body. My mother didn't want to remember her son lying still and aged beyond his years. She did not want to see his lifeless, damaged body, silent in a wooden box. She wanted to remember her son as she knew him; when he was roughhousing with his younger brothers, mowing the lawn, heading out the door with his friends and running proudly through the finish line tape at a cross-country meet. This is how Mom wanted all of us to remember him.

Aunt Barbara and Annie Laurie went together into the funeral parlor room where the casket stood waist high on the metal gurney. They walked up to it with its lid open, both made the sign of the cross as they looked upon their nephew. They saw that it was Johnny.

"I want to be able to tell my sister that it was him, twenty years later," Annie Laurie told her son Johnny, in tears, when she returned to Grandpa's house after this difficult task. These were the first tears fifteen-year-old Johnny Gallagher had ever seen fall from his mother's eyes. The next time he would see her cry was a few days later, as the Taps played.

- - -

Uncle Mike explains to me that the military sealed the casket due to the fact it was shipped from Vietnam.

"How did they seal it? It wasn't like wrapping the body?" I ask

"Oh, God no," Uncle Mike says.

"It was like a glass top."

Aunt Diane tries to remember. She says my mother was not able or willing to view Johnny's body.

"Annie Laurie said, 'well somebody's got to, ya know, make sure it's him,' and all that," Aunt Diane tells me.

- - -

I wanted to know if my aunts and uncles saw Johnny before he had been cleaned up for the public. I wanted to know what he had looked like then. Was there distress on his face? Were his skin and hair stressed from the existence this twenty-year-old boy had lived for the past six months? Uncle John had heard stories about the land mines put together by the Viet Cong. Some were intended to blow apart the lower portions of a human body. They were much more vicious than a bullet. Since he only viewed the top half of Johnny's body, Uncle John wondered if Johnny's bottom parts had been peppered with explosives that only maimed him and did not kill him. He was concerned his nephew may have suffered greatly before he died. He knew many died just as much from shock as any explosives.

I learned from Dick Barry that the military took care of the body preparation before it was sent to the family. I learned from Philip Caputo's A Rumor of War that the Marines will thoroughly document the wounds of the KIA (killed in action) before leaving Vietnam. Oddly, this knowledge offered a slice of closure. If I really want to, I thought, I can research enough to know exactly what wounds Johnny had and exactly what they did to his body. I could know exactly how bad it was for him. In the past I would probably have done so, had I known this. Today—no.

I often wondered if Johnny suffered. Thirty-seven years later, I visited Vietnam. There I walked past a Bouncing Betty and a Daisy Chain booby-trap on display in the touring area of Ho Chi Minh's Cu Chi tunnel district. I noted how primitive they appeared and would not allow my mind to think more than that. Because Jim Hornsey shared his account with my family, I now know Johnny died instantly, without suffering.

Mrs. Heeney, as the funeral director, did not want to let Denise view the body, but Denise insisted upon it. She needed to confirm it was him. What if it wasn't Johnny, she thought. This would mean he was still over in Vietnam, lost, most likely a POW. She had to know so she could initiate a search for him if it wasn't his body. Mr. Racky and Mrs. Heeney accompanied Denise into the room where Johnny's body lay in the casket. That glass sheet was placed above him preventing her from touching him one last time. He lay there in his dress blues, the white Marine cap on his head. A flash of memory went through her mind of when she had knocked that cap off of him right before they embraced at the Iowa train station. It was him. She had no doubt. She saw him for only a moment and then collapsed, caught by her dad and Mrs. Heeney on either side of her. Denise went home and slept. Sleep was how she got through this time. She had no need to take any tranquilizers. Her body put her in a natural state of sedation.

- - -

As Uncle Mike recalls viewing the body his thoughts go to Denise:

"I just felt so badly for this kid. I just can't imagine the thousands of young couples . . . I don't know if they were semi-engaged or if they were breakin' up or I don't know what it was but she really, really got hit hard by this thing."

- - -

Uncle John had been occupied with college and the seminary in Johnny's later teen years. He was not aware that Johnny had a girlfriend, especially not a fiancé. At the time, most of us did not know how important Denise was to Johnny. Yet, my parents recognized the significance of Denise's relationship through Johnny's letters and honored his heart loudly in the tiny print of his obituary notice:

Lance Cpl. John A. Guldan, U.S.M.C. died in action in Viet Nam, Aug. 3, beloved son of John, DDS and Eileen…, fiancé of Denise Racky.

Throughout his twenty years, Johnny had established relationships with strong bonds. He learned from my parents the value of friends, community, and a good partner, as he built his own life. The relationship he had built with Denise was one of trust, loyalty, and deep friendship. Denise and Johnny exchanged over one hundred letters in the six months Johnny was in Vietnam. In those letters to her as well as the letters Johnny wrote to my parents and others he often spoke of plans to marry Denise.

Along with Johnny's body came a single Marine to act as a bodyguard for his fellow Marine until he was laid to rest. His name was Ron Berquist. He was a blonde version of Elvis Presley. As a young girl in 1970, I had watched all of the Elvis Presley movies. Ron was quiet and reserved, like Elvis was in his movies. He even wore his hair like Elvis.

Dad had told this Marine he could keep Johnny's long, formal Marine wool overcoat. Mickey remembered how nice of a coat it was when Johnny had worn it home in January. He heard Mom get upset with Dad because he had given the coat away. "One of the boys could have worn it," she told Dad. This was the least the U.S. Marines could provide her. Ron then gave my brother Chris Johnny's helmet. A Marine gave an eight-year-old, the youngest of many brothers, something special. This meant a lot to Chris. He took it and kept it and guarded it as if it was the Holy Grail, for over forty years now.

While performing his duties for Johnny, the Marine Berquist stayed at the Bansley house. My cousin Anne was curious about this man in uniform. She snuck into his room while he was out at the funeral home with my parents. She checked out his stuff noting how neatly his toiletries were arranged on the dresser. The razor, hairbrush, toothpaste, and gloves were laid out neatly, too neatly, side by side, the same spacing between all his items. Anne felt there was something really weird about this. But she was just a kid. Aunt Barbara and Uncle Jim did not think there was anything weird about him at all. They recognized this Marine's kindness and support for our family, a family he had only moments to get to know under a very difficult circumstance.

Margie and Eileen and Patti all tried to hold things together during this time, with little thought left to take care of themselves. They took care of us, they took care of Mom, and

340 | T.M. Guldan

Patti kept an eye on Dad. Maybe this distraction helped my older sisters to get through these weeks.

- - -

"I was always holding onto Bonnie because Mom was so distraught," Eileen says. "Were you worried about Mom?" I ask.

"Yeah," Eileen says without hesitation.

- - -

To add salt to the injury, Johnny's July 31 letter arrived home. My parents opened it with the knowledge that the words on its paper were the only living piece left of their son. They held the paper with the knowledge that it had been touched by their living son's fingers as he folded it and placed it in the envelope. At the same time, my father's last letter had arrived in Vietnam. These two letters passed through the mail system, as Johnny's life was taken away. Like the fingers on the Sistine chapel ceiling, desperately close, reaching out for each other as an opposing force pulls them apart.

Another Long Day

Never let them see you cry.

—Princess Grace of Monaco,
to Princess Diana of Wales

That August day on which we received the news became the longest day in each of our lives. The second longest day was the day Johnny was waked two weeks later

Mom wanted us to look good at the services. She picked out our clothes and dressed all twelve of us. She made sure we all had clean clothes, clean shoes, and clean faces. She borrowed suits from cousins for the boys and had shopped for dresses with the girls.

"Why do we need to get a dress?' Eileen had asked.

Eileen was mad at Mom for having us buy a dress for the funeral. She did not want to dress up and be on display. There was a sense of confusion around the celebration aspect for us kids. Yet it wasn't the celebration my Mother was addressing when buying new outfits. It was the impression of strength. Jacqueline Kennedy was my mother's role model because she was able to pull herself together with a stylish outfit and have her children well-dressed at her husband's funeral. This signified strength to my mother.

A host of people lent a hand throughout the days leading up to the services. There was our babysitter, Pauline; there were the neighbors like Mrs. Heeney and Mrs. Barry; there were the aunts and uncles; and there were my older sisters. Mariann did Mimi's hair. Mom asked her to brush it and pull it back off Mimi's face the day of the wake. Mariann was having a difficult time with this as Mimi sensed. Her scalp ached from Mariann's rough brush strokes. Mariann was quiet as she brushed hard through Mimi's tangles. Mimi stayed quiet too, trying not to cause any more of a problem. Mimi tried with all her might to remain still. She became faint after sitting for what seemed like an hour. Mimi remained quiet. Luckily, Mariann finished in time for Mimi to drink some juice and revive herself.

On Thursday, August 13 at two p.m., the funeral home began accepting guests to view the casket and greet the family. "Be strong like soldiers and don't cry," my mother told my sisters Mariann and Patti. The oldest were to set an example for the rest of us. The twelve of us lined up, spanning the length of the room, with my parents and the lone Marine alongside the casket. Framed photos of Johnny sat on top of the closed casket, draped with the American flag. We stood ready to receive each guest.

Uncle John looks so sad, Johnny Gallagher thought as soon as he walked into the funeral parlor with his parents. Sad or not, we all looked presentable, my aunts and uncles thought, and were amazed my mom could arrange that. It wasn't long before the younger ones were allowed to go in the back room to eat something and visit with our cousins. There we sat on comfortable couches and enjoyed our cousins' company. And there was food, more food.

My mother and my father stood with the lone Marine for hours upon hours beside the casket while the line of visitors continued. It was unbearably hot for those waiting in the line outside the Heeney's Funeral Home. It was one block long, curving around the corner on 95th all the way down to 94th Street. And it stayed that way all night. Uncle Mike's roommate at Marquette, George Kearney, who was also the guy that fixed him up with Aunt Diane, stood in line almost two hours. Then Raibo Carsi and Danny Garby, two guys that he taught and coached with at De La Salle High School and had known Johnny at Marist, stood in line a long, long time. Uncle Mike found this out days later. It meant an awful lot to him.

During this greeting of friends and relatives, Annie Laurie mentioned to Aunt Barbara how long and curly Johnny's hair had looked when they viewed his body. Aunt Barbara replied in astonishment, "Annie Laurie, he had his Marine cap on. You couldn't see his hair!" That's odd, Annie Laurie thought. She distinctly remembered how his hair had looked while he lay in that coffin. At my mother's request, the casket was closed. She wanted us to remember him the way he was. I, on the other hand, wanted to know he was dead. I wanted proof of it. Even today, I wish I had seen him lying peacefully in that casket. For forty years, I thought about the possibility that only half of Johnny's body might lie in that casket. Never seeing Johnny's body enabled me to continue the delusion I was having that my brother was not dead. I fantasized he was a prisoner of war, thousands of miles away, in a strange land, continuing his heroism. Those who passed by saw a few photos of Johnny placed on top of his closed casket: his high school graduation photo of him in a jacket and tie, and another one of him smiling while at the farm. They had the wrong person in there, I thought. The concept of death was outside of the limits of Margie's understanding, too. She never thought it would happen. The closed casket allowed her too to believe it was a mistake—the Marines had made a mistake. This way of thinking helped us through, I suppose, in the same way the prescribed drugs may have helped my mother through.

Grandpa was a proud man, and he was especially proud of the relationship he had built and nurtured with Johnny, his oldest grandson. He talked with his daughter, Annie Laurie, about Johnny's short life while they sat together on one of the love seats

344 | T.M. Guldan

placed around the viewing room. In order to communicate after his throat surgery, Grandpa kept a writing tablet with him. 'I have no regrets about my relationship with Johnny,' he wrote for Annie Laurie to read.

"What a wonderful thing to be able to say, Dad," she told him.

Grandpa looked around and made sure everything and everyone about the wake was respectable of his grandson. He used his writing tablet to communicate to Aunt Diane that she should change her outfit. Aunt Diane was approaching her third trimester. Due to the high temperatures she was wearing a light weight, loose fitting maternity dress. Grandpa Bansley indicated to Aunt Diane that her dress was see-through. She left, got a slip, and then returned to the wake to continue standing with her husband, Uncle Mike, and the rest of us.

- - -

Aunt Diane laughs while recalling this and says, "He was so darling. He said it in a real cute manner. I so remember him there and just tons of people and then the soldier that was standing by his casket. "

- - -

Mickey sat in a chair, not far from my parents and the older brothers and sisters standing by the coffin. The Marine caught his attention. I too was caught by this vision as I walked from the back room toward the casket. I saw the Marine guard standing at attention, always near the body, dressed in his formal Marine attire. I sensed he was there to help my parents and I liked him for that. He stood by my parents and that box filled with all that was left of their son, providing strength. Ron Berquist was a significant, positive memory of all who mentioned him. He exemplified all the strength and compassion associated with the image of a Marine protecting his comrade. There was a nonfiction movie made about a lone Marine escort played by Kevin Bacon, called Taking Chance. Ron Berquist was our Kevin Bacon.

- - -

The image of Marines guarding Johnny's casket at the wake stays in my brother Bill's memory and heart.

"I remember Timmy Hanson stood there all night. He had already been home from a tour in Vietnam. He wore his dress blues and then they had the honor guard. What was his name—he was real nice?" Bill asks.

"Ron Berquist," I answer.

"Tim and him stood there aaaalll night long and all I remember is, uh, uh, we'd all have to stand there in line. Mom made us all stand there and stuff. And then, uh . . . people. Just a line of people from, I think it was from three o'clock, two o'clock or sumpin,' till nine, nine at night. Nonstop people. The wake was only gonna be one night and it was at the old Heeney Funeral home on 95th and what was it, Hamilton, or whatever. It was across from Waxman's Pharmacy." Bill says.

- - -

Waxman's Pharmacy was an icon of our youth. It was the neighborhood pharmacy that delivered our prescription medicine on a Harley motorcycle. Whenever that huge black and silver machine appeared in our driveway, the mysterious driver with helmet and goggles brought a small white bag of medicine to my mother. During the midst of the wake service, I crossed the busy 95th street, with an adult, to get some refreshments. Before this, I had never seen the Waxman Pharmacy store. This small place, crammed with shelves of merchandise, was where that cool motorcycle rider came from. His myth was a bit destroyed.

Although it had only been one night it seemed to Mickey we had been at the Heeney funeral home for three nights and each night there were lines and lines of people waiting to visit the body and pay their respects to our family. My brother Mickey knew some of those that were in this long line. His teachers Mrs. Milan and Mrs. McCarthy came. He couldn't believe how they waited in that long line for his brother, for him. For my brother Jim it was not so positive. Jimmy wanted to protest this wake, this funeral, and all its related activities. He stood in the receiving line while people passed by him and Johnny's closed casket, surrounded by elaborate floral displays and photographs. Many of our father's patients and friends paid their respect.

"I'm so sorry," one of them said to Jim and a few of us nearby.

"Yeah, right," Jimmy responded.

This unfortunate man got a burst of some of that steam escaping Jim like an overworked boiler. Dad must've heard because he came over to Jim.

"They're here to show their respect," Dad explained.

"I don't want to be here. This is all a bunch of bullshit," Jim said.

"You have to be here," Dad replied.

I couldn't believe he used a swear word towards my dad and my Dad stayed calm. A firm, clear direction was what Jim needed. And at that moment that's what Dad provided. My mother, the one we all typically flocked around, could not be there during this time of need. Dad was now the compassionate and caring one. He stepped up to the plate and became the pillar we needed. He may have been silently blamed for the death of his son, a blame he took and wore like a scarlet letter across his forehead, but he did not strike out in defensiveness or numb himself with medications or alcohol. He carried on.

The people that came through the line to pay their respects and offer condolences to my parents and the rest of us often had difficulty when trying to find the right words to say. Well-meaning visitors passed by with the intention of saying something that was comforting to my mother. Sometimes their good intent did not come across as positive.

"Isn't it wonderful that you have twelve other children," one friend said.

My mother, fiercely defensive of the life of her son, responded, "I love them all equally."

Another visitor said, "This is terrible. Why doesn't this happen to bad kids."

"I wouldn't wish this on any mother," Mom replied.

Another awkward visitor that day was Bruce DaCosta, Mariann's boyfriend. Bruce did not have the respect from my family he would have liked. But he cared very much for Mariann and wanted to be there for her. He never did receive a phone call from her the day the news arrived, nor did she tell him about the services. Mariann was in shock, he surmised, and was not thinking clearly. Bruce looked up the details of the services himself and found his way to the Heeney Funeral Home.

My father had asked my uncles to keep Bruce out of the wake. So when Uncle Mike was given notice that Bruce was in the line that snaked outside of the funeral home, he went outside. Uncle Mike found Bruce and told him that this was not a good time for him to be there. Bruce stayed in line. When he got to the door of the Heeney Funeral Home, Uncle Jim greeted him.

"Not a good idea to come in," he said to Bruce.

Bruce turned around to go back to his apartment, with the intention of staying clear of our family and Mariann for the next few days. But he did not leave without first putting up some resistance. "I'm just trying to—" Johnny Gallagher heard Bruce say. Then many heard Uncle Mike's booming voice, as we sat in the funeral home's foyer with our cousins. The foyer was another spot of refuge, along with the back room, during this long arduous day.

Uncle Mike led Bruce to one of the waiting rooms in the funeral home.

"Just sit there and I'll get Mariann for ya," Uncle Mike told him.

Uncle Mike went to find Mariann. As he walked, head down, back to the viewing room of the funeral parlor, trying to think what was the right thing to do, Uncle Mike's mind reeled with different ways he could approach this delicate situation.

- - -

"Did he go inside?" I ask Uncle Mike.

"Yeah, Yeah. I brought him in but not into the parlor itself. There are different waiting rooms that ya have in Heeney's. And I said, 'You go in there,' so John and Eileen would never see 'em," Uncle Mike recalls.

I try hard to imagine this exact scene at the funeral home, relieved to momentarily escape the thought of Johnny lying in his coffin.

"That was a very volatile time, with Mariann and her life and your mom. Not only that situation but Bruce was the definition of hippie. Someone you would expect to be demonstrating against the Vietnam War," Aunt Diane says.

- - -

I didn't understand what fed the anger my parents had toward Bruce. Could it possibly have been his afro and bell bottoms? I was aware of only a small part of the adult life that was going on all around me. This U.S. phenomenon, the dichotomy between the generations, the conservatives and the liberals, was reflected right within our own family. It was mixed in with the cyclone of debris heaved about from Johnny's traumatic death. Since Bruce was clearly a liberal, my aunt and uncle naturally assumed he was a war protestor. He was a pacifist but he supported our country and the war to some degree. Bruce, youngest of a Bronx family of six, had brothers that served in the armed forces. He respected their choices and did not participate in any war protests. Going to war was just not a choice that he would have made.

Margie's boyfriend, Jeff Belinger, was a completely different experience for my parents. He was athletic, tall, reserved, and polite. Jeff had shown up at Johnny's wake with his mother, whom Margie had not met before. Both mother and son approached the closed casket as they waited patiently in the slow-moving line to pay their respects. Margie was appreciative that both of them came.

"Hi. How are you? I didn't recognize you with clothes on," my mother said.

Prior to this, Mom had only seen Jeff in jeans and t-shirts at our house. She sometimes said things a ditzy blonde might say. I think she did this to make us laugh. Margie had had a bad reaction to an antibiotic, which turned her face beet red. Margie had the advantage of her medication's reaction, so no one noticed as her face turned an even darker shade of red. No one except maybe her triplet sister Eileen, who saw and felt everything that happened to Margie. Eileen was the middle triplet by two minutes. This is an important fact for a multiple-birth child. It is a defining feature. Having been named after my mother gave Eileen an added advantage. Yet, Eileen never used this card to trump her womb-sharing siblings.

Margie and Eileen's girl friends came to Johnny's wake and giggled about how the Marine pallbearers had tried to pick them up. Johnny's friends Beatty and Pachol commented to Eileen and Margie how Johnny would turn over in his grave if he saw all these good-looking girls here for him. Although, a week prior, Margie would have been interested to hear such tales and laugh along with them, now she was light years away from these types of concerns. How could they be so insensitive to care about such trivial things when I have suffered such a loss? Don't they see me with my heart broken, Margie thought. There was one friend, Pug, who did understand. Pug's real name was Rosemary Coakley. She had written Johnny letters while he was over in Vietnam. Margie felt she could share some pride, rather than shame, with this particular friend. Pug shared something very intimate with Margie and Eileen, she also had a brother in Vietnam. Pug's brother was in the Army at the same time Johnny was in the Marines. Pug's brother made it back.

Margie and Eileen didn't talk about Johnny's death and the Vietnam War, not to their friends and not even between themselves. Their close friend, Sue Stanton, stood by them during the wake. Sue was out of range as someone they could confide in about their feelings. Margie knew the Stantons did not support the war and could not differentiate between this attitude toward the war and their opinion of her brother fighting in it. Margie began to feel ashamed when she was around such people. There was no difference between the public opinion of the war and the public opinion of Johnny. Yet those who opposed the war hated it even more with each good soldier it took. It was confusing.

Most of Eileen's friends viewed his death as she did, as a sacrifice for their freedom. Although most did not go to the wake. There were tons of people. She didn't know who they all were, saying to her, "sorry about your brother." She appreciated that they seemed to care. She didn't want to see his body but thought she probably should have because for weeks after she kept dreaming that he was still alive and walking down the long hallway that separated his second-floor bedroom from hers.

The back room of the Heeney funeral home was for the family members. We spent time with our cousins in this back room. It was our refuge, a small room that offered refreshments and a distraction from the reason we were there. A huge sheet of frosted brownies was in this room. Mimi didn't care much for the nuts on these brownies but they were easy enough to pick off. These treats and that room were comforting to six-year-old Mimi. She enjoyed all the company the cousins and children of our parents' friends provided during the many hours she stayed in that back room. It was like a party, Mimi thought.

As the long, long day was nearing an end, Aunt Diane sat in one of the chairs facing the casket to rest her weary feet. The baby she would soon deliver was weighing heavy on her that night. She looked over at my mom from time to time. Mom stood there with the Marine guard and my father, late into the night. Aunt Diane stayed until the end and watched as the Marine held my mother up. Then he walked her out of the parlor and to our car. Aunt Diane was moved by the unbelievable look of grief and sadness on my mom's face. Seeing how my mom could hardly walk, Aunt Diane figured the day had been a huge blur to her.

The vision of my mother leaning on the soldier may have served to help Aunt Diane through her own grief eight years later when Aunt Diane would lose her oldest son to illness, also at a very young age. God may have been preparing Aunt Diane long before the agony of loss struck her life. In my mid-forties, I began reading a chapter in the Bible every night. I read through it sequentially. As I was having a particularly rough time in life, with a move to a new state, a new job that was not going well, and a very difficult relationship that was finally ending, I was crying as I read the Bible that night. It didn't help that I happened to be reading the *Book of Revelation*, a dark and foreboding section. I was on a chapter seven, which was usually uplifting with white robes and chosen ones. As I came to the end, my tears falling on to the pages, I read, 'and God will wipe every tear from their eyes.' My lips curled into a smile. God was paying attention to me. Thank you Lord and forgive me for not realizing you had my back. I didn't do anything special to deserve it. It was just there, His love. Possibly, Aunt Diane received this special attention at the moment when she memorialized the vision of my mother leaning on the soldier. She needed that vision when it was her time of suffering.

Funeral

This is how he died, leaving in his death a model of courage and an unforgettable example of virtue not only for the young but for the whole nation.
—2 Maccabees 7: 30-31, *Martyrdom of Eleazar, New American Bible*

The wake culminated with an 8:30 PM service, allowing my parents little sleep that night. Yet they rose early the morning of Friday, August 14. Pauline was at our house. Emma, Grandpa's maid, was there too. Grandpa made sure of that. Pauline and Emma got us all to rise, wash, and dress sooner than we would have wished for on a typical summer day. They prepared a lot of scrambled eggs and bacon with buttered toast in a heap on the table. Maybe it was pancakes or French toast. I actually don't remember. My sister Patti would have been helping to get us all organized so there was not a chance we would be late. Maybe Dr. Gallagher even came by to help drive us all back to the funeral home. None of us remember much of this morning. It would have been quiet there, my parents speaking in hushed voices, because that's how you speak at funeral homes, to Mrs. Heeney, the funeral home director. From there we loaded into the two big black cars. There was not one car large enough to hold us all, so we had to be separated. The girls went with Mom in one car and the boys went with Dad in the other car. I slid into the roomy back seat with my sisters and got lost in it. We headed to the church, trailing the hearse.

A sea of people stood outside the church as the hearse pulled up to the few steps leading to the large, brass-framed doors. There were school kids in uniform lined up along the

354 | T.M. Guldan

sidewalk holding flags. We sat in the car and the people were all silent. The Marine escort, Ron Berquist, and several Marine pallbearers were standing close by the hearse. My mother had the choice as to whether she wanted Marines as pallbearers, or family members. She chose the Marines. She thought Johnny would have wanted that. Her son gave his life for our country to protect everyone at his funeral. These brave, young men reminded us of this sacrifice as we said good-bye.

- - -

"It wasn't so sad until the funeral day," Mickey states.

He describes what he remembers of the arrival at the church and pauses a moment to mentally pull down the screen showing this scene in the theater of his memory.

"The funeral day was sad, because when we went to Christ the King, you saw all the people." Mickey had to take a moment's break when emotion overcame him. "There were a lot of people. ...people were in the balcony [of the church] and cars were lined up and the people that were all outside even before we came into the church."

- - -

Grandpa Bansley walked over toward our limo to see Mom. He was worried about her. Grandpa had suffered terribly from the surgery and chemo treatments. He used to walk around the block of Kellogg school while I played four-square on the playground during recess. When I'd see him, I stopped playing and yelled, "Grandpa," and ran up to him. It was so hard not to gag as he bent over for me to give him a kiss. I could see the inside of his neck and his head would wobble like one of those toys you see on a car dashboard. I don't mean to make fun but that is exactly what it reminded me of and it made me feel bad for him. I kissed him for my mom even more than I did it for my grandpa. It was so important to her. He was so important to her. Mom was sitting in the front seat of the long, black, funeral car. The window was down, her hand holding on to the door as if it was her life raft on a churning ocean. Grandpa approached the car. The cane in his hand had aided his stiff legs. He reached out to my mother's hand on the door and gently covered it with his. Their eyes locked on each other. Tears ran down her face as she reached out desperately for her father's loving support. Patti watched Mom from the back seat of the limousine.

"Dad, Dad," Patti heard her softly call out.

Grandpa's eyes glistened with tears, his neck exposed from the throat cancer surgery, not able to speak. No words were needed. Someone opened the door to the car I was in. The heavy church doors were propped open as we all filed out of the big, black cars. People were all around. Berquist and the Marine pallbearers moved the casket along with us.

- - -

"How was Mom?" I ask Bill.

"Depressed," Bill begins to cry again as he answers.

"She just kept walking and kept moving?" I ask.

"Yeah. But I can't say I ever saw her cry, Terri," Bill said, still crying.

"Yeah? I didn't either," I tell him.

"Never saw her cry," Bill repeats.

"How 'bout Patti and Mariann? Were they the same like Mom or were they..." I ask Bill.

"No. No. Patti and Mariann were cryin' a lot," Bill says, still crying.

- - -

By 10:00AM the outside temperature was already at eighty-seven. It was on its way to a high of a humid ninety-one degrees. The sun blazed relentlessly outside, while inside the air-conditioned-less church filled to capacity. Johnny's good friend Neal Beatty sat in the first row of the balcony, a little off to the left. There the air was so stuffy it was hard to breathe. He watched as the Marines carried the heavy oblong box, smothered by the U.S. flag, moving down the long aisle, the same aisle he and Johnny had walked several times when filing into the pews for mandatory mass during school days. He met Johnny when he transferred to Christ the King in the middle of seventh grade. Seated in front of Johnny, they chatted, and began walking home together each day. A new friendship quickly formed. Although they went on to different high schools, they remained best friends. Neal endured the lengthy service and the heat for the chance to say good-bye and honor his dear friend. "Why had we lost someone who was such an inspiration, a friend, a brother, a warrior?" Neal asked himself as he looked down on the packed church. He was sad for our family and for Denise. He had lost many close to him by age twenty, one of which was his father. Now he had lost his best friend. It was the saddest day of his life.

- - -

I ask Neal about his memories of the funeral. He has a difficult time going back to those years. It was best for him to be alone when he thought about it so he wrote it out.

"I am shaking a bit and tearing up trying to answer this. There is so much to say and such a flood of memories. Nothing had ever brought on this much hurt, or sense of loss in my life as this event did. I felt anger and loss. There was so much going on at that time in our lives, and so much to look forward to. For me personally, John's loss has stayed with me. It is one thing that I cannot seem to find a point of closure to. I talk with him often, and think about him more often. He comes in my dreams, and also in conscious and unconscious actions. I am blessed to have earned his friendship, and so value the part of my life that we spent together. The mark that his life and his death have left on my life is the most pleasant of mysteries."

- - -

Both sets of our grandparents and their friends attended the funeral. Johnny's young friends and classmates all attended. We had lots of family with lots of friends. They all filled the large church. The Marines carried the body in. Denise sat down with her mother in a pew up close to the altar. Mrs. Racky leaned over to her daughter and whispered, "Act like a soldier." Father McKenna spoke of forgiveness and war in his homily. There were several priests on the altar with him. He told us all how Johnny gave up his life for his friends. He didn't know Johnny, Denise thought to herself. It felt impersonal. Father McKenna's words added sparks to Jimmy's simmering anger. Jimmy felt as if he were in a carnival's house of mirrors, distorting the truth one hundred different ways. Jim shut out the rest of what was said on the altar of Christ the King church that day.

Our Pastor, Father Meyers, was on vacation when all of this occurred. In his absence he had sent a heartfelt letter to the parish, dated August 1970, which he wrote from his vacation home in Petoskey, Michigan. He made it clear with his few words there was not much he could say to help at this time. He praised the parish for their strength, their community, and their faith and wrote that it had been a summer of tragedy for our little neighborhood. Father listed three parishioners, in addition to Johnny, who died all within a 100-day span. They were all young men with close families. Our misery certainly had company. Up until that time there was little else that served as news within the boundaries of Beverly other than marriages and the birth of children.

After the mass, as we departed the church. The pallbearers were skittish, as they slid the casket into the hearse waiting right outside. They had been shot at while at another funeral. We saw that the grammar school children were lined up along the church drive and sidewalk. My family and I got back into the two big, black, cars parked behind the hearse. From the back seat, I peered out of the closed window that sealed us all in silence. Each student held a flag in his or her hand as they stood shoulder to shoulder in their maroon and white uniforms. Many were my age. The stream of them began outside the big stained glass doors and trailed down the steps on each side of the circular drive in front of the church. Their disciplined line continued down the sidewalk and along the street curb. We all looked out the window at them as we drove by. It was visions like this that gave our family strength that day.

- - -

Mickey remembers: "Our friends were holding flags. I remember Pat Cavanough holding a little flag. He was our neighbor from across the street."

Chris remembers: "There was an issue with all the Christ the King kids hangin' flags. I remember that bein' an issue where there was riots and stuff. Ya know? I remember Mom and Dad talkin' about it and stuff."

- - -

The funeral procession drove through our neighborhood streets, past our home. There were people lined up along the streets, with their hands over their hearts, as we drove by. As the procession headed on to the cemetery, we passed a construction site where the workers had stopped working, taken their hard hats off, and put their hands over their hearts. Eileen gazed out the back window of the car. She was upset to think someone would shoot at Marine pallbearers. She saw the line of cars that had come from the church, following us to the gravesite. There were lots of cars. She wasn't sure if this was normal since this was the first funeral she had attended. It certainly didn't appear normal to her as she stared at the infinite line of cars following on 111th street, as our car turned into Mount Olivet's gated entrance.

We all quietly filed out of the two black funeral cars at the cemetery and filed into a shed-like chapel. The family and those that could fit crammed into the little chapel surrounding the flag-draped casket. While the rest of those that followed stood outside its open doors. Chris stood by our cousins Matt, Danny, and Michael Gallagher. He noticed Mike Gallagher was crying a lot and thought, "Why is he crying?" He looked around him and saw others crying. He couldn't understand it.

- - -

"Now, every time I think about it, I tear up," Chris says.

I confess to Chris that I did not get it either. I told him how I was convinced that Johnny was a prisoner of war since we didn't see a body.

"He was boxing them all," I say to Chris.

"Really?" He laughs. I laugh. They were instantaneous, real laughs.

We continue talking about how we felt that day. We realize we had both been confused about others' reactions to Johnny's death because we were not able to react ourselves. Chris and I talk more about our indicators of denial and acceptance from the moment of receiving the news through the funeral and over the years.

- - -

Father McKenna stood at the head of the casket speaking some heartfelt words. My sister Eileen stood alongside the casket in that crowded chapel listening to the priest's words when she caught a glimpse of Denise. Eileen's attention turned to a silent wish that Denise was pregnant with Johnny's baby so that part of him would continue on. Johnny Gallagher stood a row or two of people back from the casket. He looked past the casket and noticed his Uncle Gene for the first time. Uncle Gene was an ex-Marine. He stood, with a stone face, at attention. This picture of his Uncle Gene was unsettling because seeing him there so serious seemed unnatural. Yet Johnny thought how nice it was for him to come since he was not an uncle from this side of the family. Johnny's eyes settled on my mother, his godmother, engulfed in my father's arms. They were all that was holding her up at that point. Then Johnny looked to his mother, crying hard as she watched her sister. She grabbed Johnny's hand and squeezed tightly.

"Don't ever forget this," Annie Laurie told him.

Without warning, the twenty-one gun salute came. Seven rifles went off right outside the chapel door. Then a pause. Seven more. Then again. For years after, I hated the sounds of the fireworks on the Fourth of July. The reaction these gun shots ignited in Mariann was unique to the rest of us.

- - -

"It startled me. I started to laugh uncontrollably. That was my reaction. I knew it was odd but I think it was a release. It allowed me to release to some degree," Mariann tells me.

- - -

Following the twenty-one-gun salute, one Marine played the Taps. The intensely sad melody filled the small structure we were crowded into. That is when all of the tears came. Mariann's laughter quickly turned to tears. Mickey burst into tears so abruptly at the first note from the horns that a wad of snot shot out of his nose onto the nicely pressed slacks of Marine Berquist. Mickey felt terrible. He thought Johnny would have been disappointed in him that he had done this. Up until the Taps played, I was able to accept what was going on around me by making up my own story. I had parted the sea walls of reality and walked through the past days with a sense of imaginary safety. The Taps carried a reality that chased me like the Roman chariots charged the Israelites through the dry sea bed. It was like the gunshots startled me awake to hear that clear sad horn melody resonating from the lips of a nearby Marine. God must have known it was time for the waters of the Red Sea of reality to come crashing upon me. I cried. The tears came and I couldn't stop them. I watch the Lake Michigan waters rising and receding up and down the sandy beach near my west Michigan home and it reminds me of the emotions that have occurred in processing my brother's death. They seem to ebb and flow to the surface of my child heart like the waters on the shore.

My mother was able to participate in the funeral. With the Marines and my father by her side she was able to walk down the long aisle of the church, follow the casket in and sit in the church pew throughout the service. Then she walked back down that long aisle, following the coffin out, got out of the car at the cemetery. She was able to go into that shelter, crowded with mourners. She was able to stand close to the flag-draped casket of her son as more prayers were said, the twenty-one-gun salute was performed, and the Taps were played. The Marines folded the flag lying on the coffin with precision and handed the resulting triangular form of stars and stripes to my mother. She was able to accept the flag. She then followed her son's remains once again, to their final resting spot, where prayers were said at the gravesite. She endured these traditions.

- - -

Eileen remembers Mom and Dad supporting each other during the wake and funeral period. She thinks she saw them hugging the day we all received the news.

"She never brought up about how she was going to blame him," Eileen says.

My interview with Aunt Barbara and Uncle Jim took place on December 22, 2007, the ninth anniversary of my mother's death. It was only natural our discussion went back to the day she passed. Aunt Barbara tells me what she remembers. When my mother was missing that night, my father called the Bansley house for the second time, and Aunt Barbara and Uncle Jim contacted their son-in-law, Dave Maroney. Dave was a state trooper with access to all traffic incidents. He called in for the night's reports and received the notice, "one fatal," Aunt Barbara tells me. I immediately think how the Marine log from August 3, 1970 was similarly brief and anonymous. "Two KIA," it read. My mother and my brother both died sudden and explosive deaths. Her heart stopped in an instant after an air bag exploded from the steering wheel she sat behind. His heart stopped with a piece of shrapnel shooting into it. Their wakes and funerals were also similar with long lines of people and lots of heavy hearts. When my mother died, twenty-eight years later, in the Palos Hospital that dark December night, my sister Eileen and I both felt the strong pull to look at our mother's lifeless, cold body. We knew from experience with Johnny's death that we needed to see her. This time we did—we saw a body. Her face was bloody and her leg was twisted under her as she lay in that dank, claustrophobic room in the hospital's emergency department. I went into that bare room over and over again. I couldn't get enough of her. This time I did not create a story in my head. Instead, I kissed her cold, pale, forehead for the last time.

- - -

After the cemetery, everyone was invited back to Aunt Barbara and Uncle Jim's house for a party. I did not understand why there was a party, nor did I like it. I remember all of the adults, the crowd. I had to squeeze between people to get anywhere. I would not go into the backyard for fear of those bees. I remember being small because everyone's waist was at eye level. There were hips to hips, slacks, dresses all there in the living room. I was angry people would celebrate when my brother was gone. We should be out looking for him. How could these people be having fun, I questioned, yet I never asked anyone. It was another thing that added to my confusion.

Bernie Trout was a young man who worked at Grandpa's accounting firm in 1970. He was considered an accounting prodigy because he passed the CPA exam with only a high school education. He never went to college. He didn't value education. He spoke his mind and he often had a large opinion to speak about. Grandpa and the other men at the firm tolerated Bernie because he was a good accountant and an asset to Bansley & Kiener. He attended the post-funeral party. Bernie sat on the Bansley back porch with a few other adults, including Annie Laurie. Many children were in the yard, playing on the one-year-old swing set Johnny had helped Uncle Jim build.

"We should not have been in this war," Bernie Trout declared.

Most looked up from their Chinette™ plates, filled with mostaccioli and beef, as if one of those crazed bees had suddenly invaded their dinner space.

"Look what it does. It takes good people, like John," Bernie concluded.

The others weren't ready to hear such an anti-war concept, yet no one argued. They all kept eating. Those listening had heard that statement before, "We should not have been there," but not from within their own social tribe. They heard it from other crazy hippies that were on the television, in the newspaper, from rioters and protestors. Families and friends were often silently divided between pro- and anti-war opinions.

- - -

"The war brought it [the dichotomy of attitudes] home. When Johnny got killed, yeah, you looked at the war a HELL of a lot differently," Uncle Mike says.

"And they didn't get a good welcome when they came home from Vietnam," Aunt Diane's voice goes into a higher pitch as she finishes this statement.

"That was absolutely atrocious. DeLaSalle [high school] lost sixteen kids in that war. Twelve of those kids I either taught and coached or taught or coached," Uncle Mike says in a steady, deep voice.

- - -

The death of a young Marine touched this small community the way smallpox touched families in the 1800s. It was a matter of isolation for those who were exposed to the deadly disease, albeit close friends and loved ones who were daring enough to come into our home and share in our suffering. It separated each one of us from our friends, putting each one of us in our own isolation.

IV. The Aftermath

"A dead soldier causes suffering to so many other people—his father, his mother, his siblings, his relatives, his friends."

—Christian G. Appy, *Patriots,*
Lun Huy Chao interview, NVA pilot

1970-1975

My father's last letter to Johnny was returned in the mail a few days after the funeral services. It traveled from my father's hopeful heart, to his pen, to the small pages, through the postal system, over to Vietnam, and back again to my father's broken heart. My father put it away before my mom could see it. He kept it in a safe place. Unopened. And life went on.

My mother said nothing of the package she had sent Johnny at the end of July, if it had also been returned. No one talked about Johnny's letters that trailed in, yet I'm sure we all felt the pain with each one occupying his space in our home. The war had taken Johnny piece by piece and yet he was able to send himself home in pieces with each letter he wrote. He did not come home an amputee or blind. He did not come home half a man, but he did come home in his letters. Letters we have today to read over and over again.

The day after the funeral, Uncle Mike and Grandpa went door-to-door thanking people for hanging their flags out in respect for Johnny and our family. Grandpa used his notepad to communicate his gratitude to his neighbors. "Thank You," he wrote with tears in his eyes and pride in his heart. My cousins and I adhered the stamps to the addressed envelopes for the thank you notes to all of those who attended Johnny's services and sent flowers or food. Patti and Mariann assigned and supervised this task to us. We sat in assembly line format at the large table in the kitchen of our Oakley home. Eileen and Patti wrote the notes, while Margie and Mariann addressed the envelopes. My cousin Anne put a stamp on upside down. Patti fixed it.

My mother did not write most of the thank you notes. But I think she felt a little better once they were sent. In this way, wakes don't make sense for the family who is suffering and emotionally drained. The family stands alongside their loved one's dead body for hours greeting others who are saddened. Then they have to write all of these thank you notes. Since the wake takes away from the focus of ourselves it is a good tradition. The thank you notes also helped to distract us during the initial shell shock of our loss. Sending the notes helped us to focus on something that was productive and helpful to others.

Monsignor Gleeson came by the house a couple of days after the service. He blessed those who were home and our house. My parents spoke briefly with Father Gleeson. Although he had offered counseling, it was not accepted. Jim heard only hushed monotones during Monsignor's visit. This he interpreted as adults going through the motions so they could feel they'd done their job. They did nothing as far as Jim was concerned. If someone asked if he wanted to talk, Jim retorted, "No. Leave me alone." Jim felt like he was on the outs with most of us. A part of him sympathized with Mariann and Bruce. Jim could relate to Mariann's rebellion He had his own skin he wanted to wear and needed to try it on too. After Mariann moved out and was living with Bruce, he felt like he had lost another sibling.

Jim wrote to Mariann in 1971:

> *It seems to me that everyone around here is messed up. It's hard for me to understand the things that go on around here. . .*
>
> *I think I'm going to transfer into a public school, because I can no longer get anything out of St. Rita. Freshman yr I really dug that place, Sophmore [sic] yr, when John was killed I slid by barely. Now I can't stand it. I need change I guess or I'll go insane. I don't talk to [sic] much around here to anyone except Bill. . .*

Jim continually found himself wrestling between his peace and anger over Johnny's death for the next thirty years. Jim cared. He admired and loved his big brother Johnny. He did not know how to identify his feelings and especially did not know how to articulate them.

- - -

After thirty-seven and one half years, Jim begins to cry as he talks about the day he was told of his brother's death. During the regurgitation of these memories, he needs help. His Manhattan in one hand, beer in the other, serve him like marathoner's GU over a 26.2-mile trek. I watch him choke back the tears, yet he does not hesitate to remember and talk and describe. Jim does not, for one moment, question whether he should hold back. Johnny would have been very proud of him.

- - -

Within a few days of the funeral, Johnny's personal items, which Ron Berquist had delivered with the body, were divided among the boys. Jimmy was given his clothes and boots. The first thing Jimmy did was put a large peace sign on Johnny's fatigue pants. Jimmy wore these proudly until Bobby Sapp put him in his place. Bobby slapped Jimmy around when he came to his house with the defaced fatigues of his friend John. He told Jimmy it was disrespectful to his brother and to the country Johnny fought for and made my brother run around the block until he dropped. Mickey fought with Chris over Johnny's t-shirts. Being the youngest, Chris did not win this battle. But Chris had won out with Johnny's helmet. He had the Marine Ron Berquist to thank for that.

The Bansleys went on a two-week vacation they had delayed until after Johnny's funeral. I am certain I was very lonely while they were gone. It was still summer and there was no school or cousins to occupy our time. I would typically be at Jean and Anne's house or doing something with them or my best friend Lyn. Lyn, who lived across the street, was in Brazil with her family. Her father was sent there for work for the year. I was truly on my own, with an emptiness where my heart belonged. Maybe this was when I began writing.

My mother asked Patti to encourage us to talk about Johnny and share our memories of him. Patti assumed Mom had told us the same thing. Thirty-six years later, Patti was surprised to find out that Mom had not said anything to the rest of us about Johnny. I thought my mother had forgotten all about me. She had not forgotten. She just couldn't get to it. So she asked Patti to help with that responsibility. Patti carried a lot of responsibility on her shoulders. There was no time for her to address her own feelings about her brother's death. This probably explains why Patti was business as usual throughout our interview. She had to be. It was expected of her.

Patti's friends, like herself, were a responsible group of kids who did well in school. Herb, one of those friends, said to her, "The war was a mistake. Johnny should never have been there."

"You're saying my brother died for nothing?" Patti asked him.

Patti was upset by Herb's proclamation. He hadn't meant to correlate the senselessness of the war to the integrity of his friend's brother. It was as delicate as brain surgery to differentiate the two. He said he was sorry.

For Jim it was not so much this confusion that kept him from talking much about Johnny's death to his friends. Jim had experienced the violent and sudden death of a brother. They had not. Jim figured that they did not want to hear about it. The topic was like a calloused sore. Why pick at it, Jim thought.

My father's office was situated a few blocks east of the cemetery where Johnny was buried. Since our home was in the opposite direction Dad did not drive past the cemetery to get home. Yet I imagine he felt the presence of that plot of manicured land as he turned left onto 111th, as he arrived and left his office each day. One of these evenings, a week or so after the funeral, he did not head home. Instead, he headed for the Australian embassy in Chicago, with Eileen in the front seat beside him. He had instructed Eileen not to schedule patients in the last two appointments of the day so that they could make it to the embassy before it closed. He was determined that no other of his sons would have to go off and fight in a God-forsaken war. Eileen followed him into the embassy building and watched him collect the needed forms, thinking about how her life was going to drastically change, even more than it had in the last month. Yet after they got home and he presented the forms to my mother, she would not agree with the move. My mother wouldn't leave.

She could not leave her bedridden mother and her sick father whose comfort she needed more than ever. Those were the early days after Johnny's burial.

Letters from Others

I took his gear and replaced it with mine. I wouldn't let them just toss it aside. I'll have that gear til the day I leave this place. It means an awful lot to me.

—Jerry E. Butz, platoon mate,
August 3, 1970, to my parents

A handful of letters from the government and Johnny's comrades and friends began to arrive after Johnny had been laid to rest. They came sporadically, addressed to my parents. On August 9, a typewritten letter of sympathy was sent from Ronald D. Kincade, Captain, U.S. Marine Corp:

John received the last rites of his faith shortly after his death from Lieutenant F. X. Metzbower, Chaplain, U.S. Navy. In addition, a Battalion memorial service was conducted in John's honor so his many friends in the Company could offer their respects.

I wonder if Captain Kincade had any idea how very important it was for our mother to know Johnny had been given the last rites. If my mother did not know whether her son's life was in vain or sacrificed for some political stupidity, this August 3 letter would have assured her there was value to his time in 'Nam:

I didn't know a man that couldn't get along with the "Professor" as I called him. He was definitely one of the most likeable men I've ever known. Your son was someone new "boots" could look up to. In the time he was here, he established himself as one of the finest Marines of Mike Company. John had knowledge of all situations he might have encountered. Men under John knew this and respected him highly. His men would follow him anywhere...

To me, John was like a brother. I had known John before coming to the Nam. Many times John and I had very serious talks. . . . John helped me with problems and also kept me out of trouble at times. We had to split when we were given separate squads to serve in but we still kept in touch.

...I can look at John in only one way now: He'll no longer have worries. John is free, happy and at peace now. He served his country in the highest possible manner. He didn't disgrace his family as some boys do when they evade the draft. John gave his life for the things he loved and believed in. He wouldn't have had it any other way, I'm sure. John was definitely a great man and I respected him so.

Sincerely,

Jerry E. Butz

The following letter was written by a classmate of Johnny's who must have been only twenty when he wrote it.

Dear Mr. & Mrs. Guldan,

After I heard about John's death I began reminiscing about the high school days when we ran cross-country together. . . He worked so hard at everything he did. . . .

We all got pretty tired and ached a lot after practice, John probably more than the rest of us because he never "dogged it." But all you ever heard coming out of his mouth was some silly wisecrack or song "She Wore Red Sweatpants" in the showers.

Well thinking about how great a person Johnnie was and how he always was making someone laugh, I came across a poem in our 1967 yearbook . . . the last stanza struck me as being particularly true of him. It says:

LET ME IN THE END BUT COME TO PEACE
AND LET PEOPLE SAY OF MY PATH:
THIS PLACE IS BETTER, IT KNEW HIS LAUGH.

. . . I'd like to thank you both, also, for bringing him into this world. . . . I really can't understand why he should have died but the one explanation that seems to fit best is that he did such a wonderful job of just being that God gave him his eternal reward a little early.

Sincerely,
Mike Celeski

My parents kept these letters with Johnny's letters in a wooden box under their bed. Mom told Joe that if he ever wanted to see the letters from Johnny, they were there and he was welcome to read them. Joe was twelve when Johnny was killed.

- - -

"I didn't know why he was there or what the purpose was," Joe says.

"Do you remember wanting to know that, or even being aware enough to think about it?" I ask Joe.

"Apparently not. I guess I would've asked, huh? I don't know. I was in my own stupid world," Joe replies.

The bits of Joe's memory are like pieces from different jigsaw puzzles trying to fit together. They look like they might connect, but when he brings them together the colors are all off and the shapes are not quite right. It is frustrating for him.

- - -

On August 13, Colonel G.E. Lawrence sent a letter with the casualty report and an instructional booklet on personal affairs. On August 19, we received a letter from a Phil Lamm, a cross-country teammate of Johnny's. Phil sent another letter on August 24, after receiving a response from my parents. General Lewis Wall sent a letter of sympathy on August 21. Major General C.F. Widdecke sent a letter of condolences on August 23. On August 30, a Marist Brother who had coached Johnny sent a letter to my parents praising Johnny's outstanding character. On August 31, General Creighton Abrams sent condolences from the U.S. Army. On November 6, General Chapman sent the Bronze Star with a letter from the President's office.

Not all letters were uplifting. Three months after Johnny gave his life for our country in the service of the U.S. Marine Corps, he was awarded the Bronze Star. A letter was sent home with the medal and its certificate. The letter was from a William K. Jones, representing the President. Although it included a detailed citation with a lengthy paragraph of Johnny's duties and actions, it could have been written for anybody who was in the war. Words such as "Throughout his period, Lance Corporal Guldan performed his duties in an exemplary and highly professional manner, working tirelessly, he expeditiously accomplished all assigned tasks and consistently provided his unit with outstanding communications support..." Did this make my parents feel any better?

I can't put into words the gratitude I have for those who put their feelings about Johnny in writing and shared them with us. I know it helped my parents because they kept these letters. It helps me to put Johnny to rest as I read them now. It's like I am putting his body back together and can lay it in the grave.

Back to School

Teach me to bear my loneliness

With a cheerful and courageous spirit.
—Mother's Petition To Mary

Going back to school that fall was like reentrance into life. As high school students in large schools, located in neighborhoods far from home, most of their classmates did not know Bill, Jim, Margie, and Eileen had a brother that was just killed in Vietnam. Yet, for myself, Joe, and Mick, going into sixth and seventh grade at the small school across the street from Christ the King, the kids and the teachers all knew what our family had just been through. I was not yet ready to get into the flow of normal life. The foreignness of a new classroom, a new teacher, new books and topics, each fall was magnified ten times over this year. Joe and I were beginning sixth grade. After Joe was held back in third grade we were in the same grade together and often the same classroom. Joe and I filed into our new sixth-grade schoolroom. I was assigned a desk in the first row, right in front of the teacher.

This was perfect for me because I loved asking and answering questions. Joe sat a few rows back. The first day of school, the Vietnam War came up. Immediately, I heard students mumbling. It felt like someone had reached inside me and squeezed my stomach. Then the teacher stood right in front of my desk and said, "We all know Joe's brother was killed in Vietnam." Joe's brother! What about me? It was almost as confusing and painful as hearing Johnny was killed, all over again. She didn't even look at me, right in front of her. Did she not remember I was there? I was one breath away from shouting out, "He was my brother too!" Yet, I said nothing. That teacher never said anything to me about my loss.

The principal of Kate Star Kellogg had half of the school go through an exercise together. All students from the upper grades were lined up in the hallway. Joe, Mick, and I were the few standing at the end of this activity. The principal asked a question and told us all to step forward if the answer was yes for them. The questions asked were; "Who has a family member that has been in a war? Who knows anyone in the Vietnam War?" Mickey stepped forward. Joe and I looked at him and followed. We weren't quite certain of this exercise, so Joe and I watched what Mickey did. It was strangely obvious to Mickey how the three of us stood out from the other students at the end of this exercise. Mickey believed this principal was trying to point out to the rest of the school that we had gone through something extraordinary, and they should be aware of that.

Mimi entered second grade at Kellogg that year. Her teacher, Mrs. Fogarty, did not acknowledge Johnny's death to her as she entered her new second-grade class early in September. It was not talked about. However, on that first day Mrs. Fogarty lost her fake teeth. They dropped to the floor when she was talking. What was that? Mimi wondered.

- - -

I watch as Mimi sees this vision in her mind's eye as she is telling me.

"Poor Mrs. Fogarty!" I say.

We both laugh. This was an enjoyable snippet of Mimi's memory.

- - -

Everything felt different. Everything we did, we did it with the knowledge that our brother was never to be a part of it. Washing the walls had been one of Johnny's chores. Mom quietly cried as she scrubbed, "He did a good job when washing the walls . . . and he never had to be told twice." Even Snowball brought on memories that troubled her. Not long after the funeral, a man with a van of dogs took Snowball away. When I asked where they were taking her, my mom just said Snowball was old, not feeling well, and wouldn't be coming back.

- - -

"We had to get out of the house because she would cry. She couldn't handle being in the house," Margie remembers.

- - -

Margie wanted desperately to talk about her brother, to be proud of him, to share her pride of him with her friends. She would not bring up the topic of Johnny to our mother. Margie didn't want Mom to be upset, so she didn't say anything. She held it in. In September 1970, Margie was beginning her junior year of high school. The song "I Feel Like I'm Fixin' To Die" by Country Joe & The Fish, was a song that hurt, every time Margie heard it. This popular single was played at a sock hop dance held early into the school year. Country Joe, a Vietnam veteran, wrote these lyrics:

> *Well come on mothers throughout the land*
> *Pack your boys off to Vietnam*
> *Come on fathers don't hesitate*
> *Send him out before it's too late*

The last stanza of this song goes:

> *Be the first one on your block to have your boy come home in a box*!

Margie was aware that our family was the first in our neighborhood to have "our boy come home in a box." She watched her friends and others laugh and clap as the song played while out one night. Margie ran in the bathroom and cried. She was angry. She pulled away from her girlfriends. Margie felt they could not relate to her because she was now aware of something bigger.

- - -

"Every time I met a Vietnam vet, even though I didn't know him, I'd say thank you," Margie tells me.

- - -

A simple thank you from a cute teenage girl must have been a ray of sunshine for a returning Vietnam vet. At the age of twenty-one, Margie married a Vietnam veteran, Jerry McAloon. Jerry was several years older than her and, like many vets, he would not talk about his experience in Vietnam. Margie often woke him from his nightmares about it and still he did not utter a word about his time in Nam.

Joe Heeney was a returning veteran who understood the isolation Margie felt with her friends. Joe stood about six feet tall.

When he had left for Nam, he weighed 225 lbs. He arrived home safely at the svelte weight of 147 lbs. Johnny refers to Joe's "cushy" life in his letters. It may have been "cushy" compared to a bush Marine, yet Joe's tour involved a constant state of sleep and nutrition depravation. When Joe was sent home, he went directly to Okinawa where he spent three days. He was then sent on to Hawaii, then to Edwards Air Force Base in California, then reentrance to civilian life in Los Angeles LAX airport. His travel from Okinawa to Los Angeles was within a 24-hour time span. There was no debriefing. Even the military did not seem to care what he had seen or what he had learned in his thirteen months in Nam. They were done with him and that was that. After Joe arrived back in Chicago, he rarely left the apartment he shared with his mom. Joe was compelled to stay close to the TV because of his buddies that were still in Vietnam. He watched news continually. He often felt antsy. For years after, he suffered anxiety attacks and experienced a sensation of being uncomfortable in his own skin.

On the bulletin board in Margie and Eileen's bedroom they pinned a photo of Johnny next to a magazine clipping with the words, "The good die young." I went into their room and stared at these items. It helped to see that they believed my brother died. Yet, I did not like the saying, "The good die young." It was so confusing. If I was good, was I going to die young? And if I didn't, then was I bad? What about my parents? They were good. They were old. What about Moses? He was one of God's favorites. He certainly did not die young. If you think about anything too much, it eventually doesn't make sense.

Mickey had dreams about Johnny. In some of those dreams, he forgot what Johnny looked like. In one, he was angry at Johnny for not coming home. He believed Johnny was still alive, missing in action. Once he awoke to a slap on the head and no one was there. Mickey believed that was Johnny's doing for being mad at him.

- - -

"At thirteen you think stupid things like that. I never went through the right kind of closure because Mom didn't want us to see his body. I think, as a kid, from I don't know how old, it isn't easy to see someone dead but ya gotta let them see someone dead. Ya know, I mean it's just that simple. That's part of the closure process," Mickey tells me while reflecting on those dreams.

- - -

That fall of 1970, the house was left to my mother and Bonnie. Most of us went off to school each day, Dad to work, Patti and Mariann were at college. During this time, Mom went to Johnny's gravesite almost daily. Bonnie was with her. None of us were aware Mom was going to the cemetery so regularly. To Bonnie this was normal. It was what she knew.

It didn't take long before our visits to the farm were enjoyable again, at least for Mickey, Joe, myself, Chris and Mimi. Bonnie was too young to know whether she enjoyed it. The older kids had friends and responsibilities back in Chicago that rarely lost out to a trip to the farm with us younger kids. I was a baby when we acquired the farm. As I grew, the farm became a part of me. My dreams were often set with adventures on the farm. I loved to roam its back fields, discovering new valleys, woods, and streams. They never ceased. Yet my father stopped haying and buying more animals. I think it was the summer of '71 when Dad auctioned off all of the farm equipment and remaining cattle. My parents held on to the land and horses, but it was no longer a working farm. We continued to go there for a week at a time or long weekends, but no longer for the whole summer.

Things changed, but no one talked about it. Not even when the opportunity came up when the U.S. government offered my parents professional counseling services. They declined. Mickey and Jimmy were aware of this offer and our parents' refusal. According to Jim, Mom and Dad simply did not have a clue about life. Jim turned to heavy drinking, smoking pot, and questioning authority at every turn. He felt he had only his peers to learn from during his high school years.

- - -

"Their communication style was inadequate as far as I'm concerned, looking back. Making mistakes in life that I didn't have to—I could've been more productive and less self-destructive had I had the opportunity to communicate effectively with a mentor or parent or somebody . . . whatever. I don't remember talking to Mom at all," Jim says.

- - -

Tom Wernig, Johnny's foxhole buddy, arrived at our house in his dress blues in the spring of 1971. This was a few months after he was discharged. Tom had wanted to meet his buddy's family whom he had come to know through Johnny and his letters. He and his family continued to stay in touch through letters and visit each other. Even Tom's parents and my parents became friends and visited each other for years after. The second time Tom came to visit, he drove to Chicago with three of his five brothers. It was summer 1971. Tom and his brothers arrived at our house all wearing bell bottoms. They teased my brothers about their stove-pipe jeans. After their visit, I made myself a pair of bell bottoms by adding bandana material between the seams and did the same for my brothers. If I had known Johnny swore never to wear bell bottoms, I probably would not have done it.

Denise

One never does get over the experience of war. Residual inner conflicts from such an experience stay with one indefinitely.
> —Robert Jay Lifton, *Home From the War*,
> Andy Murphy obituary

Denise continued to listen to Johnny's tapes over and over again, up in her room, alone. It was very difficult for Denise's mother to see her engulfed in such despair. Her daughter was at an age where decisions are made that ultimately set your path for life. Denise would most likely make pivotal choices while influenced by this tragedy. This is the ripple effect of war.

In the fall of 1970, Denise went back for her second year at Ottumwa College. She got to be good friends with an Ottumwa classmate named Marcia. Marcia stole the master key that fall. Denise and Marcia used the key to sneak into the cafeteria at night and steal food. Soon Marcia got a little bolder and stole a test from one of the faculty offices. Denise knew this was going overboard yet went along with it. The school authorities went all out to find the current owners of the master key. Teachers stayed up all night and staked out locations they thought the thieves might visit next. It was not long before Denise and Marcia were caught.

It was right after Christmas break when Denise placed the hardest phone call she ever had to make. She called her parents to tell them she was kicked out of Ottumwa College. Mr. and Mrs. Racky were so very disappointed. Denise did not go back to live at home. It was a fresh year for 1971 and she tried to make a go of it in Iowa City with her new friend Marcia. Denise and Marcia roomed together and were able to get odd jobs to pay the bills. Their plans were to go back to school at an Iowa public college, not Ottumwa. Yet Denise's motivation to return to school in Iowa was lukewarm at best. The year and a half she had spent at Ottumwa did not produce the grades of a good student. This struggle alone won over her desire to try to make it on her own in Iowa.

Denise returned home and enrolled in a local college. She was twenty-one years old. It was upon this return to the Chicago area when Denise met Mark Page, a Vietnam veteran, and moved in with him. Mark had a drug addiction and physically abused Denise. Denise took the abuse for only so long and one day left. She went back home, bruised face and all, with the promise to her parents to go back to school and maintain a job at the same time so that she could pay them rent. No sooner had Denise unpacked at home, when she received a phone call from an old high school classmate, Terri Archibald. Terri was calling with a plan to go to nursing school. Chicago Public Schools was offering a licensed practical nurse (LPN) degree through Holy Cross. Denise signed up and completed her degree.

Denise got her first LPN gig at a long-term care facility in Oak Forest, Illinois. There, Denise gained valuable clinical experience. In the early seventies, LPNs were treated like glorified candy stripers with an hourly wage. The defining moment that gave Denise the impetus to continue her education in nursing was during a particular busy period at the Oak Forest facility. Denise was running from room to room trying to get the patients fed. They were understaffed with a full house. Denise asked nurse Aurentz, one of the RNs on duty, if she would help feed the patients.

"RNs do not feed patients," Mrs. Aurentz responded.

That was all Denise needed. Inspired by Johnny's work ethic and positive attitude to never give up, she continued her education and received her Registered Nursing degree in 1977, at the age of twenty-eight. Denise has stuck with nursing and is currently working toward her master's degree.

In 1970, Denise was considered by most a beautiful, vibrant young girl, with a full life ahead of her. Yet, to this day she has not married or had children. She does not know the whereabouts of her high school ring and never saw it again after she mailed it to Johnny before he went to 'Nam. It didn't matter to her. At one time, she had a grenade ring that Johnny had mailed. This was a metal pin with the circular end that is inserted into a hand grenade and pulled to detonate the device. It was his symbolic ring for her. She didn't know where that was either. Johnny had also given Denise his Marine ring and his Marist High School ring. She didn't have any of them. It was like her life fell into a sink hole with Johnny, rings, motherhood, and all. She climbed out of that sink hole after a few years, when realizing she would never have a fairy-tale life without Johnny. With the thought that she had to make a life on her own, Denise found a good career in nursing. She's had jobs, cars, boyfriends, homes, even a fiancé at one time, but nothing has ever truly been a part of her the way Johnny was. As the years have gone on and my family celebrate births, weddings, holidays, and deaths, Denise has been a part of these events. She has been like a sister-in-law.

- - -

In January of 2007, I talk to Denise about the period of 1969 to 1970 for the first time. I know it may still be an untouchable topic for her. This is an unplanned interview. I don't have questions laid out or a tape recorder present. I ask only a few questions. Our second interview is conducted in the spring of 2009. Denise had responded to my email inviting her to visit me in Michigan, saying that May 23 would be a good weekend for her, adding, "It will be a good birthday." It is Johnny's birthday.

It is almost 8:30 a.m. I sit on my deck preparing when I see my first Monarch butterfly of the season. It flies right over my head, big and beautifully marked! Moments later Denise comes out and joins me. We sit, drinking coffee, on the large wooden deck off the kitchen of my Grand Haven home. A light breeze is coming off Lake Michigan a quarter mile away. I seize the opportunity.

"Denise, would you mind if I asked you some questions about your life following Johnny's death?" I ask.

"Now is the perfect time," Denise replies.

Tears begin to form in her eyes. I want so much to know her story and how, after forty years, she has lived with this chasm in her heart. The tears alone, forming so quickly at the slightest mention, are almost enough in the way of words.

"I'll try to keep away from the real emotional stuff," I say.

However, everything is emotional, thirty-nine years later. I frantically write, knowing there is no recorder to back me up. While I write and listen I think of the next question, hoping it's one centered on bringing her loss to light. I tell Denise about the twenty-year-old Iraq War widows I had watched on the news that weekend. These women had formed a support group for widows of the fallen Iraq War soldiers. Most of them were close to twenty years old. There is a stereotype with widows, the reporter explained, that you cannot truly be one unless you are old. The young war widows did not find much support or understanding for their great loss. Others thought that since they had their whole life ahead of them, their loss was not considered significant.

"I didn't have any support, not even my mother," Denise tells me.

She says this quietly while looking past me, not focusing on anything. I feel as if she is somewhere else. I am somewhere else. Watching the tears fall down her cheek brings me back to those raindrops on the car window. However, these tears were running free and not being chased like the raindrops on that cold January night in 1970. One tear establishing residence on her cheek boldly remains there throughout the interview.

After the weekend visit, we hug tightly as we say our good-byes.

"We have to talk some more," Denise says.

I am relieved to hear that, not only for this book but for Denise.

On Wednesday, April 14, 2010, I have my third of four interviews with Denise, still without a tape recorder. We meet on Van Buren and Paulina Street, just west of Chicago's Loop. Denise has just come from a dental appointment on the Rush campus. At one time Denise had worked in Rush's OR (operating room) and she continues to go back to the doctors at Rush for her personal health care. Denise waits in her little black Toyota Corolla in front of Moretti's restaurant until I arrive. When she sees me, she gets out of her car and we walk into the restaurant together. There are only a few customers. We settle into a large booth next to a west-facing window. The five p.m. sun pours in. We begin catching up right away, mostly about doctors and health issues. Then I pull out my notebook and ask her if it is all right if I ask her a few questions. Denise knows that this is a reason we meet. But I ask her again, just to make sure she doesn't have second thoughts.

"I have some specific questions, to fill in some of the detail around what we talked about last time," I say.

"Go ahead, what are your questions?"

Denise puts her hand on my open notebook and turns it slightly in her direction. I take this action as an attempt to convince herself she could do this. I start with some pretty simple questions.

"What's your middle name?"

"Marie."

"Where did you grow up, what was your address?"

"107th and Campbell."

"Did you attend St. John Fisher first through eighth grade?"

Denise begins nodding her head before I finish the questions.

"Did you go to Longwood High School?"

"Yes."

After this exercise of verifying basic information, I am confident Denise is ready to talk. We are off... One of the last questions I ask Denise is if she thinks she would have married had she not met Johnny. Tears fill her eyes again, and I watch these tears drop over the edge of her eyelids. Her bottom lip quivers as she answers in a barely audible tone.

"I wonder about that myself," she answers.

We hug tight. I walk away with a deeper understanding of the cost of war. It cost this beautiful young woman, with her whole adult life ahead of her, a family of her own. Denise has carried a sense of guilt her entire life, believing that all she had to do was say, "don't go," when Johnny asked her what he should do.

Denise's advice to others is to seek out support. Unlike back in 1970, so much help is available today.

Denise now lives in Evergreen Park, Illinois, only a few miles from the home where she grew up. She lives alone yet has a very busy life advancing her RN education, working multiple jobs, and maintaining long friendships. Denise and Neal continue to be friends. They live in the same neighborhood and run into each other often. For a while, they went for fast-paced walks together in the mornings. Denise listened to Neal's life trials and Denise informed him of events in hers. They even had moments to laugh together again.

Mariann

I am really confused about that whole period, Jimmy. I truly believe Johnny enlisted in the Marines because he wanted to "seek truth and liberty and justice for all." I also believe he thought by enlisting he could prove himself to Mom and Dad. I don't think they have the capacity to try to understand that or the ability to even consider it. Or maybe, it's just overwhelmingly painful

> *for them to contemplate. Someday I hope I might be able to talk with them about these feelings and what it was like for them—to understand who they are as people and as parents. I keep trying to understand.*
>
> —Mariann Guldan DaCosta, *May 18, 1995,*
> *to Jim Guldan*

Like Denise, my sister Mariann had an especially hard time with Johnny's death. Yet, Mariann's reaction was one of rebellion rather than withdrawal. I did not understand Mariann's feud with my parents. This difficult dynamic between Mariann and my parents was magnified with the impact of Johnny's loss. Mariann had not liked the way Dad treated Johnny. His dreadful life in Vietnam and death there added gallons of fuel to that fire.

- - -

I sit with my Uncle Mike and Aunt Diane in the sun room of their brick bungalow in Evanston. They recall Mariann during 1970.

"I think Mariann had a tough time," Aunt Diane says.

"She would have been going on 19. She was born in '51, in December of 1951," Uncle Mike adds.

Uncle Mike knows everyone's middle and confirmation name in addition to their birthday. He can usually recall an anecdotal story with the birth of each niece and nephew. He amazes me in that way.

"As I remember, Eileen (my mom) was talking to Mariann once and Mariann had said, 'Mom, it's happened. That's the way it is, you gotta move on.' And Eileen said, 'Well Mariann, what would you do if you were in my position? Just what would you do?' And Mariann just really didn't have much of an answer for her because Eileen got so upset, ya know. . . . I don't know if there were words between Mariann and Eileen. I don't know if they were necessarily, ya know, bad. And she [Mariann] was, ya know, right next to Johnny in age so she would be the one that was suffering too," Aunt Diane recalls.

"Yeah. That's right. Sure," Uncle Mike says as Aunt Diane finishes.

"That changed your mom for life," Aunt Diane says.

Mariann speaks with me about this time in 2004, thirty-four years later:

"I thought maybe I was responsible. If I had been a better person, good, then Johnny wouldn't have had to die. I couldn't say that to my parents. I couldn't risk having them say the words that made it true. I kept it all inside and withdrew further and further from them. I know I was in a state of denial and shock over losing Johnny for several years after he died. He was my hero and our country needed his help. He was important and so very special. I kept making up stories in my head about him being on a secret mission and under cover. The ending was always the same. He always returned and we lived happily ever after. That didn't happen. To this day, I'm still trying to come to grips with that time. It unleashed so much fear and anxiety in me, not that it wasn't there already. I didn't know how to cope with the loss, so I turned to someone, anyone, who could offer me the slightest attention and understanding. Someone who made me feel special because I thought that was love. It sure felt like love."

This love was Bruce.

- - -

Bruce was at our house to take Mariann back to school in the early fall of 1970. Mariann and "this guy" did not say much to my parents. They didn't talk to any one of us or laugh or joke. The rest of us might well have not been around. It seemed they wanted to leave as soon as they could. Mariann was starting her second year at Mount Mary College. She had never been excited about attending Mount Mary. Johnny had known that through her letters to him her freshman year. It was not long after she started her sophomore year she found a reason not to continue on at Mount Mary. Mariann, one month shy of nineteen, dialed Beverly8-2370 with a bold finger and the emotional support of Bruce by her side. She knew what to expect on the other end of the phone line and was not surprised at my parents' reaction.

"You did this to spite us! Why, why would you do this?" Mom spat out.

It was a Saturday afternoon and my cousins and I were in the basement rehearsing a play I had written when we heard my mom yell out upstairs. The three of us stopped and looked up. I had never heard her sound like that. I went up the stairway to check it out. The door was open. I saw my mom on the phone and my dad nearby. My mom was very upset. Her ears got red when she was excited, and her ears were very red. My father stood in the kitchen, not far from the phone. He did not seem to need a detailed explanation from my mother to know what prompted that response. He took the phone.

"Come home, Mariann," Dad said.

It was because of Mariann my mom yelled out. I didn't know what she had done. I didn't know my sister Mariann very well, and she seemed like a troublemaker, but not mean, not a bad person.

"Don't get married. Come home, have the baby, and put it up for adoption," Dad told her.

Dad talked calmly to Mariann. He was quick with advice for her to live at home until she had the baby and then put it up for adoption. On the other end of the phone, apart from a world I was able to understand at the time, was Mariann. She was insulted and infuriated that Dad would ask her to give up a baby. She could not fathom giving up another life after losing her brother. Now Mom and Dad wanted her to suffer another loss. The thought of living at home was as unthinkable as adoption.

Through the crack of the basement door, I watched my parents in distress, again. The anger and bitterness I saw in my mother's face at that moment were not originally part of her, yet she was now a casualty of war. I wanted to beg Mariann to not do whatever it was that upset them so, to not hurt them. But instead I closed the door and went back to rehearsing, telling my cousins that Mariann was on the phone. With just that explanation, they understood the commotion.

Mariann left Mount Mary College and home, eighteen and pregnant. We received little news of her. Most of us were not aware that on January 30, 1971, Bruce and Mariann got married at Eastern Illinois University, where Mariann was enrolled. Patti was the only one from our family who attended, with my mother's blessing, not Dad's. Denise, Neal, Pachol, and a few more of Mariann's close friends were also at the ceremony held in a dark, dank chapel on campus. Mariann finally attended the school she wanted. She completed one semester there before her child was born. Mariann named him John, after Johnny and asked Denise to be his godmother. Bruce and Mariann would not talk about Johnny's death for four or five years.

- - -

"Mariann wouldn't even accept he was dead for several years," Bruce says.

Bruce recalls his feelings during his and Mariann's tumultuous beginning as if reading them off a slip of paper he had tucked in a shirt pocket over his heart. Their world revolved around the loss of Johnny. Bruce, admittedly, wanted to make it better by agreeing to name their first son after Johnny.

"I don't believe I had a choice. I just wanted to please her," Bruce says with a tired note of acceptance. And then he adds, matter-of-factly, "Mariann really didn't want to be married. I thought: I'm in love with this girl. I want her to love me. I wonder what I can do."

Bruce tells me and figuratively tucks those feelings back in that pocket. He adds, "I was a twenty-two-year-old kid trying to figure out what the hell was going on."

- - -

Mariann focused her undivided attention on her son John. He grew up amid the pressure to live up to an icon he had never met and in competition with his own father for his mother's love. Mariann filed for divorce thirty years later, while in the midst of her battle with breast cancer. Although Bruce never received the much-desired love from my sister Mariann, "they shared a lot mentally," Bruce had once told me. Mariann and Bruce's union left a positive impact upon this earth. They raised three kind and intelligent sons. And Bruce continues to enjoy many grandchildren from that bond.

In 2006, while caring for Mariann during the last days of her battle with breast cancer, my sisters and I found a poem she had written in 1996. In it, she spoke of a life enveloped with sadness and despair after Johnny was killed. These feelings were a significant part of her life the thirty-six years after his death. In Louise Hay's book You Can Heal Your Life, Hay states that a probable cause of cancer is from a deep hurt, a deep secret or grief, eating away at the self. Mariann's writings, discovered after her death, revealed the unknown depth of her heartache:

Now to have things alive and interesting it must be personal, it must come from the "I": what I know and feel. For that is the only great and interesting thing. That is the only truth you know, that nobody else does.

In order for me to write, I need to know and feel that I am important. That I have interesting things to say. I am important.

Denise and Mariann did not stay close. They did not get together to share their feelings of loss. Johnny had been a part of them and now it was too hard for the two of them to be with each other and not have Johnny there. This brought on a feeling of isolation Mariann wrote about in her poem, *Blown Apart*.

Blown Apart

You can feel the wind blow through your insides. It's cold. It makes you walk in a hunched up manner. You try to pull your skin tighter to your bones to feel warmth again. You pull everything that is part of you close. You become a miser and hide yourself from strangers that pass you. You're trying to become invisible because if no one can see you, then the hurt must not be there either.

To the outside, your body looks normal, except for the dropped shoulders and the eyes that don't see and the face that's scrunched up like the skin of a raisin. You may look a little smaller to others. Your gait appears a little out of step as you tiptoe around the shadows thrown by people passing. Someone reaches out and you vanish. You become like one of the shadows you are trying to avoid.

Your heart feels like a ghost town or Japan after the atom bomb was dropped on its cities and people melted and the earth became bare. All that's left is the cold and constant wind that blows through the eerie landscape and holes of your soul. Dust moving, never landing. Meaning is gone and like the dust you scatter in the wind, not touching but avoiding.

Mom worked the rest of her life trying to fix her relationship with Mariann. Twenty-eight years later, my mother and I talk about Mariann while we stand in my kitchen. She tells me how she and Patti and Mariann had gotten together for Mariann's son's wedding. They all went out shopping for dresses. I watch my mother as she looks out my kitchen window onto the empty street. She tells me she thought it was a good visit and things were on the mend.

5 Minutes of Sorry

Ten million soldiers to the war have gone,
Who may never return again.
Ten million mothers' hearts must break
For the ones who died in vain.
Head bowed down in sorrow
In her lonely years...

—Alfred Bryan,
I Didn't Raise My Boy to Be a Soldier, 1915

My mother was forty-three years old when her eldest son was taken from her violently and senselessly at a tender age of twenty. She continued to raise the other twelve of us along with the burden of her son's death. Five of the twelve remaining children were teenagers, in the '70s, no less.

During their weekly phone calls to each other in the fall of 1970 and into the winter, my mom and her sister Annie Laurie talked about their memories of Johnny and how he was a good example to the younger cousins. They believed in the theory that the day you will die is written by the time you are born, possibly as early as when you are conceived. They also believed that the way you die is determined by the life you live. As they applied this to Johnny, they knew he had died with honor, doing an honorable thing, and therefore lived an honorable life.

We were told we weren't going to celebrate Christmas of 1970. Instead, Mom and Dad took the ten youngest to Arizona in a rented Winnebago to visit Dad's cousin in Tucson. Dad drove the whole way, there and back. My parents said the rosary each morning as we got on the road. We needed every bead they prayed. It was a treacherous trip. One night, while some of us were asleep in a motel room, a drunk plowed into the wall of the motel, inches from our parked Winnebago where others were also asleep. Several of us that had been startled awake ran out to the motel balcony. We watched as the drunk got out of the car stumbling and confused. He was holding a brown paper bag. He started to run and my dad chased after him. I screamed for my dad to come back. The police came and everything was fine except for the noise of fixing that hole in the wall.

Then Dad took us to see Hoover Dam in the Winnebago. We drove over a mountain pass much too narrow for that beast of a machine. Dad skillfully maneuvered past a truck hauling a horse trailer along the narrow, two-lane road, bare of any guardrails. This road coiled around the mountain like a lasso dug into a heifer's neck. I'll never forget that little yellow Volkswagen I saw when I looked out the side window of the Winnebago. It was smashed against the cliff wall about fifty yards down, almost directly below us. I wondered about the people in that car as I tried to determine how long ago it had happened. Based on the brightness of its yellow paint, it seemed recent, and I breathed deep. Dad exuded confidence, which gave me confidence we would not be joining that Volkswagen. Staying calm, he talked instructions to the driver of the truck pulling the horse trailer, as they slowly passed each other. Dad had rolled down his window and the driver of the horse trailer had done the same as they coached each other through this dangerous maneuver. The two of them were like mission control talking the astronauts through a lunar landing. I figured it was the rosary that guided us to the inside lane and got both vehicles through safely.

This trip continued to present challenges for my dad. The first time it rained, we discovered the windshield wipers didn't work. It rained so hard that Dad kept pulling to the side of the road to wipe the windshield with a special solution. It was the material he used on the little mirror he stuck in his patients' mouths to keep it from fogging up, he explained. I thought he was so smart. Watching my dad during that Christmas time, when our lives were in such upheaval, made me feel we could get through anything.

After we returned from our Christmas trip, Grandpa landed in the hospital for continued treatment of his throat cancer. Grandpa felt Chicago was a great city, offering the best hospitals and doctors. He felt if he couldn't find a doctor in Chicago to cure him, no doctor could. He chose Wesley Memorial Hospital. Although it was located in Chicago, same as us, it was still quite a drive for my mom when she visited him there. Dealing with the death of her son, the pregnancy of her teenage daughter, and the illness of both her parents, Mom found companionship in Aunt Barbara during their two hour round trips to Wesley.

"Oh my gosh, Eileen, I thought I'd never get out of the house," Aunt Barbara told my mom as she accelerated on to the Dan Ryan expressway. Mom was in the passenger seat with Aunt Barbara at the wheel of Grandpa's 1965 Oldsmobile 98.

"Was it the dogs or kids?" Mom asked.

"Jean and Anne were fighting again. Leaving both of them in charge may not be the best of ideas. They need to be quiet while Jim is sleeping. That weekend night shift is murder on him after working all week," Aunt Barbara said.

"I have the same problem with Margie and Eileen from time to time. They are just too close, in every way. They'll be the best of friends when they are our age." The kids were all back in school and restless on these long weekends that were spent mainly indoors. "Barb, I know what a sacrifice this trip is for you each Saturday. I can't tell you how much I appreciate it," Mom added. She stared out the window into the brightness of the just-risen sun glaring on the concrete and cars surrounding them. It was just past the holidays, cold and barren outside. Mom and Aunt Barbara, neither of them complainers by nature, took this time as an opportunity to air the negativity of their lives and kiss it away.

"Margie and Eileen are my saviors for taking care of Bonnie while I'm gone. Although I wish she was with me. I know she can be a handful and that would make it difficult to spend time with Dad, but having Bonnie around brings a happiness I can't explain. She's a little trouble-maker but so adorable with her tangled hair and toothless smile. And she loves her go-go boots! Margie and Eileen bought them for her. They'll all be watching

American Bandstand today and will be dancing with the Go-Go Girls, boots and all. She wears them everywhere, even to bed, if I didn't make her take them off!" The mood lifted. Aunt Barbara was relieved to see my mother smile.

- - -

"Your mother was very sad at this time. She was suffering," Aunt Barbara says as I interview her and Uncle Jim.

- - -

It was during these drives that Aunt Barbara learned how my mother endured the death of a child. My baby sister Bonnie was her beacon in the harbor as Mom floated through this sea of sadness in her life. Aunt Barbara learned Bonnie was not the only way my mom made it through.

"How do you get through the hardest days?" Aunt Barbara had asked during one of these drives to the hospital.

"I allow five minutes a day to feel sorry for myself," my mother replied.

Most of us never saw these five minutes. Joe did, on a few occasions. It was always in the laundry room. The laundry room was like a ship's galley. It was enclosed area in the basement with doors at both ends and a wood plank floor you had to step up onto. In addition to the washer, dryer, and laundry chute, there was a triple cast-iron utility sink stood below windows that had glass you couldn't see through yet let the light in. Mom spent a lot of time in the laundry room. I think it was her haven. Joe caught her eating her dinner down there once. Occasionally, I caught Mom talking to herself in there. I thought this was her way of arguing back to my father. Although, I often wished she would give it to him straight to his face. Not that I wanted his feelings to be hurt. I just wanted her to feel better. I suppose she believed this was how a good Catholic wife should behave—obedient.

Mom's visits to see Grandpa at Wesley Hospital came to an end. He was eventually brought back home. There was not much more they could do for him. On the morning of February 23, 1971, I went into my parents' bedroom to see if anyone was awake. I was an early riser. Mom and Dad were still in bed. I reached out and touched my mom's shoulder while standing at the side of their bed. Her head had been turned away. She slowly turned toward me. Her eyes were filled with tears.

"Grandpa died," she told me.

I had prayed so hard for God to stop Grandpa from suffering. I knew that might mean taking him to heaven. I couldn't tell my mother that. I felt terrible. I turned and walked out of their bedroom.

Not long after Grandpa's funeral, Joe walked into the laundry room on a Sunday afternoon and saw Mom quietly crying as she sorted piles of dirty clothes. He turned around and walked out. Joe didn't want to upset her more by asking what she was crying about and what he needed to ask her was not that important. He headed back upstairs. If she was crying about Johnny, Joe did not want to hear about that. If she was crying about Grandpa, Joe wouldn't know what to do. He might start to cry with her.

A lot of things stayed the same between my parents after Johnny was gone. Dad continued to have his occasional outbursts at our mother, screaming about a missing check entry in the checkbook. One day Mickey had an idea. He thought he could stop Dad's outbursts. He would talk to Mom the next time Dad yelled at him. Once she heard what Mickey told her, he knew she would put her foot down and tell Dad he should not talk to his children like that anymore. Joe realized change was needed and was willing to go along with Mickey's plan.

"Mom, Dad said I was lazy because I didn't bring the garbage out. He said he was going to belt me next time!" Mickey told Mom.

Mom was in the laundry room loading the washer and mumbling things to herself about conversations she needed to have with the milkman, the grocer, and most likely her husband when he got home that evening. With all of this thinking going on in her head, she was still able to hear what Mickey said.

"Your dad is hard at work, earning money for you to have plenty of food and wear the shoes you have on. Listen to what he tells you to do and he won't spank you!"

Mom continued right on shuffling laundry from one machine to the next.

"Well that didn't work!" Joe exclaimed to Mickey.

It was then Joe realized the respect our mother had for our father. Our parents kept any marital stress that may have been caused by Johnny's death from the public. That included us kids. It wasn't until I was an adult that my mother told me her and Dad almost divorced. She didn't say what it was that made her hang in there that allowed time to dull the memory and soften the edges on the bayonets of blame she aimed at my father.

- - -

I talk with my brother Bill in 2009 about how our parents were toward each other after Johnny's death.

"I know it probably took a toll on 'em." Bill chuckles the type of chuckle one does when trying not to cry.

"I think Mom tried to be strong and not show any emotions. But I think when she was alone—" There is silence on the other end of the phone, "...it tore her up." Bill is crying as he finishes.

"Your mother rested in you kids. No need to disturb that peace." Uncle John tells me this in a separate interview with him.

- - -

Uncle John purposely did not talk about war and religion with my father. They were both opinionated men and their opinions around these issues did not travel in the same direction. Yet it was for different reasons now that Uncle John did not talk about Vietnam or Johnny's reason for joining the service to my mother and father. Uncle John stayed silent on any topic related to Johnny because he respected it as a "topic of silence." He knew my parents were suffering. He didn't want to poke his opinions into their field of pain.

- - -

I had never asked my mother or father for their memories of this time. Was it out of respect for their determination not to talk about Johnny's death and their suffering around it that I remained silent? Was I doing what my Uncle John did consciously: honoring a moratorium on the whole topic, keeping it buried, while now it is safe to exhume? Or is it simply because I am ready?

Twenty-eight years later, weeks after Mom died, Bonnie spoke briefly with our father about these very days. He was distraught over Mom's sudden death, crying often. Bonnie watched him struggle. She wanted to help pull him out of his emotional stupor.

"How did you and Mom deal with Johnny's death, that terrible tragedy, that grief?" she asked Dad.

"We hugged a lot. We didn't cry much," he said.

I was listening to the audio book titled *Lean In,* by Sheryl Sandberg, while driving to work in 2014. This book is about achieving corporate success for women and has nothing to do with the topics in my book, yet when I heard, "Ignoring the issue is a classic survival technique," I thought—that's us. That's what we were doing when we didn't talk about it—we were surviving.

Move to Suburbs

An occurrence in which many white people move out of a city as more and more people of other races move in.
—Merriam Webster,
definition of white flight

The summer of 1972 brought the first steps toward ending the "Vietnam Conflict" and the Watergate break in. For us, it brought a move to the suburbs. Two years earlier, when Dad had brought up the idea of moving to Australia, my mother had not wanted any part of it. She didn't want to be far from her parents and the neighborhood where she grew up. I imagine she also had not wanted to leave the home Johnny was yearning for when he returned from Vietnam. Our Beverly house now bore the constant memories of Johnny. His laughter was in the walls, his footprints on the floors. Now, both Johnny and her father were gone and her mother growing weaker, not expected to live much longer. After all of that loss, my mother was willing to move.

Dad told us the reason we were moving was because the neighborhood was changing and that we had to get out. We moved west, to the suburb of Palos Park. My parents took the first offer for our house. They sold it for $25,000, the same price they had paid for it fourteen years earlier. Our beautiful brick bungalow with its leaded windows was replaced by a modern house, half the size, for more than twice the cost. Even at thirteen years old, I was aware that it was a bad move financially. They didn't seem to care. We packed up our furniture and personal items and left our Beverly home. Aunt Barbara referred to our move as "the downsizing." I think she was referring to more than just the size of the house.

Moving to the Palos house brought a different aspect to Johnny's death. Mimi, Bonnie, and Mom continued to visit Johnny's gravesite often. Although it was now several miles further from our house, my father's office was still only a few blocks away. When going to Dad's office, Mom stopped at Mt. Olivet Cemetery, with Mimi and Bonnie in tow. She often picked up the checks patients had made out to Dad and deposited them into the bank. Now in Palos Park, my father drove past the cemetery on his way to work in the morning, and again as he headed home at night. Yet, he never pulled in. He looked straight ahead, paying attention only to traffic.

One of the first things Bonnie did in our new home in the suburbs was get to know the operator. She learned that she could dial 0 and have somebody to talk to. Her conversations didn't last very long. She did this repeatedly when Mom was not in earshot. She took the phone off the receiver, pushed the button zero, and when the operator said hello, Bonnie replied with, "Shut up!" and hung up. She knew those two words too well for a five year old. Bonnie repeated this several times from a wall phone in the garage, when Mom was not in earshot. She climbed up onto the washing machine, right below the phone, and sat on it to conduct this drill. Eventually one operator called back. Bonnie answered and hung up on her. The operator called again. This time my mother answered. After the operator informed her what had been going on Mom said, "Oh no, you must have the wrong house. I'm right here with my daughter. She couldn't do that." After hanging up, Mom looked at Bonnie, who then admitted to the crime. Mom was more impressed than angry with Bonnie.

Bonnie's antics and the effort in caring for her took my mom's attention away from her pain. But there was more than this. Bonnie, now my window into viewing our mother at that time, saw her in private like no one else. No one saw her grieve like Bonnie saw her. Her grieving was the gravesite visiting ritual. Her grieving was her quiet moments, with slumped shoulders, thoughts a million miles away. Only Bonnie was with her during these times. I don't know exactly when my mom came back to us. It was a slow process. Sometimes when I caught her mumbling to herself I asked who she was talking to. She said, "God." Years went by and she didn't talk about Johnny or her feelings to anyone —maybe not even God. I guess getting us all settled into a new house and new schools was enough to fill her days and thoughts.

This new house had fewer rooms and only one floor! It was modern with a green shag rug and a cathedral ceiling. I felt like I was in the Brady Bunch house. It was a fresh place where we all could have a fresh start. However, I was entering into eighth grade when we made this move and I did not want anything to do with this fresh start. My parents had left their parents and their church in Beverly. They were now in a smaller, newer home with more space between them and their neighbors. Did they feel like fish out of water in Palos Park, as I did?

I was devastated by this move. The first day of school, Joe and I had to walk down this endless, busy road. The cars were going so fast and there were no sidewalks. We had to walk in a ditch off to the side of the road. An unleashed German shepherd protecting a big white house on a hill barked and barked at us. We kept our eyes glued on it, ready to I don't know what, if it decided to run across that road to get us. Once we were at school, hundreds of us piled into one large room and we were assigned to our homeroom teacher. I went with Joe but I was in the wrong homeroom. By the time I finally got to the correct room, I had missed the beginning of class. Then we had to find our next classroom. I wandered into the gymnasium where the PE teacher helped me. After a long day of switching classes and sitting with strangers for lunch, I had that long treacherous walk home. I lay in bed the rest of the day with a splitting headache. I was sick to my stomach. My mom kept coming in to check on me. She said I had a migraine. I cried and cried and begged her to move back to Beverly. Mom gently rubbed my head and calmly said, "We'll see." She looked at me with her head tilted to one side and her brow furrowed. She was very concerned. My mom's family had moved from an area where the Dan Ryan expressway now runs through, to Beverly, when she was a young girl of fourteen. This was the same age I was as my mother nursed me patiently through my migraine.

I returned to school the next day and the rest of the week. I soon figured out we would not be moving back. I wanted to be in my home on Oakley, close to my cousins and my best friend, Lyn. In the suburbs, I felt removed from real life. There was no discussion of Johnny among us. I wanted a connection to our life when he was in it, the way it was before. A connection did come with us to Palos Park however. There was a small, wooden box under my parents' king-size bed. This wooden box was full of Johnny's letters. They were letters to my parents and to others, all from Johnny. There were also letters from others addressed to my parents.

"You should read Johnny's letters," my mother told me.

I wasn't that interested. I read only a few. I only wanted to know what it was like for him to be in war. Now, over forty years later, reading through this box of letters, I find the details I wanted. I am grateful my parents saved these.

After the 1972-1973 school year began, Marines came to our door once again. This time they delivered medals Johnny had earned. Bonnie was five years old. She watched these two men in uniform as they sat on the couches in front of the fireplace and talked quietly with Mom and Dad. Bonnie was worried these men would make her mom sad. The medals they brought my mom hung on the wall, in a frame, for years to follow.

Mom's gravesite visits continued. She was quiet at the graveyard with Bonnie. There was prayer, but little to no tears. Bonnie squabbled for Mom's attention from the dead. Mom shushed her and told her to pray. When they got home, Bonnie looked at Mom and thought the air had suddenly deflated from Mom's body. She wrapped her little arms around our mother. Mom attempted to assure Bonnie that she was okay, hugging Bonnie back and whispering, "It's okay." Bonnie knew this sadness was a result of the Santa man being gone. This man whose visit had made everyone so excited was now gone. Bonnie didn't question where he had gone or what happened to him. At five years old, she was concerned only with the fragility of her mother.

- - -

I ask Bonnie if she was ever worried for Mom.

"Yeah!" Bonnie says.

Tears begin to accumulate on the brim of her eyelids. She continues, "Well, I remember it mostly at home. She would just stop what she was doing and sit down on the bed."

- - -

During the many drives in the car with just Bonnie and Mom, stillness often settled in. Bonnie sat trapped in her car seat in the back and paid notice. She tried to talk to Mom to bring her out of her lonely state. Mom was far away, in a trance, sometimes murmuring to herself.

"Mom!" Bonnie called from the back seat.

She knew instantly when Mom went into this other world and was aware not to upset her during these episodes. When the car stopped and Mom unstrapped Bonnie, she held our mother's face between her two little hands and turned Mom's head to look at her, their faces inches apart. This little girl was worried her mother wouldn't come back if she strayed too far into this unknown that Bonnie could not see. Mom mourning over Johnny was mostly what Bonnie knew of our mother during her preschool and elementary years.

- - -

"I don't remember a time of her not being like that. As long as I remember, we were always goin' to the grave, all the time, several times a week. On the way to the office, on the way to taking me to the orthodontist, anything. . . The other kids would be at school, we'd go all the time."

This declaration is devoid of blame and full of strength, indicating a degree of inequity. Bonnie has a right to feel a sense of injustice about what was lost to her. Her response is expressive, it is healthy. This is the saddest interview I have done.

- - -

I first learn of Bonnie's visits to the cemetery with Mom when I interview her on August 16, 2008. Bonnie is now forty-one and married with children of her own. Our interview occurred on a weekend when Matt, her husband, had taken their three boys up to their lake house in Sturgis, Michigan. Bonnie married her high-school sweetheart, Matt, also the baby of a large family. Matt is an ophthalmologist, and Bonnie stays home to raise their six children and large yellow Labrador. Bonnie has decorated every inch of their beautiful, newly built home. She has impeccable taste and is very organized. This is a far cry from Bonnie's childhood appearance with her knotted hair, carrying her puppy, Pretty-Ugly. We have a fairly quiet interview, save a few infant screeches and gurgles, the phone ringing, the dog barking, and an occasional order thrown at her oldest daughter, Molly.

Bonnie watched our mother's sadness continue. Miraculously, Bonnie never felt responsible for this sadness of our mother. She was the light in my mother's valley of darkness. By the time she reached second grade, Bonnie expressed her feelings about being involved in loss on a funeral home calendar that hung in the kitchen:

I hope I never have to go there again, she wrote on it.

Today, Bonnie often goes to the gravesite where Mom, Dad, Johnny, Grandma, and Grandpa are buried. She was not repelled after visiting the cemetery time and time again as a small child and seeing her mother so sad at this place. Now the gravesites comfort her. She feels at home there, where she learned to commune with loved ones.

End of War

Vietnam, we have reached the end of the tunnel and there is no light there.

—Walter Kronkite, *CBS News* anchor

By 1973, Annie Laurie had begun her teaching career with her youngest now in school. Her life in Michigan was very busy. She did not pay much attention to what continued to happen in Vietnam or the politics around the war—at least not until her oldest son, Johnny, received a draft number. It was a terrible feeling to know her son might suffer the same fate as her sister's son. Then the Vietnam War ended. Their family was spared.

Back in Beverly, my cousins continued their daily life without me. It was past the midway point of the school year when my cousin Anne's school mate said excitedly, "Happy Peace Day!"

"What do you mean?" Anne asked.

"The war ended. You didn't hear?" said the girl.

On January 23, 1973, President Richard Nixon finally announced a ceasefire to the Vietnam War. "Peace with honor," he called it. I called it "bullshit." I had heard the news myself while lying across one of the twin beds in my Palos Park bedroom. My feet dangled over one side, my head hung over the other, while I listened to the radio on a nearby nightstand. I heard the words "Vietnam War" and my ears perked up. We had moved to the suburbs to get away from that war and it had followed us to Palos Park, right into my bedroom. I almost turned it off, but then I listened. My gut tightened as Nixon declared an end to the Vietnam War. Big, damn deal, I thought. As an eighth grader, I did not know much politically but I knew enough to be quite cynical of this presidential decision. I rolled over, got off my bed, and went on about my day.

There had been little to no recognition of the Vietnam War in our home other than the news broadcast of this subdued ending of the war by Nixon. It was like the war that had taken my brother was easy enough to end but the president waited until the year of his re-election to do so. How much sooner could he have done it? How many lives could have been spared?

The same day, Margie was listening to the car radio when she heard Nixon had ended the war. Margie was in her freshman year at the local community college. Her English teacher assigned the class an essay on something that confused them. Margie wrote on the purpose of Johnny's death. That confused her a great deal. Her words resounded so strongly with this instructor, an ex-Marine that had fought in Vietnam, that he kept the paper with her permission. What was confusing to Margie was that we were told for so many years that the Vietnam War was necessary and then it just ended for no apparent reason. Did we get strung along? She questioned. Did Johnny get strung along, right into that daisy chain?

The whole situation became even more confusing because of the fact that troops remained there, war continued, obituaries were still littered with young men in uniform until 1975. All those protestors and hippies were right about the war being wrong, I thought.

- - -

"I specifically remember when Nixon ended it. I was so angry. I felt he [Johnny] died for nothing then. I was all confused about that," Margie tells me.

"You know I just feel that the government squandered Johnny's life, like they squandered the fifty thousand other lives.

Even Kennedy wanted out of that war. If Kennedy had lived. . ." Uncle John's voice grows stronger.

"I was a Republican. I was glad when Nixon got elected after Johnny died. I wanted him to end it. I remember writin' Nixon a letter. I wrote, 'You don't know me but I just thought you would like to know my brother was killed.'"

Eileen laughs as she tells me this and realizes now how childlike her letter must have seemed to those at the White House.

"It took a long time for me to feel normal again," Eileen offers.

"Like how long? Two years?" I ask.

"I'd say at least five," Eileen says.

- - -

At nineteen years old, Eileen was just starting to feel like an adult, in charge of her life. She had gotten her driver's license and bought a convertible MG midget. I thought it was the coolest little red sports car . . . when it ran. She began attending classes at Moraine Valley Community College while working for Dad. When she arrived home from classes one day, several months after she had written to President Nixon, there was a letter from Washington addressed to her. She was excited and opened it quickly. It was a form letter with the president's stamped signature. Eileen had hoped for more. She reread the letter, thinking she missed something, anything, indicating a personal notice of Johnny, of her loss. It was all very general, as if the same letter could have been sent to everyone in our neighborhood or the state of Illinois, or our country. She folded the letter and placed it back in its envelope, leaving it on the counter.

- - -

"They did say sorry. But they did send me somethin' back. I thought that was cool." Eileen laughs again at herself. She doesn't remember what she did with that letter. It could've gone out with the day's trash back in 1973.

- - -

I was saddened to learn of the disrespectful attitude many of the returning veterans were getting from their fellow American citizens. During his visit in 1971, Tom Wernig told us about a couple of "fisticuffs" he had gotten into as a result of anti-war sentiments. On top of that, Tom had survivor's guilt for being on R&R when Johnny was hit. I heard him say this more than once. Tom had insomnia and fitful sleeping since his tour in Vietnam. Through learning of the torment within Tom Wernig, we were not only silently suffering from the pain of Johnny's death, we were suffering the torment of his life in Vietnam, as we were still learning about it. I reconciled in my own heart that it was best Johnny was taken suddenly, while over in Vietnam. I tried to convince my mom of the same. We were in the kitchen of our Palos home. I was buttering toast I had just taken out of the toaster oven. Mom was busy flipping eggs over the range and setting out dishes at the same time. Neither of us were looking at each other when I said, "If Johnny came back, he would have been really messed up, Mom."

She didn't say anything.

While news of the end of the war that took her son was being broadcast throughout 1973, my mother delivered her fourteenth child. It was a little brother. He was born dead. My sisters Margie and Eileen named him Charlie. I asked my mother if she was sad. She was surprised by my question. I was surprised by her response.

"Of course! I could feel him inside me. He was alive," she said to me.

I learned later there was a burial. I assumed my mother was present. I don't know who else attended. We kids were not included.

The topic of the Vietnam War oozed into our lives continually even after its final end in 1975. The Time-Life books for example: During my brother Chris' high school years he developed an interest in this series that covered the Vietnam War. Mom would do anything to encourage the boys to read, and seeing these books spark an interest in Chris, she ordered the whole set. Chris had a yearning to know where Johnny had been in Vietnam and what happened when Johnny was there. He even borrowed the books about the Vietnam War from the Palos Park library. Reading and writing had been a struggle for him. Today, I am impressed with his knowledge on this topic. He patiently answered my questions as he gave me a brief history lesson on this war.

Dad tried to help Jimmy with finding an interest to pursue. Using connections he developed while attending Northwestern University, Dad asked a friend, who was now in Congress, to get Jimmy into West Point. After graduating from Carl Sandburg high school in 1973, Jim tuned down the opportunity to apply to the prestigious military academy. 'Screw 'em. I don't want to be part of this government,' Jim thought to himself when presented with the offer. Dad didn't push it.

Jim's eyes had been set on another Point, Stevens Point. This was a university in a small town in Wisconsin, about an hour north of our farm. Jim had always enjoyed the farm, just like Dad, just like Johnny. Jim thought he might study there and then go into dentistry. As time passed, Jimmy's anger metastasized to his heart, his brain, and his limbs. It controlled him for many years. He chose to use mind-altering substances on a regular basis, which didn't mix well with his professional aspirations. His lack of focus negatively affected his grades.

"You don't have to go into dentistry...Are you doing this because of me?" Dad pressed Jim.

At the time, Jim took Dad's discouragement of dentistry as a lack of confidence in his ability to make it through dental school. Jim let life take him wherever. The blanket of anger he wrapped around himself built in limitations to where that life took him. It especially kept him from the focus of a challenging advanced degree for many years.

- - -

Jim tells me he now understands that Dad's discouragement of dentistry was not a sign of a lack of confidence in him.

"Dad just didn't like being a dentist. Besides, I bombed out [of school]. So dentistry was not for me. I had to survive. So I became a life time student, so to speak," Jim says.

Jim received his undergraduate degree in 2009, at the age of fifty-five and interviewed for his first professional job. It was in corporate facilities. While interviewing, the hiring manager discovered our father had been his family's dentist. My father occasionally accepted goods in exchange for payment when a patient could not afford the bill and this man's family had paid their bill in toilet paper. Jim got the job. It was an increase of thirty thousand dollars more per year with benefits. It included paid business trips to Houston, where his daughter and grandchildren lived. For the first time in his life, he was paid for vacation.

"Dad's still pulling strings for ya, Jim," I say when Jim tells me the good news.

I hear a shaky voice over the phone as Jim indicates he has no doubt of this.

- - -

As the war was coming to an end in East Asia in 1974, a peace agreement was within reach on our home front as well. Mom visited Mariann and her grandson, John, who was now three years old. My mother had not told my father she would be visiting. He would never have allowed that. She snuck the visit in while going to see a New York plastic surgeon for Mimi's dog bite scars. Mimi was eight by this time and was along on the trip. During the day, Mom and Mimi watched Sesame Street with little John while Mariann ran errands. Mariann normally did not allow her son to watch television but because Sesame Street was educational, she allowed it. Bruce was not around during this visit. When Mariann was around, Mimi sensed the extreme distance between Mom and her big sister. It was a difficult visit.

Mariann was twenty-two, married and raising a toddler while living with her in-laws. Mom was infiltrating enemy territory. Mariann's in-laws saw her as the wife of the man who rejected and insulted their son. The DaCostas were well aware that Dad was still not willing to accept his daughter's marriage to their son nor accept their child. In their eyes, my mother was at fault for not attending her own daughter's wedding and coming for a first visit to see her daughter's child, her grandchild, after three whole years had passed.

- - -

"Mom wanted Mariann to forgive her. Yet Mom was struggling with her anger too, and Mariann's choices," Mimi tells me she can see this now, yet at the time it was all so jumbled.

"I believe it took me five years to come to the realization that Johnny was dead," Mariann says. During those five years she got pregnant, dropped out of school, got married, and had a baby.

- - -

There were subsequent visits to Mariann, few and far between, yet my father knew about them. Mom sent cards and gifts regularly. Eventually, time healed all wounds and even my father actually went to visit Mariann. This did not happen until Mariann and Bruce had moved to their own place in Tucson, Arizona. By this time, they had a second child, Danny. Chris, Mimi, and Bonnie went with Mom and Dad on this trip to Arizona. It had been six years since Mom's visit to New York.

Grandma, who had been bedridden since 1960 from a severe stroke, died in 1975. This was a blessing. Pop died in '75. We drove in from the suburbs to attend the services at Christ the King. These funerals did not have much of an impact on our lives. Perhaps we were thinking that now Johnny had lots of company in heaven.

It took a few years after Johnny was gone, but times of joy did come back. The summer of '75, Dad took all the boys on a fishing trip to Canada. Fishing was one of Joe's biggest thrills as a child, and he enjoyed doing it with Dad. Yet, there were a few stressful moments. One of those moments occurred while fishing in Canada. Joe yanked his line out of the water in a sudden reflex motion and watched, horrified, as his hook sailed past Dad's lips. It was a near miss. God must fish, Joe thought. Makes perfect sense, since His son was a fisherman.

A year later, Mickey graduated from high school. It was a time of peace for our country. And although Johnny had given Mickey advice, back in 1969, not to join the military if there was no war, Mickey seriously considered the service. He got as far as the physical, yet never signed up. A year later, graduation nearing for Joe, he told our mother about his interest in joining the Navy. She didn't seem to mind. The Vietnam War had ended and it was still a time of peace for the United States. Yet Joe felt it would be hard on Mom so he did not pursue the service.

- - -

"I was actually going to join the Marines. But I was workin' at the hospital. There was a retired Marine security guard there. He kinda' talked me out of it," Chris tells me.

Chris eventually joined the Navy.

- - -

Mariann and Bruce laid down their (metaphorical) weapons to enjoy a visit with all of us, including Dad. I have a photo of us all enjoying a moment at the farm- A picture truly does say a thousand words. Several of us are gathered around the front porch of our Victorian farm house, including my father, who is smiling. Bruce and Mariann are together as a growing family, with two sons now. Little John, about five, is sitting on my lap. Bruce is still sporting an afro and bell bottoms. Mariann looks happy. My parents look happy. I remember this. We were all in the yard, playing badminton and enjoying a beautiful summer day together. My mother was feeling quite comfortable with Bruce at this point, yet still perplexed by what he was all about. He was from New York, had different views of the world. Although she had accepted this, she was still curious to know more about him.

"Aren't you concerned when you wear your hair like that somebody will think you're like that guy?"

Bruce, sitting across the picnic table from my mother, watching his young sons enjoy the game of badminton with their Aunts and Uncles, was honestly perplexed by this question.

"What guy?" Bruce asked.

"You know. That guy everyone's always talking about."

"No. What guy are you talking about?"

"Abbie Hoffman," said my mother.

Bruce had no idea who Abbie Hoffman was. My mother explained to him that Abbie Hoffman had been a part of the infamous Chicago 7 arrested for violence sprouting since the 1968 convention. That day, Bruce learned something from Mom.

Beyond

One thing I've learned from this was not to be afraid to ask for help from those around you when your task at hand is difficult. Since Johnny's death, I never really discussed the pain I held inside. I blocked out my feelings and moved forward with my life.

—Jim Guldan, 1995,
address to family

In 1990, our family and Marist alumni returned to Johnny's High School for the first annual John Guldan Memorial 5 kilometer run. The event pulled a solid number of participants consisting of current cross-country members, past classmates of Johnny's, and family. Several of the teammates Johnny had led as captain on the Marist cross-country team regularly participated in what became an annual John Guldan Memorial Run. Mom attended every year and enthusiastically cheered the kids on, wearing the t-shirt bearing the image of Johnny crossing the taped finish line. She was very proud of this run that was dedicated to her son. She never missed attending and every year as the event approached she asked each of us if we would be going. You just knew it was important to her that we all were there with our children.

The first weekend of August, 1990, a memorial service was held for Johnny at Christ the King church. Tom Wernig, Johnny's Marine brother on Hill 55, had flown all the way from New Hampshire to attend. I picked him up at the airport and he stayed with me in Naperville. It was my responsibility to get Tom to the mass. I was new to Naperville and not familiar with directions to Christ the King. We got lost on the way and arrived at what I thought was midway through the service. Tom was visibly upset. I was devastated that he came all this way and I didn't get him to where he needed to go. This service was so very important to him. As soon as we walked into church, I slid into one of the back pews. I watched Tom walk straight ahead, toward the altar. Aunt Marilyn, married to Uncle John, was sitting in one of the front pews and turned around when Tom entered.

- - -

Seventeen years later Aunt Marilyn describes Tom's entrance:

"I'll never forget him arriving in his combat greens and combat boots. He did not wear the formal Marine dress. He wore the outfit they fought in. He walked all the way down the long Christ the King aisle, from the back of the church and got in the pew with your mother and father. I'll never forget the sound of his combat boots as they clicked on that marble floor. He looked straight ahead, very somber and very steady. That picture defined the military for me. The loyalty, the steadfastness, the discipline. It was riveting."

Aunt Marilyn says it was perfect timing when he walked in. I thank her for letting me know that getting Tom to the church late that day had some value.

- - -

Mariann drove in from Pittsburgh for this service. She stood at the podium on the altar and delivered the following dedication she had written in all Capital letters:

JOHN GAVE ME THREE GIFTS:

    A POSITIVE ATTITUDE
    A SPIRIT OF DETERMINATION AND PERSERVERANCE
    AND HE MADE ME FEEL SPECIAL
I THANK HIM EVERY DAY FOR THIS
I WANT TO PASS THESE GIFTS ON TO
    MY CHILDREN AND THEIR CHILDREN
    AND THIS WAY KEEP HIS SPIRIT
    ALIVE AND WELL
HE BELIEVED IN WHAT HE WAS DOING
    IN VIETNAM AND I SUPPORT HIS
    MEMORY FOR THAT
LOVE HIM VERY MUCH AND MISS
    HIM EVERY DAY.

This twenty-year reunion mass was a pivotal point for Jim. As he listened to Father McKenna speak once again about his brother, something inside him began to change. The anger began to dissipate. He could listen and accept that he wasn't perfect, our parents weren't perfect, our society wasn't perfect. He saw in that moment that Johnny's choice was his choice to do something for himself, something he felt was important. Something he felt was so important that he gave his life for it. Who was I to judge that? Jim thought to himself. He approached Father McKenna after the service.

"If only I had been able to listen to your first sermon I wouldn't have had so many years of pent up anger and a destructive mode when Johnny died," Jim said.

Twenty years, three children, two divorces, a few episodes of gout, and a few attempts at a bachelor's degree later, Jim's anger finally began to subside. It was clear that Jim loved Johnny. He admired him. He respected him. And for many years, he hated him for going to Vietnam.

\- \- \-

"The mind is a very fragile instrument. How well you perceive the tragedies, deal with the tragedies, is all individual," Jim says.

\- \- \-

After the memorial service, Uncle Jim and Aunt Barbara hosted a reception at their house. It was a beautiful day and we all congregated in their large backyard, where the swing set Johnny helped Uncle Jim assemble the summer of 1969 still stood. Today, Uncle Jim still lives at 9323 Longwood. The swing set is still there. Twelve children, umpteen nieces and nephews, fifty plus grandchildren, great-grandchildren in the double digits, and many neighbors have all played on it. Today, it is no longer usable, with one of its six legs rusted off. Uncle Jim will not take it down, and his children know not to suggest it.

In 1995, another ceremony was held in Johnny's honor. This one was to dedicate the street we lived on to Johnny. My parents attended this dedication but did not have much to do with its happening. They were quiet about it and respectful of the effort Aunt Barbara had put into organizing it. Aunt Barbara petitioned Ginger Rugai, a Chicago politician to get the name of our street officially changed to **Honorary** LCPL John A. Guldan Ave. There were speeches, bagpipes and a march down the street. My nephew, who was named after Johnny, stood on a tall ladder and placed a brown street sign with Johnny's name below the green Oakley sign while my brother Jim read a dedication he had written for the occasion. He had given us each a copy. Its few paragraphs were formatted neatly and a rubbing of Johnny's name from The Wall was included at the bottom of the page, in red. He started by thanking everyone involved and followed with:

"...One thing I am certain of was my brother's passion for freedom. A passion that was instilled early in his youth from his parents, his relatives, his church, and his community. It was my brother John's choice to join the United Sates Marine Corps, in 1969, to face the perils of North and South Vietnam to which his strength was equal..."

Jim's emotional reading of his speech showed that the pain from the loss of his older brother had remained with him. In the weeks prior, Jim had asked for help from all of his brothers and sisters in preparing this speech. Mariann replied to Jim in a letter:

The hardest thing for me to accept about John's death was not only his dying and dying alone in a faraway place, but he also must have had to face killing another human being. If he had any hope of surviving from one day to the next he had to do that. That's the hardest thing for me to think about so I try not to.

Mariann did not support this event, nor did she attend.

At the time of my brother's death, my siblings and I ranged in ages from three to twenty-one. Because of that and our individual natures, each of us had different concerns, different perceptions, and different coping mechanisms. Yet we had one thing in common: In some way we all changed because of it.

My mother came back to us strong. She was there for each of us when we needed her. She spent a week with each one of us after the birth of a child. While at my house, she polished my silver and folded the laundry so I could spend time with my baby or catch up on needed sleep. She was the best grandmother our children could ever have. She was my role model for coming through loss. She called me almost daily during and after the end of my marriage, helping me through it. I think she had had enough of me crying over the phone when she offered her "Five Minutes of Sorry" therapy.

"Give yourself five minutes to cry and then get on with the day, Terri."

My parents kept the family operating, getting us all through each day while dealing with their own sense of a deep loss. God gave us what we needed to get through. Although a hole had been created in each of our hearts, we learned to build around it and life went on to be good again. Johnny would have wanted it that way.

The author of Tsotsi, a novel that was adapted to become an Academy Award-winning film, comes to mind when I think about the impact of the booby-trap that took my brother's life. Tsotsi was about good unfolding after the murder of a young mother in a car-jacking. The plot steps through the positive events that occur as a result of this violent act. The moral is that when an act of violence happens, in sometimes only fractions of a second, it is what unravels afterward that matters. What happened after

Johnny's death was a working of the good in others' hearts. Like the Dr. Gallaghers, the Mrs. Heeneys, the aunts and uncles, the Mrs. Grogans, the food-bearers, all of the friends standing in line for hours, the Ron Berquists, the memorial events, and the letter writers. There have been and will be millions more acts of violence in wars like Vietnam and on the streets. If we choose to react to those acts of violence with determination to perpetuate the good and focus on the positive stories that come from those acts, then the loss from those acts of violence is not senseless. So this story does not have a climax with a happily-ever-after ending. What is important is that this story gets told, with its many heroes and angels, focusing on the good that unfolds.

V. My Journey

All that I have seen teaches me to trust the Creator for all I have not seen.

—Ralph Waldo Emerson

2003-2016

I had no intention of going to Vietnam, ever. That place took my brother from us. They treated him with hostility when he was trying to help them. Yet, as I was writing and researching this book, things happened and a trip to Vietnam seemed to fall in to place. Tours of Peace (TOP) is a nonprofit organization to help Vietnam veterans and their loved ones heal from the wounds of war. TOP took me to the area where Johnny was killed and involved me in many humanitarian efforts for the South Vietnamese people. We went to a home of single mothers with their infants and delivered much needed items, then on to a children's home, providing more items. We sang songs with the kids and did face painting. They hugged and kissed us good-bye. Through these children, I could feel Johnny ever so slightly. Each day I emailed home, sharing my experiences with my family, and many wrote back.

My brother Jim remained in contact via emails. He did not say much, yet his few words were attached to every step I took, half a world away, alongside Johnny's last steps. A couple of days before I reached the site where Johnny died, Jim sent an email request:

'If you can, grab some of the mud for me where Johnny spilled his blood!'

The day I was scheduled to visit the site where Johnny last stood, I wrote:

March 12, 2007, In Hoi An

Hello all,

It has been a wearing last two days. I have tried multiple times to get to the Internet to send a letter off and it has been foiled. It's really odd—all technological things seem to be breaking down since yesterday—Internet, camera batteries, photo memory card. A member of the group here backs me up as each thing fails. Two nights ago we stayed in a beautiful resort, again on the South China Sea, called Quy Nhan Life spa, or something like that. Once again, food was beautiful and so was the weather. So hard to imagine there was such a terrible war going on here, yet it was 40 years ago. I keep thinking about how much time has passed since Johnny was here. I knew the next day or so was going to be difficult, so before we left this resort I took a walk to the meditation garden. My stomach began knotting and my head was pounding as I started thinking more about standing on THE spot in Bich Nam. This meditation area was encased in trees and had multiple small flowing ponds. Peering out through the tress was a view of the shore and sea. I felt a comforting feeling wrap around me and say, "I'm glad you are here." I felt him say these words a few times to me. All I could say back was, "It took so long." Well that was it. The tears started flowing and they didn't stop until just an hour or so ago. Later that day we went to a home that houses adults and children that have had agent orange defects. We delivered all sorts of needed items and walked to the crippled adults and children's rooms to say hello and shake their hands. Many were so crippled they could not even shake hands. The day ended with a group meeting where I read four of Johnny's letters dated July 24th and later. The next day we went to the My Lai massacre site. There we met an 82-year-old woman who was a survivor of the massacre. She told us her story. Then we went on to Tham Ky (an area Johnny spoke of in a letter) and ate lunch where the locals eat. The dishes we enjoyed were specific to that area. We drove alongside the same RR tracks I had been watching these past few days. One of the group members, Bruce, had gotten a detailed geographical map of the area and plotted the points where Johnny was killed. Bruce had a GPS with him to make sure we were within 100 meters of the spot. We drove that big old bus up to the bridge, about 1.5 miles from the sight and discovered there was an overhead rail that the bus was not going to clear. Our plans were changed. Dai (our driver) turned that big old bus around and instead we went on to Hill 55. This is where Johnny spent much of his time and wrote many letters. The other vet with us that was stationed on Hill 55 was able to tell me about life there. We continued on to the site. Everyone (in my TOP group) was working to find this site. We then came to where the RR tracks met the river, the landmark Tom Wernig had remembered. At this point, I was having a difficult time. The walking was a little rough alongside the track and heading toward the river. I thought of Johnny marching and picked up my boots. We saw the town of Bich Nam in the distance—the town that Johnny had been assigned to as an operation just a couple of days before his death. As we approached the area, I gave my camera to a group member, Sherri, and asked her to take pictures for me. Later Sherri told me my camera ran out of pictures just as we approached Johnny's spot. Sherri's camera then ran out of batteries. We walked beside a rice paddy with lush, green rice stalks. As we were arriving a train went by on that track that had been following us the last three days. It was full of passengers and baggage. In the days prior it had appeared empty (How symbolic-carrying its baggage away). To our left was a corn field. One trip member pointed out that it is quite unusual to see corn growing in this area. He asked if it looked like our farm. I looked around and it was beautiful and peaceful. The wind was gently blowing through the rice paddies. When I looked at the cornfield, I thought it did remind me of the farm. I bent down and scooped up some dirt Jimmy had asked for in a pill bottle. Then I stood up and soaked in that sight to engrave it into my memory for all of us. Johnny was there, I was there, you will all be there when I bring home the stories and pictures. It was so very peaceful and beautiful there. Our trip guide conversed with the locals. When he arrived back on the bus he told us what they had said. The trip leader took a video while he spoke. The people told our guide that the GIs gave them candy. I wouldn't doubt if Johnny were one of those GIs. Just as the guide finished speaking the video camera batteries ran out.

I am exhausted both physically and mentally as I write this so if parts don't make sense, I am sorry. I would send some pictures but my batteries are being recharged (no pun intended).

Love you and hen gap lai,
Terri

I said the Lord's Prayer on Johnny's site, as I knelt down to gather the dirt from that ground. One TOP member noticed a pronounced breeze that came through the field. It made the rice paddy sing a soft, gentle song as if God's breath were blowing through, she said.

The Wall

Reflections of those who miss, wonder, ache, love, hate, blending into the gray carved names in block letters no more than one inch high on the shiny, black granite. All are heroes.

—T.M. Guldan, *2009 Journal entry*

My parents would not go to the Vietnam War Memorial in Washington, D.C. and they weren't interested in seeing The Moving Wall in Chicago. The Moving Wall, a half-sized replica, travels to each state throughout the year. I did not care to see The Moving Wall either, let alone travel all the way to Washington to see the "real" Wall. I appreciated the effort of those who created it, yet I felt that a panel with my brother's name on it could do nothing for me. I was wrong.

When I was a young mother, my husband talked me into going to see The Moving Wall in Chicago. At that time, it had been sixteen years since my brother's death. I didn't realize there were any emotions inside me about the Vietnam War or my brother. Then, I touched his name with my infant son snuggling close to my chest in the baby carrier I had strapped around me. A wave of emotion poured over me as if it had shot directly from his name, through my finger, up my arm, and into my heart. The tears rushed up from somewhere inside me. I fought them. How could this be, I thought. Time was supposed to heal all. After all these years, where is this emotion coming from with a simple touch to his name on a dark, cold panel. I tried to convey this sense of release to my mother. She listened, but it wasn't enough to get her there. I told her that when she was ready I would take her and my father to D.C. to visit The Wall. We did not make it there before her death in 1998. After my mother passed, my father did not travel well without her.

In the spring of 2009, I visit the real Vietnam Wall memorial in Washington, D.C. for the first time. Again, I experienced a healing power like I did with its smaller version in Chicago. Yet, this time I recognize the others. As I gently run my fingers over Johnny's name on panel 8W line 79, I think about how someone took the time to research the order in which all of these men were killed. Someone learned exactly when, to the minute, Johnny was killed, who was before him and who was after him. I look for Jack Gilbert, the young man who died with my brother. His name should have been right next to Johnny's, yet he is two names away. I am told that Gilbert had a son. His son and mother—casualties of war. The visitors around me, of all ages and colors, are quiet and reverent as we slowly walk past each black panel. Hundreds of people a day come to visit the memorial, designed by Maya Lin and dedicated in 1982, looking for loved ones that died thirty and forty years ago. I walk with the crowd. The dark, solemn slabs full of the grey names along our left lead us up from below. When it finally ends, I continue walking and find a bench to sit. I watch from afar and notice how the path rises so that the names on The Wall greet the distant sight of the Washington Monument, the symbol of freedom, for which these men believed to be fighting. Their spirits are felt.

Dream of Closure

They all therefore praised the ways of the Lord, the just judge who brings to light the things that are hidden.
—2 Maccabees 12:41,
New American Bible

Throughout most of my life, I have been driven by the search for the truth about my brother's experience in Vietnam and his death. What Johnny's body went through from the moment of that explosion until the time his body was returned to us back home was a set of images that I have imagined for many years. Did he suffer? Who was with him when he died? Who saw his body? What did it look like? Who touched it and was it handled with respect? Equally as important as his death, I wanted to know about my brother's life in Vietnam and his relationship with my father. Every word in my father's last letter, my family's memories, and Johnny's letters seemed to help piece that truth into a whole. Yet, closure came for me in the wee hours of April 2, 2014. I was in a hotel in Madison, Wisconsin, when I had my first dream of Johnny.

I was attending a two-day conference for work and hadn't been thinking about my book, let alone Johnny, when I woke from a dream at about 1:00AM. The dream was so real. It was as if he was there, with me. He was in full form. Long lines of people were walking around a large public area, with escalators in the background going up and coming down from a second floor. I stood on the first floor. There was one other person standing close by me. I didn't know this person who was preparing me for my meeting with Johnny. It happened quickly. We were standing in a small, dark circular area without a visible ceiling. The preparer directed me to a spot on the floor with footprints. I stepped onto them. The preparer said, "okay," and on cue, Johnny stepped into the circular area from darkness. Johnny stood there facing me, only a few feet away. He had on dark, casual clothes that were too big for him, although his legs were very long. A cable knit crewneck sweater in dark brown or green and jeans both hung baggy and too long on him. I could not see his hands or feet or any shoes. It was like his clothes and his body were borrowed.

"You're so tall," I said.

It was then his hands showed, only briefly, as he reached them out to his sides and then in toward his stomach while looking down at himself. He had little reaction to this odd body, like it didn't matter and he didn't want to waste time on it. His head looked like a paper cutout from his Marist senior picture placed on top of this body. He had that same hint of a smile. He had not aged.

"Can I hug you?" I asked.

He didn't say a word, yet the look on his face told me he wasn't any surer than I about this but it was okay to try. I tried to step off the spot I was on and could not move. Seeing I couldn't come to him, he reached out to me and I reached toward him. I noticed an unusually small hand peeking out from under the long sleeve of his sweater. I touched it, palm to palm, surprised at the solid, fleshy feel. I was expecting my hand to wave through his body.

"Your hand is so warm," I said.

I gently squeezed the small hand. It did not squeeze back. I let go. Johnny had not said anything. Just then, Johnny stepped forward to his right, back into the darkness. I awoke. After thinking about this dream, I realized the childlike hand I was grabbing when we reached toward each other was my own, eleven-year-old hand—my child within.

At fifty-six, I finish this book after working on it for thirteen years. I have touched Johnny's name on The Wall; I've gone halfway around the world to walk where he walked in his final days and stood on the spot where his life ended on this earth; I have read and transcribed his letters; I have talked for hours with family about his life and death. Yet, until this dream, I hadn't realized that this was my own journey in healing.

*

Follow the letter God writes upon your heart. This is my journey and I thank you for sharing it with me.

VI. Acknowledgements

Once I decided to write this story, I began by reading many books about Vietnam. I would like to thank the authors of those books. In particular, Christian Appy, who wrote Patriots, which provided a lot of background and also the idea of interviewing my family members. I thank Carl Marlantis, whose book Matterhorn explained the kill teams and ambushes mentioned in Johnny's letters. I thank Philip Caputo and his detail on the processing of the dead, provided in A Rumor of War.

I thank Danielle Trusoni, author of *Falling Through the Earth*, for encouraging me to go to Vietnam. I stood on the spot Johnny stood when he left this earth, traveled over the roads and possibly met some of the same people he encountered almost forty years prior. I thank TOP (Tours of Peace) and its founder, Jess DeVaney, and my TOP trip members, for that experience. I especially thank Bruce Logan for the hours and favors he used to find the location of my brother's "hit," and Steve, for providing me a glimpse of what life was like on Hill 55. I thank all the TOP participants on the 2007 trip for their enlightenment into the world of Vietnam during the sixties and seventies as well as their support through my difficult journey.

I thank Johnny's friends Neal Beatty and Marty Psik for digging into their school day memories.

I thank Jim Hornsey, Tom Wernig, Bob, and all of the Vietnam veterans willing to share their memories that may have been difficult to part with. Jim lives an hour or so south of Chicago. My family and I hope to meet him at the first book signing. I thank Dick Barry for painfully recalling the memories of locating Johnny's body and his wife, Cathy, for her support. I thank Joe Heeney for his memories, Marine protocol, and honesty of feelings, as well as his brother, Mike, for the funeral service protocol and details on the day we received "the news," that no one else in my family knew about.

I thank John Riffice for his publishing knowledge and encouragement as a new writer. I thank my dear friend Bonnie Petersen, who gave me the book Patriots and continually encouraged me to keep writing. I thank Mrs. Davis and York High School students, Loyola and Jesse Brown Veterans Hospital for allowing me to present my story, and my cousin Jean for attending and recording. I thank my cousin Anne for placing that branch from Johnny's tree on my dashboard as a constant reminder to keep going. That branch has traveled in two cars now.

I thank all of my aunts and uncles who provided valuable insight into those years through lengthy interviews. Uncle Jim, Aunt Barbara (in memory), Uncle Mike, Aunt Diane, Uncle John (in memory), Aunt Marilyn, and Aunt Annie Laurie, my cousin, Johnny Gallagher.

I thank Denise for the letters and personal affects she entrusted into my care for several years and for retelling her moments and memories with Johnny despite the tears she had to shed to get to those stories.

I thank my children and friends for tolerating the lack of me these last few years as I wrapped up this project. I thank every one of my brothers and sisters for their honesty, their generosity of time and effort, and their amazing bravery in cutting through those layers of scar tissue to reach back to the dark corners of their memories. I thank them for their support and trust in me throughout the arduous process of writing this book. I thank my sister Mariann (in memory) for the honest vulnerability portrayed in her writings. I especially thank my sister Margie (in memory) for handing me the letter.

I thank Sr. Helen Prejean who encouraged me as a new writer, at her book signing of *Dead Man Walking,* to follow my passion to be the messenger.

I thank my editor Helga Schier for expert insight and patience with my virgin voyage to publish. I thank my generous publisher Rosy Hugener who hung in there with me year after year saying it is almost ready. I thank Kelly, Steve, Anne, Jennifer, Mickey, Jim, and Joe, who all offered their time to read and edit. I thank Anne again, for her willingness to edit my final version twenty-four hours a day.

I thank Johnny for his abundant and beautifully honest letters. I thank my parents for keeping every letter from Johnny and the last one my father wrote. These were invaluable in my research of this book. Without them, there would be no book.

I especially thank the Holy Spirit for placing the need to tell this story within my heart.

To those whose interviews contributed to this book and were not here to read it:
Rest in peace
Mariann
Uncle John
Aunt Barbara
Margie

VII. APPENDIX

A.   The Characters

1.   John and Eileen Guldan, married June 12, 1948.
Eileen (Bansley) Guldan (1927-1998), first child of James and Anne (O'Rourke) Bansley.

John Guldan, Jr. (1925-2003), first child of John and Florence (Kennedy) Guldan.

2.   Patti
Patrice Eileen Guldan (1949), first-born.

3.   Johnny
John Anthony Guldan (1950-1970), second child, first son.

4.   Mariann
Mariann Guldan (1951-2006), third child, second daughter.

5.   Margie (Triplet)
Margaret Mary Guldan (1953-2015), fourth child, third daughter.

6.   Eileen (Triplet)
Eileen Mary Guldan (1953), born two minutes after Margie, fifth child, fourth daughter.

7.   Jim (Triplet)
        James Michael Guldan (1953), born seven minutes after Eileen, sixth child, second son.

8.   Bill
        William Joseph Guldan (1955), seventh child, third son.

9.   Mickey
        Michael Thomas Guldan (1957), eighth child, fourth son.

10.   Joe
        Joseph Edward Guldan (1958), ninth child, fifth son.

11.   Terri
        Therese Marie Guldan (1959), tenth child, fifth daughter.

12.   Chris
        Christopher Edward Guldan (1962), eleventh child, sixth and youngest son.

13.   Mimi
        Marybeth Florence (1963), twelfth child, sixth daughter.

14.   Bonnie

Bonnie Marie (1967), thirteenth child, seventh daughter.

15.   Denise
       Denise Marie Racky (1951).

16.   Aunt Annie Laurie & Uncle Jack, married December 28, 1954.
       Annie Laurie Bansley (1929), second child, second daughter of James and Anne (O'Rourke) Bansley,

       John J. Gallagher (1930-2003).

17.   Uncle Jim & Aunt Barbara, married September 4, 1954.
       James Anthony Bansley (1931), third born, first son of James and Anne (O'Rourke) Bansley.
       Barbara Wynn McCann (1932-2009).

18.   Uncle Mike & Aunt Diane, married September 4, 1965.
       Michael Garrett Bansley (1935), fourth child, second son of James and Anne (O'Rourke) Bansley.

       Diane Head (1939).

19.   Uncle John and Aunt Marilyn, married July 25, 1981.
       John Ralph Bansley (1937-2009), fifth child, third son of James and Anne (O'Rourke) Bansley.

       Marilyn Hopkins (1934).

B. Photo of The Letter

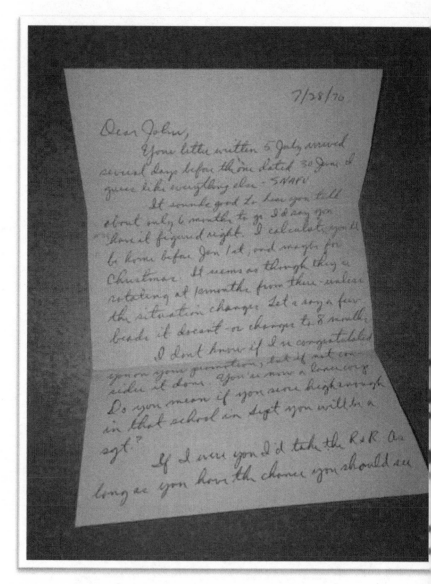

Just follow.

Page 2 and 3

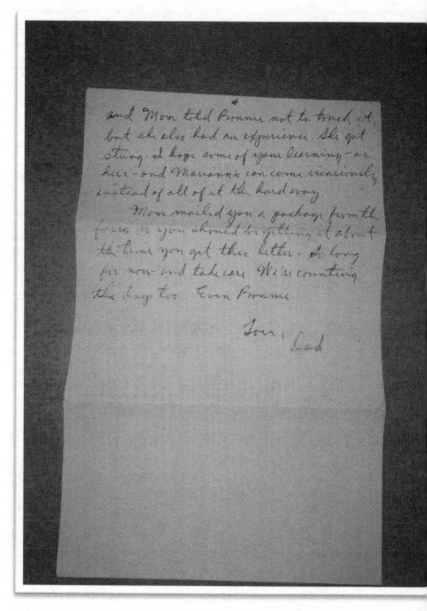

Page 4

C.   1970 News

The following facts were obtained from
http://www.thepeoplehistory.com/1970.html.

- Average Cost of new house is $23,450.

- Cost of a gallon of gas is 36 cents.

- U.S. postage stamp is 6 cents.

- Paul McCartney announces that The Beatles have disbanded.

- Apollo 13 mission to moon is abandoned.

- Japan becomes the worlds "fourth space power," after the Soviet Union (1957), the United States (1958), and France (1965).

- First Earth Day celebrated.

- The U.S. Environmental Protection Agency begins operation.

- Boeing 747 makes its first commercial passenger trip to London.

- The United States invades Cambodia.

- 100,000 people demonstrate in Washington, D.C., against the Vietnam War.

- The U.S. population reaches 205 million.

- The United States lowers the voting age to 18 from 21 when President Nixon signs the bill into law on June 22.

444 | T.M. Guldan

- California becomes the first U.S. state to adopt "No Fault" divorce law.

- Controlled Substance Act passed part of the Comprehensive Drug Abuse Prevention and Control Act of 1970.

- Chicago Seven defendants found guilty of intent to incite a riot in 1968 (later overturned)

- Dow Jones drops to 631.

- National Guards fire on and kill 4 protesters on May 4 at Kent State University.

- Brazil wins their third world cup with Pele as the captain.

- The Isle of Wight Festival takes place. 600,000 people attend the largest rock festival of all time.

- Jimi Hendrix dies of barbiturate overdose in London.

- Janis Joplin dies in a cheap motel from a heroin overdose.

- The first New York marathon is run in New York.

- Simon and Garfunkel release their final album together, Bridge Over Troubled Water.

- Popular Films and Music
  - M*A*S*H
  - Patton
  - Woodstock
  - Hello, Dolly!
  - Catch-22
  - The Beatles, "Let it Be," released on May 8
  - The Jackson 5, "ABC" and "I want you back"
  - Edwin Starr, "War"

D.   Cu Chi Tunnels

The Cu Chi Tunnels, referred to in July 22 entry, had a significant part in the Vietnam War. I include here for background.

The district of Củ Chi is located 40 kilometers, or about 25 miles, to the northwest of Saigon. The Cu Chi tunnels are one of the most famous battlegrounds of the Vietnam War. They are an immense network of connecting underground tunnels, part of a much larger network of tunnels that underlie much of the country. The total network spans almost 250 kilometers or 155 miles. At the height of the Vietnam War, the tunnel system stretched from the outskirts of Saigon all the way to the Cambodian border. The Cu Chi area tunnels, a 75-mile-long underground maze where thousands of fighters and villagers could hide, were used by NLF (National Liberation Front) guerrillas as hiding spots during combat, as well as serving as communication and supply routes, hospitals, food and weapon caches, and living quarters for numerous guerrilla fighters.

The tunnels themselves are undeniably impressive; built over a 25-year period, starting in the 1940s. Throughout the war, the South Vietnamese Communists, or Viet Cong, continually expanded the three-level network, which included mess halls, meeting rooms, an operating theater, and even a tiny cinema. Sleeping chambers, smokeless kitchens, and wells were built to house and feed the growing number of residents and rudimentary hospitals created to treat the wounded. It was an underground city with living areas, storage, weapons factories, field hospitals, and command centers. Most of the supplies used to build and maintain the tunnels were stolen or scavenged from U.S. bases or troops.

The medical system within these tunnels serves as a good example of Vietnamese ingenuity in overcoming a lack of basic resources. Stolen motorcycle engines created light and electricity and scrap metal from downed aircraft were fashioned into surgical tools. Doctors even came up with new ways of performing sophisticated surgery. Faced with large amounts of casualties and a considerable lack of available blood, one man, Dr. Vo Hoang Le, came up with a resourceful solution. "We managed to do blood transfusion," Vo said, "by returning his [the patient's] own blood to the patient. If a comrade had a belly wound and was bleeding, but his intestines were not punctured, we collected his blood, filtered it, put it in a bottle and returned it to his veins."

By the early 1960s, the NLF had created a relatively self-sufficient community that was able to house hundreds of people and, for the most part, go undetected by large amounts of American troops based, literally, right on top of the tunnels.

Underground conference rooms where campaigns such as the Tết Offensive were planned in 1968 have been restored, and visitors may enjoy a simple meal of food that NLF fighters would have eaten.

The tunnels are between 0.4 to 1m wide. In places, they were several stories deep and housed up to 10,000 people who virtually lived underground for years...getting married, giving birth, going to school. They only came out at night to furtively tend their crops. The tunnels consist of three levels, up to twenty-three feet deep, were dug out of hard, red clay, and were surrounded by booby traps. People dug all this with hand tools, filling reed baskets and dumping the dirt and hard clay into bomb craters. They installed large vents so they could hear approaching helicopters, smaller vents for air and baffled vents to dissipate cooking smoke. There were also hidden trap doors and gruesomely effective bamboo-stake booby traps.

The Americans were never able to take these tunnels even after some of the most intense bombardments of the Vietnam War. Forty thousand Vietnamese people perished here. It was only when captives and defectors talked that the extensiveness and complexity of these tunnels became slightly more clear. But still the entries, exits, and even the sheer scale of the tunnels weren't known until years after the American war. Chemicals, smoke-outs, razing by fire, and bulldozing of whole areas, pinpointed only a few of the well-hidden tunnels and their entrances. The emergence of the Tunnel Rats, a detachment of southern Vietnamese working with Americans small enough to fit in the tunnels, could only guess at the sheer scale of Cu Chi. By the time peace had come, little of the complex, and its infrastructure of schools, dormitories, hospitals, and miles of tunnels, had been uncovered. Wells provided the vital drinking water to the three-tiered system of tunnels that sustained life. A detailed map was not possible for security reasons. It required an innate sense of direction to guide the tunnelers and those who lived in them. Many routes linked to local rivers, including the Saigon River. Their top tier soil was firm enough to take construction and the movement of heavy machinery by American tanks. The middle tier was safe from mortar attacks and the lower 8-10 meters down was impregnable. A series of hidden, and sometimes booby-trapped, doors connected the routes, down through a system of narrow, often unlit and in-vented tunnels. At one point American troops brought in a well-trained squad of 3,000 sniffer dogs, but the German shepherds were too bulky to navigate the courses. One legend has it that the dogs were deterred by Vietnamese using American soap to throw them off their scent. More often pepper and chili spray was laid at entrances, often hidden in mounds disguised as molehills to throw them off.

The tunnels allowed guerrilla communication and surprise attacks, even within the perimeters of U.S. military bases. Water was pumped through known tunnels, and engineers laid toxic gas. One American commander's report at the time said: "It's impossible to destroy the tunnels because they are too deep and extremely tortuous." But the Americans were never passive about the tunnels, despite being unaware of their sheer complexity. The U.S. retaliated with large-scale raiding operations using tanks, artillery and air bombs, eventually turning the region into what writers Tom Mangold and John Penycate called "the most bombed, shelled, gassed, defoliated and generally devastated area in the history of warfare."

Today, the trees and bushes have grown back. And since 1988, two sections of tunnels have been open for tourism. They remain unlit and mostly unreconstructed, which means chunky Westerners shouldn't even try.

D.   Bibliography

Patriots, The Vietnam War Remembered from All Sides, Christian
    Appy, ISBN: 0 14 20.0449 9, Penquin Books 2004

A Rumor of War, Philip Caputo, ISBN: 0-03-017631-X, Holt,
    Rinehart and Winston, New York 1977

Home From The War: Learning from Vietnam Veterans, Robert Jay
    Lifton, ISBN-10: 1590511689, Other Press 2005

My Stroke of Insight, Jill Bolte Taylor, Ph.D., ISBN: 978-0-452-
    29554-4, Plume 2006

Masters of The Art, A Fighting Marine's Memoir of Vietnam,
    Ronald E. Winter, ISBN: 0-89141-879-2, Presidio Press
    2005

The Ice Beneath You: A Novel, Christian Bauman, ISBN-10:
    0743227840, Touchstone 2002

Up Country, Nelson DeMille, ISBN-10: 0446611913, Vision 2003

www.merriam-webster.com/dictionary - Simple definition of
    White Flight

www.capmarine.com - Combined Action Program (CAP) mission
    statement

Wikipedia 12/31/2012 - White flight among other topics

Life magazine, June 1969 issue published 242 photos of those killed in "Vietnam conflict" in one week'

I Didn't Raise My Boy To Be A Soldier; Alfred Bryan, 1915, WWI famous war ballad.

E.   End Notes

(1) Monday's Child: First recorded in A. E. Bray's Traditions of Devonshire (Volume II, pp.287-288) in 1838 and was collected by James Orchard Halliwell in the mid-nineteenth century